Cinema and Fascism

CINEMA AND FASCISM

ITALIAN FILM AND SOCIETY, 1922–1943

Steven Ricci

UNIVERSITY OF CALIFORNIA PRESS

BERKELEY   LOS ANGELES   LONDON

University of California Press, one of the most
distinguished university presses in the United States,
enriches lives around the world by advancing
scholarship in the humanities, social sciences, and
natural sciences. Its activities are supported by the UC
Press Foundation and by philanthropic contributions
from individuals and institutions. For more
information, visit www.ucpress.edu.

University of California Press
Berkeley and Los Angeles, California

University of California Press, Ltd.
London, England

Library of Congress Cataloging-in-Publication Data

Ricci, Steven.
   Cinema and fascism : Italian film and society,
1922–1943 / Steven Ricci.
      p.   cm.
   Includes bibliographical references and index.
   ISBN 978-0-520-25355-1 (cloth : alk. paper)
   ISBN 978-0-520-25356-8 (pbk. : alk. paper)
   1. Motion pictures—Italy—History.   2. Fascism
and motion pictures—Italy—History.   3. Motion
pictures—Social aspects—Italy.   I. Title.
PN1993.5.I88R48   2008
791.43'094509041—dc22   2007019336

Manufactured in the United States of America
17 16 15 14 13 12 11 10 09 08
10 9 8 7 6 5 4 3 2 1
This book is printed on New Leaf EcoBook 50, a
100% recycled fiber of which 50% is de-inked post-
consumer waste, processed chlorine-free. EcoBook 50
is acid-free and meets the minimum requirements of
ANSI/ASTM D5634–01 (Permanence of Paper). ∞

For Diva

Contents

Illustrations

Preface

This study began when I first encountered pre-neorealist Italian cinema in 1978. While working in the UCLA Film and Television Archive, I almost literally stumbled upon Mario Camerini's *Darò un milione* (1935). The print was part of the Twentieth Century Fox collection of studio prints that had been deposited with the archive in 1972. Fox acquired the rights to the Camerini film in order to make an American version with either Gary Cooper, Tyrone Power, or Don Ameche in the role originally played by a young Vittorio De Sica. When I put the film on the Steenbeck, I was immediately struck both by what was and by what wasn't there.

Darò un milione presented certain compelling mysteries. How could such an accomplished film go unmentioned in virtually all of the English-language and much of the Italian-language scholarship on the history of Italian cinema? After all, it was directed by Mario Camerini, whose storied career spanned the silent, fascist, neorealist, and art-cinema periods. It starred a thirty-two-year-old De Sica and was written by his neorealist partner-to-be Cesare Zavattini. The film's charm and Sturges-esque populism were as worthy and convincing as any comedy of manners produced by the Hollywood studio system in the thirties. Most of all, I wondered, where was the ominous black shadow of fascism?

These and other "small" mysteries launched a journey of intellectual curiosity, revision, discovery, understanding, and misunderstanding.

They made for a map of research plotted along numerous dotted lines that converge in the present volume. I have been able to connect these lines of inquiry, in significant measure, because of groundbreaking work by certain new historians who have begun to rethink interwar Italian culture. Gian Piero Brunetta's fundamental study of Italian cinema history and Victoria De Grazia's analysis of leisure time during the Fascist period were particularly influential.

At different times and for different reasons, my research into earlier, pre-neorealist, pre-Fellini/Antonioni, pre-Leone/Argento and pre-Pasolini/Bertolucci cinemas moved from the front to the back burner. (Describing these as "earlier" cinemas already sets up an unfortunate reverse teleology.) Although one can always propose narratives of delay, occasioned by other projects and professional horizons, such scenarios sometimes lack convincing explanatory force. In this sense, the concept of "back burner" offers a more nuanced and not entirely inaccurate metaphor for the book's evolution, since it participates, arguably, in the best tradition of slow-food cuisine. My investigation of Italian cinema under fascism has continuously evolved, not unlike a risotto cooked ever so slowly and with the occasional addition of fresh, locally produced ingredients. However undeserved, I prefer the culinary metaphor.

Since I began my research, a number of important studies on Italian culture during the Fascist period have appeared. I hope that this book will make a contribution to that critical and historiographic dialogue in light of three compelling questions. First, a recent wave of scholarship has shaken to their core traditional approaches to national identity. Simply put, we are challenged to find new theoretical paradigms in order to account for concepts of nationality and nationhood in light of a seemingly borderless globalization. Whether they are postcolonial, diasporic, transnational, or virtual, how are we now to speak about cultural agency and identity when they almost inevitably function both locally and globally? Second, some trends in contemporary cultural theory have tended to devalue ideological analysis. In our context, for example, the specific relationship between Fascism and the Italian cinema has avoided political analysis by discussions locating it within the broader historical dynamics of modernization. In general terms, how are we to speak in material and coherent terms about the relationship between culture and power when our very notions of both materiality and coherency are fundamentally questioned by the postmodern? Finally, how can historical study of such relationships enable our understanding of, resistance to, and reappropriation of cultural identity in the contemporary setting? Although the economic conditions and the structure of the contemporary mediascape are quite different from those of the pre–World War II era, the troubling hyper-concentration of media control by international conglomerates such as Murdoch's Fox and Berlusconi's Mediaset make investigations into the historical precedents for the nexus between media and political power very compelling today.

ACKNOWLEDGMENTS

This volume would not have been possible without support, advice, and encouragement from a substantial number of colleagues, friends, and institutions. For their generous assistance, I am indebted to archives both in the United States and Italy: the UCLA Film and Television Archive (Charles Hopkins, Mark Quigley, Eddie Richmond, and Rob Stone), Cineteca Nazionale (Alfredo Baldi, Antonella Felicioni, and Sergio Toffetti), Cineteca di Bologna (Margherita Cecchini, Anna Fiaccarini, Davide Pozzi, and Angela Tromelini), Cineteca del Friuli (Lorenzo Codelli, Livio Jacob, and Piera Patat), Istituto Luce (Andrea Amatiste and Claudio Siniscalchi), Mostra del Nuovo Cinema (Adriano Aprà, Lino Miccichè, Alessandro Levantesi, Riccardo Redi, Giovanni Spagnoletti, and Bruno Torri), and the Museo Nazionale del Cinema (Alberto Barbera and Roberta Basano). The intellectual engagement of colleagues at UCLA has enriched and broadened the scope of my research. I would like to recognize in particular Phil Agre, Nick Browne, Marga Cottino-Jones, Anne Gililand, James Goodwyn, Lisa Kernan, Leah Lievrouw, Stephen Mamber, and Howard Suber. I thank Robert Rosen (dean of the School of Theater, Film, and Television) and Aimee Dorr (dean of the School of Education and Information Studies) for their unflagging encouragement and support. From early on, this book was gifted with elegant guidance from Mary Francis at the University of California Press.

There are too many people to adequately thank for their help. A partial list of the names (which blurs the distinction between colleagues and friends) includes Dudley Andrew, Toni and Giuliana Bizio, Giuliana Bruno, Emily Carman, Roberto Cecchini, Mariuccia Ciotta, Alberto Farassino, Dawn Fratini, Alan Gevinson, Sergio Grmek Germani, Marco Giusti, Armen Gurekian, Alex Kupfer, Vittorio Martinelli, Nicola Mazzanti, William McClain, Marco Müller, Kalicia

Pivirotto, Angela Prudenzi, Roberto Silvestri, Alberta Soranzo, and Piero Tortolina. The book benefited particularly from the insight and enthusiasm of Angela Dalle Vacche, Michael Friend, Giuliana Muscio, Eric Smoodin, and Vivian Sobchack. Geoffrey Nowell-Smith's close read of the early manuscripts and his counsel at various stages were essential ingredients in its gestation and birth.

Finally, the idea of such an undertaking was unthinkable without my family, my wife, Mannig Gurekian, and my son, Giovanni Ricci. I value their support above all else. Mannig redefines the very meaning of grace, and Giovanni's genuine curiosity inspires me endlessly.

POSTSCRIPT

Inevitably, projects such as this one must encounter both roadblocks that are part of intellectual inquiry and those that are not. My thanks go to all of the people who helped me overcome a full variety of challenges. Of my more recent tribulations, it would be strange, if not rude, to say nothing. Therefore, all my gratitude goes to the voices of support that I heard so very clearly during the months of June and July 2007.

How can one thank the staff of the Neurological ICU at UCLA? How can one thank anyone for their own life? To the staff of Barlow Respiratory Hospital, too, I have trouble expressing the depth of my appreciation.

INTRODUCTION

Italian cinema is one of the past century's most influential, artistically innovative, and politically engaged cultural forms. Since the inception of film studies, few other national cinemas have received as much sustained critical interest. It has served as a frequent site for mapping debates on cultural theory and has occasioned major theoretical investigations into issues such as the aesthetic properties of realism, cinema as artistic form, historical narration in relation to historical memory, art cinema, and concepts of authorship, cultural production, and ideology. That said, on perhaps no other terrain have the terms and conditions for such investigations shifted as radically as they have in the historical accounts of Italian cinema during the Fascist period.

Over the last six decades, the study of Italian cinema of the Fascist period (1922 to 1943) has undergone several paradigm shifts, each of which points to larger changes in critical and political cultures. The differences between contending schools of thought could not be more pronounced. At one extreme in the spectrum, a good portion of Italian cinema histories (written in the postwar period) seek to repress accounts of the cinema in relation to fascism. These studies paradoxically dismiss this historical relationship insofar as the national cinema in this period *must have been tainted* by its unavoidable association with the regime. Simply put, cinema during the time of fascism *was fascist* and, as such, unworthy of enlightened critical scrutiny. And yet, as I will discuss later on, repressed memories often return as structuring absences

1

that shape conceptions of historicity. In fact, even as early studies on Italian film history are sown with major lacunae and apparent paradoxes, such is the long-term impact of the experience of cinema under the Fascist state that its "presence" always remains just one step beyond the historiographic horizon.

At the other end of the spectrum, where fascism's influence is actually taken under consideration, certain more recent studies attempt to depoliticize the cinema's specific relationship to the regime through a nostalgic redemption of what is thought to be an unfairly condemned past. Thus, the Italian cinema was indeed tainted by its relationship to fascism—but only insofar as film history itself has ignored the period's actual artistic achievements. Underlying this approach is a conceptualization of culture that defines cinema as essentially pluralist and democratic since *quality* always supersedes *politics*. For these scholars, therefore, the historiographic error lies in the very notion of a "fascist" cinema, since great works of cinematic art cannot be reduced to any political or ideological judgment.

Both ends of the spectrum are informed by unresolved questions about the nature of Italian fascism and its cultural policies. One ongoing problem is that numerous definitions seek to reduce fascism to essentialist properties, ignoring both its internal contradictions and its dynamic evolution over time. How, for example, does one square the dictatorship under Mussolini with its German and Soviet counterparts? Was Italian fascism influenced more by a reactionary traditionalism or by aggressive "modern" social engineering? How do we reconcile the regime's antiurbanism with its massive investments in modern communication and transportation technologies? Did fascist culture mean monolithic and monumental aesthetics, or was it more opportunistically pluralist and eclectic? Over time, what balance did it achieve between the avant-gardist practices of futurism and the agrarian-based traditions of Italian folklore?

For previous generations of media scholarship, these troubling questions about fascism exist in a tension between *too little* and *too much* history. In cinema studies, the extraordinary distance between the two (almost epistemological) positions is embedded, for example, in the very titles of two symptomatic books. Whereas in 1952 Leopoldo Zurlo wrote *Memorie inutili: la censura teatrale nel ventennio (Useless Memories—Theatrical Censorship of the Twenty Black Years)*, by 1979 Adriano Aprà and Patrizia Pistagnesi were writing *The Fabulous Thirties!*[1] This tension presents us today with substantial challenges to the writing of a more nuanced picture of cinema over time. Although the cinema's ideological relationship to totalitarianism has been the subject of extensive study and major revisionist rethinking in the German and Soviet contexts, intriguing and largely unexplored questions about Italy remain. What agencies mediate between political and cultural practices? How do they act upon a government's attempts to regulate cinematic affairs and the cinema's *autonomous* production of film texts? And here, which historiographic models best account for both the economic and the ideological qualities of that regulation and that autonomy? In addition to traditional scrutiny of industrial practices, genre codifications, and institutional discourses, what other terms help us to periodize film history? For example, might shifting conditions of readership—that is, the manner in which audiences live their experiences of the cinema—provide explanatory force and clarity on a par with the more common categories?

What does it mean today to speak of a national cinema when so many aspects of a given national cultural experience include the inescapable presence of non-national productions? For example, we know that, with the exceptions of the United States and India, film exhibition in most countries is never dominated by locally produced titles. Indeed, how can we apply the very concept of national cinema in light of recent writings on globalization that militate against the concept of stable, unitary categories of nationality? This last question is of particular importance when we consider contemporary intellectual shifts in the study of nations, nationalisms, and national identities. One need only think, for example, of the spate of recent historical writing that is modeled upon Benedict Anderson's conceptual framework in *Imagined Communities*.[2]

To address these questions, this project examines the Italian cinematic institution from 1922 to 1943. Its core question is: what was the relationship between the rise of fascism and the experience of cinema in Italy? While the bulk of my analyses of film texts draws from the period 1929–43, I begin my account in 1922 because the early evolution of the film industry and the cultural forces at play in the twenties profoundly influence most aspects of Italian cinema in the thirties and early forties. And, starting in 1922, the state introduced social initiatives and cultural iconographies that formed a lexicon of images and imagined topoi that were the shared background of filmgoing throughout this entire twenty-year period. While 1922 signals the beginning of the fascist state, 1943 closes my period of study for a number of geopolitical and cultural reasons. All in the same year, Mussolini is forced from office, the Allies land in Sicily, and the Partisan movement takes hold. Moreover, Luchino Visconti's *Ossessione* (1943) provides a persuasive symbolic break with the previous organization of cultural life under the fascist regime.

In 1922, the Fascist party seized control of the Italian government. Whereas a fully formed "fascist" cinema did not spring up as an immediate consequence of this event, the development and implementation of fascist cultural policy are indispensable coordinates for any historical account of cinema in this period. The same year also coincides with a number of key economic and institutional changes in the Italian cinema industry. Specifically, the characteristics of the industry's crisis and virtual collapse in the very early twenties directly impact both the relatively slow introduction of sound technologies and the cinema's overall institutional reconstruction in the thirties—that is, what many historians refer to as the "rebirth" of Italian cinema.

The case of the Unione Cinematografica Italiana makes this point clear. Representing Italy's first attempt at industrial consolidation and vertical integration, the Unione Cinematografica Italiana (UCI) was founded in February 1919. UCI was a confederation of several major production companies, including Cines, Ambrosio, Caesar Film, and Tiber Film, that sought to deploy national strategies for film finance, distribution, and exhibition. Yet for many reasons it was unable to halt the industry's vertiginous decline in film production. One of the clearest reasons for its failure was the near-total disconnect between film production and exhibition. For example, less than half the total number of films produced in 1920 were actually released in either 1920 or 1921. Film production itself continuously declined for the next ten years. In 1931, only two feature-length Italian films were released, one of which had completed production in 1927.[3]

With the failure of the Unione Cinematografica Italiana in 1922 and its formal dissolution in 1923, it can be argued that the newly formed government inherited not only an industry in shambles, but also a virtually clean industrial slate. Given the cinema's anemic institutional base, the new state was in a potentially ideal position to radically reorganize the entire industry. At the same time, if the state were to seek such reorganization, one of the major factors that would have to be addressed was the massive presence of Hollywood cinema. The penetration of American films into the Italian marketplace, a process that began immediately after World War I, was in fact consolidated by the establishment of an MGM distribution office in Rome in 1923. The presence of American films in Italy informs not only Fascist cultural policy but also the textual practices of Italian cinematic production throughout the period.

One of the principal axes along which previous studies on fascism and film have been plotted is the continuity/discontinuity between the cinemas of the fascist and neorealist eras. This study, however, does not search out neorealist filmmaking practices in the interwar years.[4] Neither do I attempt to rehabilitate the period through a consideration of the period's better film authors. In larger historiographic terms, I try to avoid any reductive or determinist account that might simply equate cinema under fascism with "fascist cinema." Conversely, I intend to pursue an investigatory path that navigates between historiographic models that lead to either determinist explanations *(too much history)* or idealist ones *(too little)*. From this perspective, the political acquisition of state power by the Fascist party in 1922 would fundamentally alter the relationship between the cinema and its cultural context. One preliminary outcome of this alteration was the state's primary role in the reconstruction of the film industry after its precipitous decline in the early twenties. But even more importantly, this study addresses a necessarily complex dialectic between the single-party state, its cultural philosophy and practices, and cinema. I will argue that the social conditions within which films were read by Italian audiences offer a revealing perspective on all sides of this dialectic. I also hope to demonstrate that accounts of such conditions make for valuable conceptual tools with which to periodize cultural history in general.

The social experience of cinema during the interwar years participated in at least three major cultural paradoxes. First, while early Fascist philosophy embraced certain aspects of modernism, it also spoke through an antitheoretical and reactionary "historicism." As many of the regime's intellectuals put it: "Fascism makes history, it does not write it." At the start of the 1930s, the protofascist exaltation of action over theory gives way to stabilizing institutional policies and bureaucracies.[5] We see this transition, for example, in the transformation in the representation of Mussolini from a figure whose moral authority emanated from various demonstrations of strength and virility to one whose stature derives from his skill as an international statesman. Second, the fascist state theoretically possessed immense authority to regulate cultural production, but appears to have applied that authority in less than totalitarian ways. Critics and historians are surprised, therefore, by the extremely limited representation of state officials, uniforms, and monuments in the period's fiction films and equally by the state's modest application of censorship laws. Thus such scholars expected fascist culture to be a repressive, panoptic prison house but were confounded by the commercial cinema's appearance as a pleasure palace. Third, while many fascist writings articulated an extreme opposition to pluralist mass culture, the state clearly, through both economic and institutional practices, supported the production of a popular, genre-based film industry. There is, therefore, a continuous asymmetry between the state's general propositions about the role of culture and the state's specific support of a commercial cinema. In one particularly important context, for example, the cinema had to navigate between the state's ideological predilection for cultural autonomy (and later, its xenophobia) and the actual presence of foreign cultural sources.

This last contradiction compellingly illustrates the complexity of the dialectic between Italian cinema and government practices. A mainstay of Italian fascist political economy was its drive for *autarchy,* that is, for economic self-sufficiency and independence from foreign cultural influence. The question of autarchy is a particularly revelatory site for tracking the explicit relationship between fascist economic and cultural discourses. For example, the Fascist regime explained its invasion of Ethiopia in 1936 in terms of Italy's economic need to extract basic raw materials. The regime then attempted to justify the satisfaction of Italy's economic need for self-sufficiency by orchestrating a multisite ideological campaign that depicted African culture as naturally inferior. The "civilizing" character of Italy's colonialism depended upon essentialist formulations on the home front, of a hypothetically indigenous, noncomposite, and pure Italian national culture. The regime's political propaganda also sought to justify its expanded territorial claims by invoking other traditions of European colonialism. In a word, if the English empire could extend its dominion over a non-Western map, then certainly Italy could lay legitimate claim, if not to a modern Roman Empire, then at least to a new *mare nostrum.*[6]

And yet throughout the *ventennio nero* (literally, the "twenty black years") the Italian cultural landscape remained heavily populated by the visible presence of American, English, French, and German cultures. In the cinema, almost two-thirds of the films seen by Italian audiences during the fascist period were foreign titles. How do we explain the totalitarian regime's apparent neglect of this fundamental imbalance? In other words, how can we speak of a nationally specific Italian cinema under fascism when most of what cinema audiences saw wasn't produced locally?

Such evident contradictions make it crucial to take into account the entire network of cultural practices within which both film production and viewing took place. Andrew Higson's seminal article on the construction of national film histories is particularly insightful on this point:

> To explore national cinema in these terms means laying much greater stress on the point of consumption, and on the *use* of film (sounds, images, narratives, fantasies), than on the point of production. It involves a shift in emphasis away from the analysis of film texts as vehicles for the articulation of nationalist sentiment and the interpellation of the implied national spectator, to an analysis of how actual audiences construct their cultural identity in relation to the various products of the national and international film and television industries, and the conditions under which this is achieved.[7]

Higson's suggested focus on consumption in the context of both national and international industries leads us away both from the purely economic or determinist models *(too much history)* and from apolitical interpretations of film texts that are fundamentally polysemic, are, that is, texts that construct potentially endless chains of meanings, without accounting for the material, social practices through which such meanings are encoded and decoded *(too little history)*. My study, therefore, is not intended as a chronological history of the period's films. Rather, it describes the key cultural practices and discourses surrounding these films that suggest a range of socially distributed heuristic codes for their reading. I contend that the cinema experience in the period was indeed fascist *in the manner* and *to the extent* that the state's intervention into cultural affairs regulated processes of reading. As such, I offer a historical account of the relationship between such codes and the construction of the social authority specific to fascism.

The concept of *reading* is at the core of our approach and, as a complex matter for critical theory in general, requires some explanation. It usually leads to extensive considerations of both the production of specific meanings through *interpretation* and the positioning of subjects through processes of *identification*. But for the purposes of this project, I use it here in a different sense and draw particularly from the theoretical frameworks provided by Mikhail Bakhtin and Michel de Certeau.[8] I mean it to describe the processes engaged in by audiences/subjects in order to bind together references (figures, exclamations, citations, and allusions) both inside a given text and between that text and other sites of cultural production. In this way *reading* is not employed as an explanation of the cognitive processes whereby audiences come to understand specific meanings. Instead it traces how the fluid network of connections between references affects—that is, how it expands or delimits—a range of possible understandings. The approach also suggests that insofar as these connections are compiled by real audiences over time, the *network* of connections is describable in material, historical terms.

My concept of readership comes from a particular tradition in reception studies. Janet Staiger summarizes this tradition in the following way: "It is not a way of interpreting works but an attempt to understand their changing intelligibility by identifying the codes and interpretive assumptions that give them meaning for different audiences at different periods. Another way of putting it is that reception studies try to explain an event (the interpretation of a film), while textual studies are working towards elucidating an object (the film)."[9]

Keeping in mind the distinction between interpreting and intelligibility, context-activated readership (as opposed to either text- or reader-activated readership) has three historical requirements. To begin with, competent or coherent reading requires that audiences recognize the topology of filmic texts. This is not merely a question of mimesis, of how given texts may or may not *look like* the pre-filmic world, but instead speaks to levels and types of familiarities. Thus, since Italian audiences in this period were not familiar with the iconography of the Western, for example, since images of the American frontier were not available within locally produced mappings, the films could only be read by taking up positions of curiosity or fascination regarding an imagined other. This is not to say that transnational figurations such as "the frontier," "the trail," and "the showdown" were entirely unintelligible to these audiences. It does suggest, however, that disparities between condensed textual representations and lexicons of available discourses outside of given texts significantly alter the background for readership and thus for interpretation.

Next, while individuals, however prepared (one could say *preconditioned*), can interpret textual meanings within almost limitless ranges, readership is a shared, collective activity. Interpretations by individuals are only almost limitless; they are limited because audiences, tied together by (at least) class and gender, agree upon a range of common readings. In his work on national audiences in Great Britain, David Morley describes the social differences between collective and individual reading: "The audience must be conceived of as composed of clusters of socially situated individual readers, whose individual readings will be framed by shared cultural formations and practices preexistent to the individual: shared 'orientations' which will in turn be determined by factors derived from the objective position of the individual reader in the class structure."[10]

Finally, readership positions can change very quickly. On the one hand, text-oriented accounts of meaning production insist on the malleability of certain representations. Thus the historian is surprised and challenged by the seemingly endless possibilities for interpretation given that texts themselves are fundamentally open.[11] Positions of readership are therefore always in flux and unfixable. On the other hand, the connection between the "objective position of the individual reader" and even quite malleable texts is dynamically informed by particular cultural practices over time. In addition to matters of class and gender, the relationship between reader and text is indeed dynamic but is also traceable to conditions of social organization and discourse that evolve over briefer periods of time. As we will see later on, the cinema and other arts rapidly transmogrified the representation of Mussolini. In a little under ten years, Mussolini morphs from the revolutionary leader of *squadrismo* into the highest representative of the Italian state, often compared on an international plane to figures such as Theodore Roosevelt. By 1928, Mussolini biographer and art critic for the fascist newspaper *Il Popolo,* Margherita Sarfatti asserted his greatness as statesman by comparing it to that of several generations of French political leaders: "Benito Mussolini is carrying out a gargantuan task that in France required the combined efforts of a great dynasty of many men of genius (from Louis XI through Richelieu, Mazarin, Colbert, and Louis XIV through Napoleon I, Haussmann, and Napoleon III). By mobilizing every possible means and all the nation's forces, he is making Italy aware of its unity and moral greatness through her capital's architectural unity and material greatness."[12]

This evolution of representational strategies takes place *at the same time* that early Fascist street tactics begin to disappear and the more civically oriented state programs begin to be implemented (social engineering of family practices, land reclamations, massive urban renewal projects, etc.). Taken together, the textual and the pretextual changes induce a shift in positions of collective readership, specifically from admiration of the heroic to adulation of the cultic.

Having stipulated that the text/reader relationship is based on recognizability, collectivity, and dynamism, how do we arrive at audiences' interpretations of what films mean to them? Here, Stuart Hall's explanation of the movement from readership to interpretation, as a communication process that is characterized by encoding (textually) and decoding (by audiences), continues to be useful. For Hall and other members of British cultural studies, the encoding/decoding process creates three basic kinds of readership: dominant/hegemonic, negotiated, and globally contrary or oppositional.[13] While this early formulation has been heavily criticized, given that it is possible to theorize readership positions in addition to only these three,[14] the basic idea that specific readings are limited by a finite number of historical conditions is extremely important. As Hall puts it:

> Any society or culture tends, with varying degrees of closure, to impose its classifications of the social and cultural and political world. . . . The different areas of social life appear to be mapped out onto discursive domains, hierarchically organized into *dominant or preferred meanings.* . . . The domains of "preferred readings" have the whole of the social order embedded in them as a set of meanings, practices, and beliefs; the everyday knowledge of social structures, of "how things work for all practical purposes in this culture," the rank order of power and interest and the structures of legitimations, limits and sanctions.[15]

The limits placed on positions for reading, what Hall defines as "frameworks of knowledge," constitute the historical *conditions of readership.* These (pre)conditions precede individual decodings. They are the (back)ground to the production of texts and include everything from authorial intent and craftsmanship to institutional and economic policy. They are the (fore)ground through which audiences decode the produced texts. Conditions of readership are the terms that are available in *both* texts and the visual worlds of Italian culture during the fascist period. In metaphorical terms, they make up a figural map with many of its coordinates already filled in, but without predetermined itineraries. These conditions serve to organize a view of the fascist world by giving it a history of foundational elements, articulating a system of values, and showing how these two interoperate. For the purposes of our present study, the core question becomes *upon which authorities do these conditions rely?*

This particular approach has the benefit of entirely bypassing the epistemological trap often encountered in accounts of purely textual constructions of meaning. By emphasizing the fluidity of networks of references, we can avoid a formalist orientation that recognizes meanings as the mechanized results of internal textual processes, on the one hand, and the antiformalist (postmodernist) orientation that explodes texts into an infinity of possible readings on the other hand. Robin Pickering-Iazzi's evaluation of de Certeau's work is particularly on point:

> Of equal importance, particularly in examining an authoritarian regime that sought to manage cultural life, are what Michel de Certeau calls "unsigned" forms of production. His theoretical paradigm enables us to examine everyday practices—of reading, using spaces, film viewing, or self-fashioning—in order to achieve an understanding of the different ways the *bricoleur* may implement, manipulate, or thwart the signs put at her or his disposal by dominant groups. . . . For example, impromptu plays on words, jokes, and changing the lyrics to songs constitute cultural production that . . . disrupt the symbolic order and the power relations authorizing it.[16]

Within this framework, it is possible, then, to locate textual codes that both converge upon and diverge from fascist political authority. My account of the cinema under fascism, of how its meanings were encoded and decoded, elucidates *both* parts of the equation—that is, the terms of consensus building and conformism alongside the potential for resistant readings and opposition. If we accept that it is both textual practices and a contextual cultural milieu that contribute to a given film's reading, which cultural sources do fascist-era films invoke? Which protocols are drawn upon in order to coordinate the interaction of the film text and extra-filmic discourse? (As I will demonstrate later, Bakhtin's notions of *intertextuality* and *chronotope* will be particularly useful critical tools.) If such an interaction constructs a range of coherent readings—proposing some, attempting to limit others—what are the authorities for such protocols? On what political and sexual discourses do they depend for their currency with audiences? What role, then, did the Fascist state play in the public erection and circulation of a hierarchy of texts and contexts? Finally, how can one characterize the convergences and divergences, the points of contact, denial, and exchange between a fascist rhetoric of social organization and the textual rhetoric, the modes of address and figural strategies within Italian cinema?

My project begins by retracing received wisdoms about Italian cinema history. Chapter 1 examines the manner in which many writings on that history fear and ultimately repress knowledge of that cinema's relationship to fascism. I then suggest that a set of largely unexplored institutional and economic practices through which that relationship was constructed can instead broaden our understanding of the cinema *and* of political history. I will argue that, in the context of Italy's belated industrialization and modernization, the cinema played a central role in the transformation of the public sphere.[17] In support of this hypothesis, I describe the historical framework within which the cinematic institution first attempted to address spectators, to construct its audience, and to articulate the ideological contradictions of public life. In a word, parallel to its modernization from 1910 to 1914, the Italian cinema sought to construct nothing less than a historical etymology for the newly formed nation state. And, for the Fascist state specifically, the attempt to build and maintain a theoretically unified national consciousness would be one of its highest priorities. Where its social policies attempted to fuse private and public life, the regime's cinema policies would seek to efface local issues, that is, to erect a national industry that could suppress the cultural markers of social difference.[18]

The question of its relationship to modernism has long been a central point of debate in the study of fascism.[19] In film studies, James Hay's work offers a particularly insightful set of considerations on how the institutional organization of Italian cinema, especially in the thirties, was a response to modernization. My approach differs from Hay's inasmuch as he concentrates on the more long-term processes, the *longue durée* of modernization—that is, on the circulation of mythologies that were present both before and after Italian fascism. Such historical framing has the potential to veer away from an analysis of the specifically fascist response to these processes. Thus, Italy under Fascism may have responded to the same contradictions, *and in the same ways,* as Italy did in the two decades prior to the installation of the totalitarian state. Hay introduces his critical focus as follows: "I intend instead to investigate a cultural form which at that historical moment most vividly highlighted these tensions and enabled those in Italy most affected by modernization to cope with the highly unstable nature of their cultural foundation. Although I do not wish to ignore the regime's attempts to mobilize a popular culture, I prefer to examine the complex field of cultural codes and techniques through which political and other varieties of social action and performance occurred and through which they could be envisioned."[20]

After analysis of both early and more contemporary Italian film studies, I investigate the specific institutional preconditions, the prehistory, of the state's entrance into cinematic affairs. By providing a particular vision of the country's past, the cinema helped to identify the cultural terrain upon which an Italian national identity might be circulated. In the second decade of the twentieth century, the cinema both introduced new terms and recycled previous terms of reference for that hypothetical identity. In addition, the manner in which the cinema addressed prior cultural sources effectively privileged it as *the* agency for the construction of a national civic consciousness. Not only was the film industry informed by the specifically political agenda of the country's delayed unification, it also helped to overdetermine the Italian public sphere as unavoidably political. And although the fascist organization of these processes was hegemonically consolidated during the early thirties, the legacy of their overall institutional effects continued to condition much of cinematic practice well after World War II.

The apparent asymmetry between fascist cultural theory and its institutional policies regarding the cinema requires explanation. Chapter 2 outlines the history of the specific institutional relationship between the Italian cinema and the Fascist state. When the Fascist party came to power in 1922, it inherited a cinema industry in full economic and institutional decline. As a single-party totalitarian regime, with seemingly unlimited political discretion over cultural affairs, Italian Fascism provides a revelatory and unobstructed view of a particular national response to the larger, global processes of modernization. In 1926, for example, the government created a monopoly over nonfiction film production and distribution by establishing the Istituto LUCE, a state-owned newsreel and documentary agency. As the sole producer of documentary and newsreel images, the regime set about engineering its own representation. Since through censorship the regime theoretically also regulated all cinematic representation, it could be argued (to use Althusserian terms) that fascism functioned as both ideological *and* repressive state apparatus. Althusser's distinction between ideological and repressive state apparatus is useful because it provides a single theoretical framework that contains the full range of mechanisms in which the new state acquires and applies power through cultural practices. That is, this distinction allows us to account for what might seem to be the internal contradictions of a given state and to see them instead as sets of institutional practices that are coherent aspects of that state's overall goals as they evolve over time.[21]

These unmediated circumstances provide an excellent vantage point from which we can view the fascist cinematic position vis-à-vis Italy's rapid industrialization. Was fascist cultural policy able to reconcile Italian political and economic modernization with what has been described as the epistemological disruption engendered by modernity? That is, how could the state seek to construct a single national identity that would contain both the values of a modern society and those of Italy's traditionally regional, agrarian society? How might it have simultaneously produced both the pleasure palace and the panopticon in culture? In other words, could the regime, as ideological state apparatus, extract modernism from its very own program of rapid expansion and industrialization?

This chapter also hypothesizes that the industrial organization and ideological regulation of the cinema were characterized principally by processes of exchange and mediation between the cinematic institution and two dominant authorial agencies: fascism itself on the one hand, and the Hollywood cinema on the other. Fascist cultural practices and the pervasive presence of American culture were two of the most visible components of the social lexicon available to audiences during the period. They are inextricably linked together in the *repressive* formation of state censorship guidelines and the state's political economy vis-à-vis cinema. They are also linked in the *nonrepressive* expressions of an ideal cinema—of what that cinema should look like, what it should say, for which purposes, and to which audiences. This ideal for the Italian cinema was articulated in nongovernmental discourse through the period's film criticism, the awards bestowed at the Venice Biennale, and even the characteristically American industrial model upon which the country's national film studio, Cinecittà, was built. In its own official discourse, the fascist regime's discussions of film and film policy also insistently referred to Hollywood films and to Hollywoodian industrial practices. For these reasons, we designate Fascism and Hollywood as two dominant authorial agencies. The state, Mussolini, and Hollywood were the paradigmatic authorities for both cultural production and reading in the period. Here I would like to suggest that, decades prior to the implosion of the concept of the unitary nation-state that was brought about through postcolonial theorizing of nationhood, these two putatively national cinemas cannot be separated from one another.

National film histories, even when distinguished by two governmental bodies as dissimilar as Italian fascism and United States liberal democracy, have always also been both inter- and intranational.

The following chapters analyze the structures of individual film texts in relationship to fascist social organization. They do not seek only to ascertain the extent to which the films might reflect a hypothetically stable fascist ideology. Instead, I will describe the organization of filmic texts, the extra-filmic discourses that it invokes, and both social structures and cultural practices in which the films are embedded. Each analysis attempts to build a map of intertextualities, of Bahktinian "chronotopes," in order to excavate the premises upon which readings were based. Thus my analyses describe exchanges of information and knowledges between the films and other discrete discursive sites. As a whole, they attempt to place Italian cinema within the culture-wide, transnational production and regulation of a specifically fascist heuristics.

Chapter 3 begins by examining representations of the body in the strongman cycle during the twenties. Here, the notion of action (as a purifying moral force) draws on futurist and protofascist nationalist philosophies. As we will see, this cycle of films reenacts fascist physical culture and sports. Over time, the intertextual relationship between these films and their social counterpart would evolve. By the end of the decade, the essentialist and antihistoricist impulses of the strongman cycle come to an apparently abrupt halt. They are replaced, however, by a particular resurrection of the historical epic.[22] While both the early cycle and the traditional historical genre focus on the organization of bodies in fictive spaces, the former focuses on the body as site of performance and the latter on the gathering of multiple bodies for the production of mass spectacles. What is crucial to underline is that the reappearance of the epic form takes place at the same time that fascism resolves internal contradictions within the party and definitively consolidates its control over Italian government. In dialogical terms, this historical political turn is encapsulated by the manner in which the (new) historical narration proposes to its audiences a historical teleology of fascism as manifest destiny.

The second part of chapter 2 places film texts alongside the state's organization of leisure time and looks specifically at representations of travel and tourism. Unlike the historical epic, the films I investigate in this context are clearly recognizable as popular culture and entertainment. Less overtly political than films that announce the historiographic projects of fascist philosophy, these films nonetheless chart the terms and boundaries of class identity. Here, participation in particular social strata and the general limits to social mobility focus specifically on moments/tropes of transition between the basic groupings of contemporary Italian society. Situating major narrative events in trains, cruise ships, and buses, each of these films overlays geographic travel upon movement between social strata. As with many classical Hollywood narratives, these films momentarily dislodge characters from an initial collocation in class precisely in order to return them to *where they belong:* that is, to a restabilized social order framed by an idealized family. In certain ways, the only significant intertextual difference from Hollywood is that *the departure* and *the return* in these films are achieved through the fictive evocation of the state's real organization of tourism. Since Italian audiences of this period were also likely participants in that nontextual tourism, I will suggest that this particular overlay of texts and social practices is a potentially fertile ground for oppositional readings. In the case of *Treno popolare* (Rafaello Materazzo, 1933), for example, the state could subsidize leisure-time travel but might not have been able to restrict all playful (and particularly sexual) behaviors.

Chapter 4 addresses the problem of autarchy by placing Italian filmmaking practices under fascism in their relationship to the Hollywood cinema. I begin by postulating that any cultural mapping of the fascist/Italian world had also to accommodate what was outside of "our" world. In a word, how would the basic conditions of reading achieve a balance between idealized national (self) and international (other) imaginaries? Through the textual analyses in this chapter, I propose at least three partial answers. First, the two industries were economically interdependent. Second, the two cinemas often worked in a "limited" partnership in producing the ideological effects of an overall cinema experience that was specific to this period. So, for example, it is not true (as some historians have suggested) that Italian audiences were never presented with representations of criminality during the period. When historians note this apparent absence, it is too easily explained as a result of state censorship. The fact is, however, that crimes and criminals did populate the cinema experienced by the period's audiences. It's just that either they were located in entirely invented countries or, more often, they were to be found exclusively on American soil. Thus the combined, imagined map did indeed include the kind of dystopian images that are normally associated with neorealism and the postwar period. More importantly, the figurative displacement of crime away from the Italian map served to rearticulate the state's utopian vision of an "indigenous" fascist order. Third, the institutional partnership between the Italian state and the Hollywood film industry was also lived as an extraordinary (intra)textual dialogue between the two cultures. That is, audiences viewed Italian productions within the context of a particularly thick knowledge of Hollywood. Given the economic interdependence, it might be argued that American figured as a friendly "other." At the same time, however, the Italian star system and some Italian films (particularly those directed by Mario Camerini in the thirties) also competed for position with local audiences. The question to pursue is whether or not American culture represented a substantial threat to (a crack in) fascist cultural hegemony. Put another way, could reading certain Italian films, fully activated by a fascination with Hollywood (and a mythical America), also provide the ground for resistant or oppositional positions to the fascist mainstream?

This project concerns the relationship between cinema and its political and cultural contexts. It investigates the very way in which we study such relationships through the particular case of the Italian cinema from 1922 to 1943. In chapter 5, I propose two general findings, one centrifugal and one centripetal. First, the nature and timing of the regime's interventions into cinema were heavily influenced by the industrial conditions that it inherited, by the logic of its internal marketplace, and by the requirements of the fascist corporatist state. Second, even within the context of a totalitarian regime, the overall organization of the cinema evolved over time and was always also transnational. Viewing films during the period was also predicated upon external, international intertextualities, most often personified by the American "other." Thus the dynamic interaction between (local) institutional practices and (globalized) conditions of readership enable us to describe, not only the long-term evolution of Italian national cinema, but also a specifically fascist cinematic experience. This concluding section summarizes the results of the preceding textual analyses in order to describe a range of codes, a historical codex, for reading cinema under fascism.

If it is useful to periodize cinema history in terms of such materially produced reading codes, how might such an approach lead to future research into the history of this and other cinemas? For example, we are led to ask how these codes changed with the dissolution of the fascist state and the arrival of neorealist film culture. Rather than once again trying to untangle the question of neorealism's complicated formal similarities to certain filmmaking practices from the twenties and thirties, it becomes much more suggestive to ask if the basic coordinates of readership were entirely obliterated or merely updated during Italy's postwar reconstruction. In a word, what was left of the fascist cinema's institutional role in addressing and forming new audiences? As we will see through our discussion of post- and antifascist culture, the answer is quite complex. On the one hand, postfascist Italian cinema bears *some* unmistakable marks of both the internal and the external conditions that were produced during the years of the regime. On the other hand, such markers may also point towards the potential coordinates for resistance and opposition in even the contemporary Italian mediascape.

The epilogue describes a remarkable instance of film readership from well after the fascist and neorealist periods. Here, we include an account of the 1980s film programs known collectively as the *estate romana* (the Roman summer) in order to underscore the country's persistent engagement with how audiences decode texts both culturally and politically and within both local and global cultural frameworks. The *estate romana* invited Italian audience/publics to reappropriate Roman history and to interrogate their own fascination with Hollywood film. As a prelude to a future study, I suggest that questions of resistance to and reappropriation of dominant cultural paradigms are particularly relevant to the contemporary setting, that is, to the massive consolidation of media ownership that has occurred over the past two decades. At the very least, the centralization of media control by Silvio Berlusconi's Mediaset and his government's regulation of state communications call out for additional critical scrutiny.

In this context, our attention is drawn back to the book's cover image, a poster from the 1931 sound version of Giovanni Pastrone's classic *Cabiria* (1914). The poster's prototypical strongman, Bartolomeo Pagano, bears a striking likeness to Benito Mussolini. But when one considers the more recent suppression of diversity in media expressions under the Berlusconi government, yet another resemblance seems to surface.

ONE

AMNESIA AND HISTORICAL MEMORY

Constructed in this key, fascism *is* modernization; it represents motion forward along a global continuum rather than
an aberrant, ideological regression. But in order to survive
under the new rules developed between the two wars, Italy
obsessively directed energy toward its own so-called autarchic position in the global economy through a campaign that
specifically effaced the international crisis. Thus, producing
and consuming bodies represent themselves as specific to an
Italian national context even though the graphic design styles
may derive from an international, modernist one.

Karen Pinkus, *Bodily Regimes:*
Italian Advertising under Fascism

"SOULLESS SHADOWS":
THE CINEMA UNDER FASCISM DIDN'T EXIST

It is a paradox that the study of Italian cinema from 1922 to 1943 re-
presses historical knowledge of the relationship between that cinema—
its texts and institutional practices—and political life.[1] In fact, until
the late 1970s, most national film histories conscientiously ignored
virtually everything which fell in between the acclaimed international
successes of a few Italian silent film epics and the critical esteem afforded to neorealist films after the Second World War. In other words,
there was an almost forty-year gap within the body of scholarly writing about the history of Italian films. As a consequence, films which
followed Giovanni Pastrone's *Cabiria* (1914) and preceded Luchino
Visconti's *Ossessione* (1943) have received very little critical scrutiny.

The sparse critical attention which actually has been dedicated to this in-between period routinely relegates the period's films to two theoretically simplistic categories, as either escapism or propaganda. Even more telling, the whole of the period's cinematic production presented historians with an epistemological choice between these mutually exclusive categories. Either the films did not overtly articulate the social problems of Italian life during the period (escapist), or they spoke of those problems from the exclusive perspective of the fascist state (propaganda). Thus escapism was seen to preclude oppositional reading and to encourage conformism. Blocked from a film's relationship to other textual sites and to relevant social discourses lying outside the specific fiction or genre, the audience is deprived of the means to effect alternative readings or to derive unexpected pleasures. Propaganda, on the other hand, could only produce hegemonic reading and was seen therefore as a primary tool for the construction of ideological consensus. In these cases, the audience is blocked from the possibility of playful or even disrespectful reading, since in theory the didactic authority for the narrativization of *real events* would never be called into question. Of course, one of the most serious drawbacks to this particularly harsh either/or is that it is predicated on an idealized notion of the audience as unified, monolithic, and willing. Neither category leaves room for the possibility of the audience's misreading these texts, whether for purposeful, for tactical, or simply for serendipitous reasons.

Pierre Leprohon, whose *The Italian Cinema* had for many years served as an international standard history of Italian film, for example, accounts for this entire period of cinema history in a singularly brief passage—less than twenty-five pages to sum up close to thirty years of film making. At the same time, Leprohon deploys close to two hundred pages to deal with the immediate postwar period. In addition, the book draws heavily from a group of previous Italian film histories, which similarly dedicate relatively cursory attention to the period. Leprohon depends almost exclusively upon accounts written in the 1950s and eschews consultation of documents, reviews, and historical and critical writing from either before or during the fascist period.[2]

The lack of historiographic rigor in these studies on the cinema during the fascist era stems, in part, from the way these works evaluate that cinema's aesthetic achievements. For example, Leprohon summarily dismisses the entire period in the following manner: "All in all the achievements of the Fascist cinema did not amount to much;

though more films were produced, they were mainly trifles in the style invented by Camerini, who continued to lead this field."[3] While Mario Camerini (and Alessandro Blasetti) serve as heavily qualified exceptions to what Leprohon sees as a predominantly insignificant period of cinematic malaise, he goes on to cite Carlo Lizzani as authority on the remainder of the period's filmmakers: "Dutiful camp followers such as Bragaglia, Mattoli, Brignone, Gallone and so on blurred the direct onslaught of out and out propaganda films with a smokescreen of white telephones and mawkish romance. . . . It seems unbelievable that at a time of worldwide suffering there was such a proliferation of films as non-existent, as empty and as alien to the national identity as our 'commercial' films of those years. . . . They were full of gesticulating, soulless shadows speaking a language which would be quite incomprehensible today."[4]

Such totalizing negative evaluations are also based upon extremely casual research into the evolution of the film industry and certainly did not involve systematic revisiting of the films. And yet, the cinema experience was extraordinarily vital for Italian audiences and, as we will see later, consistently represented the largest percentage of personal expenditures on culture throughout the period. The descriptions and accounts of individual texts often draw on the historian's recollection of his or her original and long-past viewings. These two decades were famously referred to as the period of the "white telephone" film, yet this dismissive judgment was formed without sustained scrutiny of the films themselves, their textual and ideological complexities. Indeed, the place of the "white telephone" film itself in the period's genre cinema is left almost entirely unexamined. Though this kind of popular genre by no means declares an intention to explicitly address issues of national identity, just how they are embedded within the social and sexual politics of the period has rarely been considered. It is for this reason that the language spoken by these "soulless shadows," as Lizzani put it, remains incomprehensible.

Perhaps even more importantly, most of the standard works on the cinema under fascism also treat the period's films as informed by what is seen as a determining collusion between the single-party state apparatus and the cinema. That is, the films either willingly conformed to or unknowingly reflected the political interests of the fascist regime. Thus, Giuseppe Ferrara, for example, offers the following reductionist historical explanation of the latter half of the period: "In 1934 the Direzione Generale per la Cinematografia was created, through whose doors passed every film project to be realized. In this way, after the release of *Il capello a tre punte,* a period of squalid conformism was initiated."[5] The Direzione Generale per la Cinematografia was a sub-ministerial national agency charged with the development and application of both economic and censorship policies vis-à-vis the cinema. It first came under the purview of the Ministry of Corporations and later under the Ministry of Press and Propaganda. The film referred to, *Il capello a tre punte,* was directed by Mario Camerini and released in 1935. It starred famed Neapolitan actor Edoardo De Filippo in the role of a governor of Naples under Spanish rule. Among other things, fascist officials were unhappy about its presentation of corruption in local government. After viewing the film, Mussolini himself ordered the cutting out of scenes depicting popular unrest over that corruption.

The unquestioned theoretical basis for this type of account is itself revealing. The oversimplification of the relationship between the state and the cinema hints at the social roots for one form of what could certainly be termed historical amnesia. The majority of the traditional Italian cinema histories were written in the 1950s and 1960s in parallel to the country's precipitous rise in the number of film festivals, cine clubs, and film journals. Throughout these two decades, critical investigations into cinema were dominated largely by discussions of divergent theories for realism in world cinema and by debate on the practices, importance, and future of neorealism in Italian cinema. The debate was carried out in film conferences, newspaper editorials, and political manifestoes and can be clearly resurrected from articles published in the two central film journals: *Bianco e Nero* and *Cinema Nuovo.*[6] And early on, the majority of its participants—film critics, political figures, historians, theoreticians, and filmmakers—came to a general agreement on at least one major issue: that neorealism represented a definitive rupture with that *soulless and squalid* past.

That past was identified, however, not with the experience of World War II and the need for social and economic reconstruction in the postwar years, but with the twenty previous years of fascist rule. Throughout the critical debate in the fifties and sixties, neorealism's past was bracketed not only by the rise and fall of the fascist regime but also by a set of aesthetic practices of a cinema which (it was assumed) must have been controlled by fascism. In this way, the discussions and writings about neorealism themselves attempted to participate in that same cultural break with the past. That is to say, having articulated an *evidently* fundamental discontinuity between the cinema under fascism and contemporary Italian filmmaking, very few studies ever sought out neorealism's cinematic antecedents. Any possible influence exerted by the "fascist" cinema on subsequent filmmaking practices was to be theoretically excluded from the discussion insofar as it might endanger the cultural and political breaks with fascism. For Lizzani, Ferrara, Leprohon, and many others, Italian cinema of the twenties and thirties had to be ignored since it was a cultural manifestation of a univocal conformity with the ideological identity of fascism, an identity that had been overthrown politically by the war and the resistance movement and culturally by neorealism itself.[7]

While it is clear that their historiographic methodologies are problematic in and of themselves, it is important to note that they also have social roots. Such frameworks are mediated by a nationwide desire in postwar Italian society to overcome the experience of fascism by repressing a memory of it. In other words, in taking a closer second look at films from the *ventennio nero,* the cultural autonomy and political integrity of the neorealist project itself might be placed at risk. And, in the often partisan political context of cultural debate in postwar Italy, a serious investigation into the specific characteristics of popular culture during fascism could incur the political liabilities of guilt by cultural association. Therefore, in this particular social context, any methodology which could have brought historians to look closely at cultural production during the fascist period would have ironically risked ideological contamination by the very subject of its study.[8]

This particular form of historical amnesia had a very real and significant effect on Italian film culture in the fifties, the sixties, and most of the seventies. By undercutting the potential validity of studying the period's films, these histories were a major factor in repressing general cultural interest in them. In the absence of an overriding mandate to look at the films, the copies languished unpreserved within the vaults of Italian archives.[9] Despite the virtual explosion of film clubs and festivals during the sixties, those films that still existed in relatively good shape were certainly never presented for public consideration.

The nature of Italian cultural studies underwent a major transformation in the early 1970s. A series of new histories began to propose a radical revision of the traditional methodologies and their accepted wisdoms. In cinema studies, the key works for such a revision were Gian Piero Brunetta's *Storia del cinema italiano: 1895–1945* and Aldo Bernardini's three-volume *Cinema muto italiano: arte, divismo e mercato.*[10] Where the previous generations of film scholarship placed severe limits on what could or should be studied, Brunetta and Bernardini dramatically expanded both the scope and the fields of information for Italian cinema study.

By way of simple quantitative comparison to that previous generation: the *Storia del cinema* dedicates over 250 pages to the cinema in the fascist era alone. As historiography, Brunetta's work is also compelling for its extensive inclusion of heterogeneous cultural sources that were new to the field of Italian film study. Some of *Storia del cinema*'s chapter headings, for example, include "The Star System," "The Origins of Criticism," "The Birth and Development of Narrative," "The Politics of the Institutions," "The Catholics and Cinema," and "The Work of the Literati." And while film texts lie at the center of Brunetta's account, he also traces the evolution of these wider cultural and political contexts in relation to the films themselves. Another way of putting this is that Brunetta's work not only takes into consideration a large number of films ignored by previous Italian film historians, he corrects that historical amnesia by locating them within their specific cultural and historical contexts.

Another key moment in the transformation of Italian cultural studies occurred in 1974 with the tenth Mostra Internazionale del Nuovo Cinema. Located in Pesaro, the Nuovo Cinema initiatives have long been an important meeting ground for filmmakers, critical theorists, and historians. This particular edition crystallized a renewed interest in the Italian cinema during the interwar years by presenting films from that period, most of which simply had not been seen in public for the previous three decades. Showing these films signaled a turning point in Italian film culture because it literally made it possible to begin a systematic excavation of an entire generation of films and filmmakers. Since then, there have been dozens of conferences and retrospectives of pre-neorealist sound films in Italy. Renewed efforts at their cataloguing, preservation, and restoration by the five major Italian film archives and, more importantly, the removal of the cultural/political taboo that had surrounded these films, culminated in a 1987 RAI (Italian state television) national broadcast of over forty "fascist" titles. Whereas the 1987 RAI retrospective was surrounded by wraparound panel discussions in which historians and critics emphasized the value of these films as historical documents, today the films are broadcast as entirely unproblematic entertainment. On the rare occasion that additional contextualizing information is still provided, such information ironically constitutes commercial appropriation of a forgotten history.

Figure 1. Early Pesaro conference: Alberto Lattuada, Mino Argentieri, Pier Paolo Pasolini, and Gianni Toti (circa 1967). Courtesy of the Mostra del Nuovo Cinema.

Current interstitial material for this kind of programming speaks of the films as *vintage* objects from an unspecified past, as objects that have now lost their tainted political charge.

The initial impulse for the Pesaro group's overall project of reevaluation had been the question of the continuity or discontinuity between fascist cinema and neorealism. The principal goal of the conference and film retrospective had been to establish the terms for a systematic and unencumbered reexamination of neorealism and its cultural project. A number of the papers presented, however, broached the subject of the cultural debt that neorealism owed to the previous generation of films and filmmakers. These presentations traced stylistic, aesthetic, and even ideological affinities between the two periods.[11] By the end of the conference, the principal focus of study had shifted away from neorealism and its antecedents to the cinema under fascism as such. The conference organizers and participants were convinced that, in order to account for the evolution of neorealist film practice, its historical roots had to be identified and more closely scrutinized in their own right. Some five years later, Lino Miccichè, the storied director of the Mostra Internazionale del Nuovo Cinema, recalled the move towards this reevaluation in metaphorical terms, as a dutiful response to a never-performed cultural autopsy:

> It was natural, therefore, in a climate of systematic undervaluation of the "text," that the characterization "not one film—not a single frame," bestowed upon Italian cinema under fascism would call for no textual verification. That it imposed the removal and concealment of the textual realities of Italian cinema up to 1943 was not only a veritable historiographic manipulation . . . [but also] . . . simply an operation of grave-digger hygienics, the removal, that is, of an old and embarrassing skeleton.
>
> But sooner or later skeletons in the closet always cause difficulty. Indeed, they normally end up by posing the troublesome and inescapable problems which one wanted to avoid by closing them in. . . . And when in 1974 . . . it appeared evident that the discussion (of neorealism) had been truncated, and that if one wanted to speak of the neorealist "yesterday" and the post-neorealist "today," one could not avoid speaking of the pre-neorealist "day before yesterday," that is, precisely, the Italian cinema under fascism.[12]

Indeed, the 1974 conference was followed by an explosion of materials and books on the fascist cinema in Italy. Each year from 1974 to 1979 saw no fewer than three major retrospectives and conferences dedicated to the topic. These "revisionist" studies self-consciously contextualized themselves as correctives to the critical amnesia that had characterized decades of previous scholarship. The films, after all, had not been publicly screened for almost three decades. It has been estimated, for example, that less than half of the roughly seven hundred films made in Italy between 1929 and 1943 still survive. And, as of 1976, approximately two-thirds of the remaining titles existed only as negatives or internegatives. These statistics are particularly alarming when we consider that it is only through a continuous regime of inspection and duplication that the long-term preservation of this cultural patrimony can be assured.

The "Pesaro" desire to fill in dramatic lacunae in historical memory was expressed in opposition to the determinist constraints of Italian ideological criticism of the fifties and sixties. Pesaro removed the cultural taboo surrounding the study of culture during the *ventennio nero* by resisting that unforgiving theoretical formula that had previously equated all of the period's cultural production with the narrowly defined political interests of the fascist state. Liberated from the potential political embarrassment of writing openly about their object of study, the Pesaro group now enthusiastically engaged in rediscovering a largely unknown or forgotten generation of cinematic activity.[13]

It is important to point out that this new approach to cinema historiography did not occur in a vacuum. What were the social forces at play in Italy that allowed this *liberation* in cultural discourse? Why was it now safe to speak of the cinema under fascism? As we have mentioned, the new histories and the Pesaro initiative take place in the early seventies, the *anni di piombo*. During these "years of lead," Italian civil society was traumatized by an insidious wave of internal terrorism from both right and left wings of the political spectrum. Tobias Jones describes the global effect of the numerous terrorist actions as follows: "Italy seemed to have reached an impasse, a confrontation between irreconcilables: a liberal country modernizing at an exponential rate, and those traditionalists and 'forces of order' who—after two decades—were still struggling to come to terms with democracy. The climate, suggested both left-wingers and foreign journalists, was self-evidently ripe for a coup. . . ."[14]

In the context of this culture-wide impasse, discussion of culture in the purposeful absence of *the political* created a semblance of a brief respite from the harsh political realities that dominated contemporary social discourse. These discussions attempted to construct a space for reflection that might avoid the bleakness of any political positioning—since for a time, none of the established political parties were able to offer coherent or effective solutions to the almost daily shock to civil society. Thus, the act of speaking about Italian films during the fascist period without collapsing them into the single political category of fascism offered a cultural liberation from the perceived hopelessness of *all* political discourse during this brief time frame.

While cultural phenomena such as Pesaro and the wider historical revisionism of fascism (De Felice) began to take place, yet another form of forgetfulness surfaced. The Pesaro project participated in what might seem to be a less insidious form of something Lino Miccichè referred to as "historiographic manipulation." Having established both the legitimacy of these forgotten films and the critical need to reexamine them, a significant portion of the work was now carried out as a search for the period's "auteurs." Adriano Aprà, the organizer of the

1975 and 1976 Pesaro film retrospectives, contextualized the project of rediscovery in the following way:

> The moment had arrived for abandoning the defensive attitudes which had characterized the 50s, when one had to search for the legacy of neorealism in every worthwhile film to the point that good moviemaking was inconceivable outside its direct or indirect influence . . . and it was thus necessary, before anything else, to see the films once again: and in this period 700 films had been made. A decision was taken to postpone a second part of the (1975) conference until the following year, and to concentrate that first year on the three best-known directors, Blasetti, Camerini, and Poggioli.[15]

Though there were notable exceptions, the value in studying the period was now also to be obtained by identifying "good moviemaking." That is, despite their appearance under the fascist regime, the films could be recuperated because they may have been made by greater or lesser authors. Thus, the new agenda for critical analysis became a question of subjective evaluation, of locating directors within a classical canon. While Alessandro Blasetti, Mario Camerini, and Ferdinando Maria Poggioli defined such a canon's upper limits, the "skill, talent, and craft" of other directors such as Augusto Genina, Rafaello Matarazzo, Mario Mattoli, and others would participate in a critical struggle for inclusion and position within the canon's hierarchy. *The Fabulous Thirties: Italian Cinema 1929–1944,* published in conjunction with the Incontri Internazionali d'Arte film series at the Museum of Modern Art in New York (the first public presentation of fascist-era Italian films in the United States since before World War II), clearly articulates this auteurist excavation.[16] The first lines from the book's biographic portraits of Carmine Gallone and Goffredo Alessandrini, for example, seek to rescue the directors from previously undeserved critical treatments:

> Alessandrini is a director who risks being undervalued because in him one recognizes more the traits of the metteur-en-scène than those of the auteur; that is those of the cinema professional rather than those of the "artist." . . . He was wrongly attributed a taste for a certain masculine rhetoric, owing to the famous (and wrongly despised) *Luciano Serra Pilota,* but the sincere delicacy of *Seconda B* is sufficient to quell any doubts. . . .
> Gallone's career is too long and complicated to permit a balanced critical judgment on the basis of the few films viewable today. However one can say that he deserves a re-evaluation and in no way the oblivion or derision to which he has been condemned because of *Scipione l'africano* and because of the prejudice that has surrounded the "artist's biography" genre.[17]

It is indeed true that both films were critically successful. Alessandrini's *Luciano Serra pilota* shared the Mussolini Cup with Leni Riefenstahl's *Olympia* at the 1938 Venice Film Festival. *Scipione l'africano* won the award the previous year. Yet the authors pointedly avoid any discussion of why *Luciano Serra pilota* was "wrongly despised" or why Gallone had been "condemned" for *Scipione l'africano*. Although each film requires further detailed analysis, the key historiographic issue at hand is that they had both been severely criticized in the postwar period precisely because of their putative support of fascist ideology. Simply put, both films had once been attacked as being "fascist" and are now rescued by shifting attention to the artistic merit of their directors. Rather than investigate how such films might be both "fascist" and "successful," this kind of study simply looks for craft, stylistic merit, and thematic consistency. Thus, for a different set of reasons, the very topic of specific *history* is once again considered a bad object.

Italian critical inquiry had now successfully removed the nagging question of continuity-discontinuity between fascism and neorealism by displacing the terms of the debate onto the terrain of *the author*. De Sica's work as director of neorealist films, for example, needs to be examined in light of his experience as an actor in several thirties films by one of the period's major directors, Mario Camerini. His much-praised postwar work, his neorealism, is inoculated from any potential contamination by fascism insofar as it can be located in a previous tradition in filmmaking craft. Yet auteur theory makes no explicit structural provisions for the historical relationships, determinist or not, between the whole of the cinematic institution and its social context. Whereas it may provide certain guidelines for describing the evolution of a director's work over time, its traditional agenda clearly seeks to "evaluate" quality rather than to "explain" history. The very desire to liberate the films from the ideological and determinist criticism of the fifties and sixties, when carried out in the name of the author, had removed the directors and their films from the specific cultural context in which they worked.

CINEMA AND INDUSTRIALIZATION

The renewed interest in pre-neorealist filmmaking practices has produced a wealth of historical information.[18] Again, Brunetta's work represents a rich source of information and analysis on the period and a particularly useful model for the writing of film history. Yet where the "traditional" histories tended to repress knowledge of the period's films because of their presumptive association with fascism, this second wave recuperates the period, in part, by extracting its great directors from that very association. Given this particular methodological orientation, a significant portion of the recent studies have indeed rescued them from ideological contamination by fascism, but at the cost of short-circuiting systematic ideological or historical examination of any sort. Many intriguing questions remain.

To begin with, the cinema has always occupied a privileged status in the Italian cultural landscape. There are, for example, more film festivals in Italy than in any other country in the world. To explain the huge numbers of festivals and conferences—that is, to locate the origins of that demand or "need" for more cinema—we must account for the privileged position it occupies. In other words, we need to pose an overriding question, one which informs every aspect of Italian cinematic production and reception: why is the cinematic institution, in the largest sense of the term, so important to the country's affairs, both cultural and political?

Even though its economic health may have varied from period to period, the cinema in Italy has almost always maintained a privileged status as a cultural institution. At the outset, we can note cinema's economic status relative to the national ensemble of cultural industries. In 1927, for example, in the midst of the industry's dramatic decline, cinema box office receipts still represented over 50 percent of the total national income for entertainment.[19] Even while its economic preeminence may have faltered in given periods, the cinema's privileged status as cultural institution remained constant.

That heightened importance given to the cinema was caused in part by a virtually uninterrupted slippage between the "cultural" and the explicitly "political." While it is generally reductive to construct these two as completely separate ontological categories, Italian cinema history has insistently intertwined them as equally pertinent categories of discourse. This slippage coincides with the birth of regularized Italian film production. It was systematized—that is, it became one of the basic conditions of cinematic culture—between 1910 and 1914. That the cinema industry had assumed a vital role in Italian social life by this time is affirmed, for example, by the first attempts on the part of the Giolitti government to regulate its textual practices in 1913.[20]

By 1908 there were nine Italian film production companies. With the exception of Cines studio and Carlo Rossi e C. in Rome, the main centers of production were located in Italy's two most industrialized cities, Milan and Turin. In 1908 these companies produced over 325 films.[21] This figure represents both fiction and documentary titles. The totals would be slightly higher if one were to make a detailed inventory of the smaller Neapolitan companies along with the foreign companies producing in Italy. The most prolific production companies included Ambrosio (Turin, 94 titles), Cines (Rome, 55 titles), Luca Comerio-Società Anonima Fabbricazione Films Italiane (Milan, 59 titles), and Carlo Rossi e C.-Itala (Rome, 76 titles). In most cases, the films were sold by the production companies more or less directly to exhibitors.[22] Yet, despite this level of productivity, these firms were never able to turn out enough titles to satisfy the needs of the Italian market.[23]

Between 1907 and 1912, most of the first production companies were completely reorganized.[24] They came under new management and sought to develop new relationships to finance capital in order to underwrite more and longer productions. With this reorganization, many of these privately owned concerns were transformed into public companies. The small businessmen who were their original founders were replaced by financiers, lawyers, and, most importantly, by industrialist aristocrats. The organizational goal of this new class of industrial leaders was to consolidate the previously loosely connected filmmaking practices into a nationally organized cinema industry that could effectively compete in both national and international markets.

A good example to consider is Alberini-Santoni, which was founded in 1905 as one of the country's first production companies. It was also the first to be rearranged by members of the Italian aristocracy. Renamed Cines, it was transformed into a public company in April of 1906, with investments from the Bank of Rome and electric-power industrialist Adolfo Pouchain Foggia. Its new executive board included Ernesto Pacelli (president of the Bank of Rome) and notable members of Italy's aristocracy, including Prince don Prospero Colonna di Sonnino and Count Francesco Salimei. In 1911, Baron Alberto Fassini became its director and chief administrator.

Throughout this period, similar shifts in company leadership effected the reorganization of both Comerio-SAFFI and Rossi-Itala. Of the four largest production companies in 1908, only Ambrosio seems to have been left unmodified. In 1908 Luca Comerio lost control of the company he had founded, Comerio-SAFFI. By September of 1909 it had been renamed Milano Films and was headed by Count Pier Gaetano Venino, Baron Paolo Airoldi di Robbiate, and Giuseppe di

Liguoro. Carlo Rossi e C., founded by Carlo Rossi in 1907, was restructured into Itala films in May of 1908. Itala's new leaders came primarily from the banking world and also included Giovanni Pastrone, who would go on to produce and direct the groundbreaking *Cabiria* in 1914.[25]

In addition, the penetration of the aristocracy into key positions within Italian film production also characterized a number of newly founded companies. In 1912, for example, Count Baldassare Negrone started Celio Films in Rome with the financial support of Marquis Alberto Del Gallo di Roccavergine. Two years later in Naples, Count Francesco Anamoro established Napoli Film.[26] In many cases, these Italian aristocrats invested their own private capital directly into film production. However, by bringing with them many personal contacts in the financial sector, they also encouraged more substantial second-party investment from Italy's national banks. Their arrival, and the subsequent infusion of new capital into the film industry, made possible an immediate surge in the overall number of films produced. The titles released by Cines alone almost quadrupled, from 55 in 1908 to 208 in 1912. For the industry as a whole, production more than tripled, jumping from 325 to 977 over the same four-year span.[27] And while some of the earliest companies went out of business in this period, the total number of production companies rose to at least fifty by mid-1914.

Perhaps even more significantly, it is in this same period that the length of narrative films began to increase, exceeding the one-reel barrier for the first time. With its reorganization in 1909, SAFFI-Milano Films, for example, began a huge project for the filming of *Dante's Inferno*.[28] Upon completion in 1911, the film was over 1,300 meters long.[29] The successful American distribution of *Dante's Inferno* in 1911 and of Enrico Guazzoni's *Quo Vadis?* in 1912 had a significant effect on the development of Italian film production policy. While Cines had already set up offices in New York in 1907, the subsequent American successes of feature-length historical costume film was one of the factors that led the major Italian film companies to concentrate on this type of production. Each of the reorganized major production companies began to plan and produce longer works. While continuing to produce a stock of short melodramas, comedies, documentaries, and low-budget serials, by the end of 1912 the companies had consolidated the practice of dedicating a relatively high proportion of their new financial resources to feature-length films. Some of the more notable examples include Enrico Guazzoni's *La Gerusalemme liberata*

(1911, Cines, over 1,000 meters); Giovanni Pastrone's *La caduta di Troia* (1911, Itala, 600 meters); Guazzoni's *Quo Vadis* (1913, Cines, 2,250 meters); Nino Oxilia's *Addio giovinezza* (1913, Itala, 1,012 meters); and Pastrone's *Cabiria* (1914, Itala, 4,500 meters). While Italy was not the only country to extend the length of narrative films in this period, it was the first to consolidate it into an industry-wide practice.[30] In fact, historian Aldo Bernardini has suggested that by 1914, Italian fiction films averaged between 1,000 and 1,500 meters in length, or roughly one hour of projection time.[31]

The birth of cinema in Italy, its reorganization into a film industry, and its corollary expansion in lengths and numbers of films produced took place in the context of the process of industrialization within the country as a whole. During the 1860s, at the time of Italy's formation as a nation-state, the national economy was predominantly agricultural. As much as 75 percent of the total workforce was in the agricultural sector.[32] The pace of industrialization was thus relatively slow in comparison to other Western European countries such as France, Great Britain, and Germany. While there had been a gradual growth both in the creation of new industries and in the concentration of capital resources, it was only in the last years of the nineteenth century that industrialization began to take hold.

The traditionally agriculture-based composition of the workforce underwent a significant shift in the first decade of the twentieth century. The 1901 national census listed a population of 32,475,000. In the same year, 15,904,000 were gainfully employed, 59.8 percent in agriculture and 23.8 percent in modern industries. By 1911 agriculture's share of the workforce had dropped to 56.1 percent, while industry's had risen to 26.9 percent.[33] This general modification of the workforce's composition was also reflected in the demographic shift from the agrarian countryside to the industrial cities. It is estimated, for example, that the population of Milan alone more than doubled between the 1860s and 1906.[34]

Italy's industrial growth was most particularly felt in its metallurgic, machine manufacturing, transportation, and hydroelectric industries. The extensive development of hydroelectric power generation has received particular attention in studies on industrialization. Italian industrial leaders had hoped that hydroelectric power would reduce the country's massive importation of coal, thereby resolving one of its raw material shortages. In point of fact, between 1896 and 1913, finance capital invested more heavily in this sector than in any other industry.

Hydroelectric production jumped from 66 million kilowatts in 1898 to over two billion kilowatts in 1913.[35]

These developments can be traced, in part, by key mergers between the steel industry and heavy-machine manufacturers, the nationalization of rail transport in 1905,[36] and the establishment of FIAT in 1899 and Olivetti in 1906. In the late 1890s, the reorganization of the structures of national finance and the infusion of new capital created the economic conditions for this rapid industrial expansion. Nicos Poulantzas characterizes these economic conditions in the following way:

> Given the importance of commercial and banking capital from the time of the Renaissance, and the retardation of primitive accumulation in agriculture, the process of industrialization was characterized *from the start* by a tendency to rapid fusion of banking and industrial capital into finance capital, and by a very high rate of capital concentration. Industrial monopoly capital did not "precede" the formation of finance capital, but was its corollary. This tendency was further accentuated with the considerable penetration of foreign capital into Italy, due to the advance of other countries and the backwardness of Italian capitalism.[37]

On the one hand, the infusion of finance capital into the metallurgic industries had made possible a rapid increase in productivity. On the other hand, it was the reorganization of the internal marketplace which allowed for steady and continued growth. For example, protectionist trade tariffs helped to deter importation of less expensive steel goods from Germany. Since the newly nationalized railroad acquired steel predominantly from Italian companies, the steel industry was guaranteed a virtual monopoly over the national market.

Despite the fact that the Italian film industry dramatically expanded its activities in the same period, it was slow to follow the economic and industrial logic characteristic of the process of industrialization as a whole. While the aristocratic owners of film production companies were initially able to arrange for increased financing of single film projects, no overall system of film industry finance was achieved. The increased number of Italian films in circulation between 1907 and 1914 did in fact help the industry to compete for preeminence within the Italian marketplace. However, that competition took place almost exclusively at the level of production and did not address film distribution. The Italian film industry was therefore never able to extend full control over its own internal/national marketplace. It is this disparity between the Italian cinema's strength in production and its weakness in distribution that seriously retarded potential economic growth and that distinguished it from the patterns of industrialization in other sectors. By itself, the production of Italian film, even at an expanded rate, was unable to stave off the importation of foreign films. From the beginning of cinema in Italy, the marketplace had been saturated by films from abroad. From 1896 to the beginning of World War I, French films in particular constituted a significant portion of the total number of films distributed in the country. In fact, as I will discuss in chapter 2, the distribution of foreign films began to form a key industrial condition for Italian cinema after World War I. By the early 1920s, when production was in steep decline, the exhibition sector exerted a dominant influence on the construction of national film policy. Thus the industry predicated its strength and growth potential on the consolidation of independently owned theaters into national chains. Ironically, this consolidation was made possible by arranging exclusive distribution agreements with American studios for a steady stream of film products.

The economic success of the Italian feature-length fiction films abroad was only momentary, since it was soon met with stiff protectionist measures, particularly in the United States.[38] Neither did it guarantee a similar success within Italian theaters. The extended length of the films had reduced the number of shows that theaters could present in a given day and thereby initially decreased box office receipts. This reduction in the number of programs was certainly one of the reasons for an increase in the cost of admission and the construction of theaters with larger seating capacities. At this time, however, for a film to recover its costs, it also needed a longer run within these theaters. Yet while many of the major production companies continued to sell their films directly to exhibitors, this arrangement was not organized on a systematic and national level. The patterns of distribution then current, therefore, did not guarantee the producers a national circuit for their locally produced films. The industry's potential income base was further weakened when the significant inroads Italian films had made into both Western European and South American markets virtually disappeared with the advent of World War I.

In the absence of protectionist tariffs on foreign films, and given that production had not yet been fully integrated with distribution, production companies could not prevent regional or even local exhibitors from freely acquiring films either from other Italian companies or from abroad. Since there were no economic incentives to show films produced in Italy, exhibitors acquired films as readily from Cines as they did from Pathé or Paramount. In fact, this relative autonomy achieved by Italian film exhibitors became one of the principal obstacles in effecting a complete vertical integration between production, distribution, and exhibition. Indeed, the only period in Italian cinema history in which the film industry was able to establish any form of monopolistic control over its own internal marketplace would be between 1938 and 1945.[39] The inability to control its own marketplace created an almost permanent position of economic deficit for the industry as a whole. Culturally, it represented one of the principal challenges that would be addressed by the fascist regime.

CINEMA AND NATIONAL IDENTITY

While in general the cinema did not follow the structural logic of Italian industrialization, it did however participate fully in the fundamental conditions of its modernization. Almost since its inception, and certainly by the time of its first major industrial expansion, Italian cinema's principal role within the public sphere was characterized by the manner in which it negotiated a set of social contradictions introduced by that modernization. The cinema specifically inscribed itself into what can be termed a cultural search for national identity.

The geopolitical unification of the Italian nation-state in 1860 did little to overcome the regional, cultural, and linguistic differences among the previous city-states and duchies. In actuality, the political unification of Italy as a nation did not include Rome and Venice until after 1870. To this day, each of the country's twenty regions has its own distinct dialect. It can even be argued that Sardinian and Friulano are actually autonomous languages. Linguistic divisions aside, the deeply rooted social and cultural contradictions between the industrial north and the agricultural south remain very much vigorous to this day.

By the turn of the century, the initial phase of Italian industrialization (the partial transformation of Italy's traditional, regionally based, agricultural economy by the infusion of finance capital) brought these divisions into sharper relief. Huge increases in the urban population and workforce and the significant migration away from the countryside signaled a dramatic reshaping and extension of the public sphere. Yet, at the same time that industrialization effected a rationalization of the internal marketplace and expanded the now nationalized system of rail transport, it also brought forth a series of new social contradictions that exacerbated the cultural differences endemic to Italian regional identities.

For the first national election in 1870, only 530,018 citizens were eligible to vote, that is, roughly 2 percent of the total population. By 1911 the voting population had increased to 3,329,147. The reform of suffrage laws in 1912 further increased the number of eligible voters to 8,672,249, approximately 25 percent of the total population. Suffrage rights had been premised not only upon educational qualifications, but also upon property ownership. Electoral reform in 1912 extended suffrage to literate males over the age of twenty-one and to veterans of military service. Another indication of the expansion of the public sphere was the establishment of trade unions, a process that led to the consolidation of several unions into the socialist-leaning Confederazione del Lavoro in 1906. During this period, labor activism, both its promotion and attempts at its containment, played a key role in the formation of national political policy. That the trade unions could fill an influential role in the construction of public policy was indicated, in part, by the number of strikes they organized. In 1901, there were 1,000 strikes with 200,000 participants. By 1913, more than 385,000 workers participated in over 800 strikes.[40]

Electoral reform, along with the establishment of national trade unions, extended to these groups the ability to participate in civic affairs at a national level for the first time. Antonio Gramsci underscored the formative national importance of the 1913 general elections, for example, in his essay "Moments of Intensely Collective and Unitary Life in the National Development of the Italian People":

> Within the context of the development of national life from 1800 onwards, examine all the moments in which the Italian people has been assigned the resolution of an at least potentially common task, when a collective (in depth and breadth) and unified action or movement could thus have occurred. . . . The nature and character of these moments may have been various: wars, revolutions, plebiscites, general elections of particular importance. . . . The election of 1913 is the first with distinct popular characteristics because of the very large participation of the peasants. . . . There was a widespread mystical conviction that everything would be different after the vote, that it was a real social palingenesis: at least in Sardinia.[41]

The problematic that Gramsci refers to, and that lies at the core of his cultural writings, is the relationship between collective political activity and the construction of the ideological coordinates for a composite national identity. For Gramsci, the attainment and legitimation of political authority is always also based on its cultural corollary. In this case, the level of participation itself in the 1913 national elections signified a crucial modification of the Italian public sphere. Extended to include a wider popular participation, the public sphere was politicized insofar as it engaged in a structural dialectic of exchange between national political life and regional cultural difference. On the one hand, national politics began to be informed by the presence of civic groups that had previously been defined by their very cultural differences not only from one another, but also from any unitary conception of *italianicity*. On the other hand, participation in elections is one example of how a sense of "nationality," above and beyond regional or city identities, was apprehended by communities that had previously defined themselves as northern or southern, Tuscan or Sicilian, Roman or Venetian.

That the nexus between the local and the national is compelling specifically in the Italian context is evidenced by the extreme linguistic differences between regions. At the time of Italian unification in the 1860s, less than 10 percent of the new country's total population actually spoke Italian, that is, the Florentine literary Italian most commonly associated with the Tuscan and Roman dialects.[42] Howard Moss sums up the problem:

> Perhaps it is not surprising that language has aroused strong emotions among the Italian political and intellectual classes. After all the Italian state began its life in 1861 without a common language among the mass of its people, and with the crucial need therefore of a national tongue to articulate and forge the national consciousness which did not exist but would need to be spread. . . . What the new Italian government was facing therefore was a situation in which, out of a population of 35 million, at least 31 million did not have a common language.[43]

The Italian cinema participated directly in the complex dialectic between national politics and cultural formations. Although its aristocrat-led "industrial" growth was not in step with Italian industrialization, its overall ideological project sought to privilege cinema as a central cultural agency within the Italian public sphere. Not only did its films explicitly address national political issues, the cinematic institution also attempted to assert its role as an agency that could recruit, codify, and circulate the cultural terms for a modern national identity. As a corrective to the approach sketched out by Benedict Anderson, David Forgacs places the role of the media in relation to the national in the following way:

> It is hard to conceive of a national identity being established or consolidated without continued *relays of information* among those who share the

identity, relays which play back to them their sense of common cultural memory or mutual belonging. . . . This all suggests that the history of nations has a peculiarly close relationship with the history of the media. It also suggests that the media do not reflect or articulate the identity of a pre-existing national community but are one of the means, maybe even the principal one, by which that community and its identity are brought into being and shaped and later (perhaps) eroded.[44]

The aristocrats who had guided the evolution of Italian film production saw themselves not so much as captains of the cinematic industry as much as patrons of a new art form. In many ways, they attempted to create for the cinema a position of privilege within the Italian cultural landscape similar to that held by opera in the eighteenth and nineteenth centuries. Brunetta summarizes their relationship to the cinema: "Above and beyond the formidable increase in capital, the presence of these aristocrats has a determining weight on the efforts towards the cultural qualification of film. Thanks to the cinema, these exponents of a society, which by now was completely marginal to the country's economic and cultural growth rediscover some reasons for gratification by finding a way to appear like an illuminated avant-garde, directly responsible for the cultural growth of the cinema."[45]

Indeed, one of their first moves was to infuse the cinema with the prestige status that could be attained by an association with representatives of already legitimated art forms. Between 1910 and 1914 leading literary figures such as Giuseppe Verga, Guido Gozzano, Salvatore Di Giacomo, Roberto Bracco, Grazia Deledda, Mario Praga, Giuseppe Adami, and Matilde Serao were recruited to write either film treatments of their own work or screenplays for new films. While their collaborations did not play a preeminent role in the evolution of narrative codes for cinematic production, their authorship was heavily publicized by the film industry.[46] In 1913, for example, Gabriele D'Annunzio was paid 50,000 lire by Itala films in exchange for writing the intertitles for Giovanni Pastrone's *Cabiria* and, more importantly, for the use of his name as author of the film.[47]

The film's producer and director, Giovanni Pastrone, had in fact already written the screenplay. Yet, as Maria Adriano Prolo has pointed out, Pastrone's name never appeared in either the film's publicity materials or in any of its critical reviews.[48] As is evident in the film's publicity posters, authorship was ascribed entirely to D'Annunzio. Despite the fact that the poet's contribution to the film was something less than definitive, Itala nonetheless consistently publicized *Cabiria* in its press

**Figure 2. Poster for *Cabiria* (1914, Giovanni Pastrone).
Courtesy of the Museo Nazionale del Cinema, Torino.**

announcements and in the libretto that was distributed to the audience
as a work *by Gabriele D'Annunzio*.

From its industrial expansion to the beginning of World War I,
the two principal sources, narrative pre-texts, for Italian fiction films
were international literary classics and famous episodes from Italian
history. Bernardini has argued that these sources not only reflected an
aristocratic taste for "noble" themes, but also satisfied the industry's

economic imperatives. He suggests that the use of such themes helped to defray the additional costs of producing feature-length films. Thus, literary adaptations and films that utilized real historic locations were less expensive than original works that required the construction of entirely new sets.[49] As such they can be generally located in the context of the film industry's economic growth, one that also led to the construction of larger theaters and higher admission prices. That is, the filmic translation of famous literature and the treatment of historical themes recognizable to both national and international audiences were designed to support wider distribution and higher box-office returns. At the same time, however, these practices also participated in a larger ideological project. They assumed for the cinema as institution many of the responsibilities of an educational mission. In a 1909 interview in the journal *Lux,* Arturo Labriola proposed just such a mission: "Why not sack the treasures of our civil history, so dramatic and so unknown to *the masses?* Why don't we give ourselves a panorama, a general picture of all of our national evolution? They say that the undying merit of Alexander Dumas consisted in rendering universal the history of France. We do not have writers who have been able to vivify and make our national history interesting for *the people.* All right, that which the writer's art did not know how to give, let the cinema give us."[50]

In trade journals and film magazines, this proposal to render the cinema a tool of historical and cultural education was quite common.[51] More importantly, the proposal converges on a set of economic, institutional, and textual practices that set forth basic coordinates for what was envisioned to become the cinema's distinctly social role. These practices lay claim, that is, to the cinema's legitimate and legitimizing participation in the construction of a composite for the country's diverse regional identities. Two decades later, the fascist state would build on those claims in relationship to its specific political agendas. As Ruth Ben-Ghiat describes it: "Fascist officials also recognized cinema's extraordinary communicative potential and granted films a central role in their attempts to transform ideologies and lifestyles. . . . Feature films proved no less important to fascist plans for a collective transformation, since they were seen as an ideal way to transmit political messages unobtrusively. As one critic commented, they could impart 'a political vision of life and the world to a multitude of persons who believe they are merely giving themselves an hour of innocent entertainment.'"[52]

As larger theaters were built, many exhibitors began not only to increase the cost of admission, but also to vary prices according to seating location within the theater: balcony, loge, and so forth. In the major industrial cities, a geographic distinction was also drawn between first- and second-run movie houses. In most cases, first-run feature programs were presented in theaters built exclusively for film programming and located in the center of the city. Second-runs (and cheaper admission tickets) were generally rotated to older establishments in the urban periphery, which also included other forms of popular entertainment. Both modifications were designed to attract and maintain audiences that might not be able to afford the generally higher prices.[53] Yet these economic practices stem not only from an evaluation of economic differences within the cinema audiences; they also enact a discursive relationship, a social contract between audiences and the cinematic institution. The act of buying a ticket was now mediated by socioeconomic distinctions within the pool of potential customers. The variable admission prices and the difference between attending first- or second-run films presented the film audience with a reminder of its social status. In the most basic fashion such differentiations address the film *audience* as a socially defined *public*.

A transformation was also under way in the manner in which film magazines from 1908 to 1914 addressed their readers. They began to refer to the audiences less frequently as customers, patrons, or clients and more to their membership in larger social groupings. Like the above-cited Labriola interview, the audience is now made up of "spectators" as often as it is of "the masses," "the people," "Italians," "the nation," or "the public." In fact, the Italian word *pubblico* signifies both "audience" and "public." Its usage in this period, however, emphasizes a more civically oriented definition over the English sense of "audience" as only a group of spectators. Although it wasn't until 1913 that major literary journals began to include articles on the cinema, they too attached social valences to the cinema as a cultural project *in relationship to* its audiences. In an article from *La Voce*, Giuseppe Prezzolini asked that the cinema do away with "facile tearfulness and imbecilic optimism in order to make way for a cinema which would make Italians know our country, its glories, its shames, its joys and its pains."[54]

The very first regular film column to appear in a daily newspaper even justified its existence in terms of the interconnection between the growing cinema industry and its public. In the column's first article (4 February 1908), the film reviewer for *La Gazzetta del Popolo* wrote:

"The continually growing development of the cinematographic industry, let alone *the public's* predilection for cinematographic genre
spectacles, have advised us to begin this current column, which aims
precisely to illustrate everything that is relevant to the cinema."[55] This
distinction between a generalized film audience and a socially characterized public is important because it implicates a social role for the
cinema. An *audience* appears and is spoken of as an undifferentiated,
ahistorical body appealed to by various intertextual strategies to enter
into the cinema. Its principal job is to watch and enjoy a given spectacle. The *public* is a social entity, an institutionally addressed and regulated collectivity that reemerges from the cinema with historical roles
and duties. Its job is also one of obligation, action, and citizenship. By
consistently invoking these differences, the extratextual practices of
the early Italian cinema provided a basic discursive premise that stipulated that the cultural exchange between the cinematic institution and
its social context is *always also* ideological in nature.

This social recruitment by the Italian cinematic institution was certainly not the only method for attracting audiences and addressing
their desires. It is significant, however, that it precedes the circulation
of other institutional forms of invitation and promise. The star system,
for example, develops later in Italy than in the United States. Its first
successes can be traced back to the performances of Lyda Borelli and
Mario Bonnard in Mario Caserini's *Ma l'amor mio non muore* (1913,
Gloria Films). The subsequent practice of circulating actors' names as
guarantors of quality, as promise of a particular form of cinematic
pleasure, would come to dominate film publicity, in fact, only in the
later half of the decade and throughout the 1920s.[56]

The Italian cinema shared this social invocation of the audience with
some of contemporary theater's institutional practices. The differen-
tiation between cost of admission and seating location, for example,
was a technique borrowed directly from traditional theater. Indeed,
before the construction of new movie houses, many films were actually
presented in rented theater halls.[57] Representatives of Italian theater
came, in fact, to view competition from the cinema as the chief threat
to its economic survival. Moreover, the question of the similarities and
differences between the two media did not escape the attention of the
period's cultural critics. On one of the rare occasions that Gramsci
wrote about cinema, for example, he refers specifically to the economic
plight of the theater. Writing in 1916, he suggested that the new film
industry was supplanting theater's hold over the public:

They say that the cinema is killing the theater. They say that in Turin
the theatrical firms have kept their houses closed during the summer
months because the public is deserting the theater and thronging to the
cinemas. . . . There is no doubt that a large proportion needs to be enter-
tained (to relax by shifting its field of attention) with a pure visual distraction. By becoming an industry, the theater has recently tried to satisfy
this need alone. It has become quite simply a business, a shop dealing in
cheap junk. It is only by accident that they put on productions that have
an eternal universal value. The cinema, which can fulfill this function
more easily and more cheaply, is more successful than the theater and is
tending to replace it.[58]

Above and beyond the intrinsic differences between cinematic and
theatrical form, Italy's cinema during this period distinguished itself
remarkably from the theater in terms of the kinds of themes that it
began to treat. Along with literary classics, one principal source for
film subjects was episodes from Italian history. In fact, the historical costume film was the chief generic form for many of the period's
groundbreaking, extended-length films. These films established what
would become the most enduring genre in Italian film production.
Over the course of Italian film history, the genre has drawn from virtually every period in Italian history. Between 1908 and 1916, however, the historical costume film concentrated primarily on ancient
Rome and the Risorgimento, that is, Italy's national unification in the
nineteenth century.

Some of the titles which employ the Risorgimento as historical backdrop to the fiction include *Nozze d'oro* (1911, Ambrosio), *Tamburino
Sardo* (1911, Cines; remade under the same title by Gloria Films in
1916), *La lampada della nonna* (1913, Ambrosio), and *Piccolo pa-
triota padovano* (1916, Gloria).[59] However, the number of films that
narrativize (Roman) antiquity far exceeded treatments of the Risorgimento. Some of the films were simply longer remakes of previous
titles. That in some cases two production companies used identical
titles in the same year indicates increased industrial competition as
well as the centrality of the genre during the period. A partial list
of these films, by production company, includes Ambrosio's *Ultimi
giorni di Pompei* (1908), directed by Luigi Maggi; *Nerone* (1909) and
Lo Schiavo di Cartagine (1910), by Arrigo Frusta; *Gli ultimi giorni
di Pompei* (1913) and *Nerone e Agrippina* (1914), by Mario Caserini; Pasquali Films' *Gli ultimi giorni di Pompei* and *Spartacus* (both
1913), by Giovanni Enrico Vidali; Itala's *La caduta di Troia* (1910)
and *Cabiria* (1914), by Giovanni Pastrone; Cines's *Quo Vadis* (1913);

Marcantonio e Cleopatra (1913); and *Caius Julius Caesar* (1914), by Enrico Guazzoni.[60]

A detailed evaluation of the ideological significance of such concentration on both Roman antiquity and the Risorgimento is perhaps more complex than it might initially seem. Bernardini has suggested that Italian nationalist fervor was the larger social context in which the films operated. "What's more, the ideology and, above all, the mentality of nationalism was taking shape and gaining strength in Italy. It depended on traditions, on patriotic memories, on historical and cultural heredity, in order to reinforce that unity of Italy and of our people which, after forty years, was still quite far from being a reality."[61]

Indeed, nationalist fervor was one of the principal political currents during the period of Italy's industrialization and has been considered a precursor of Italian fascism. Ultra-right-wing, antidemocratic, imperialist sentiments were at the core, for example, of the political journal *Il Regno,* founded by Enrico Corradini in 1903. In 1910, the nationalist movement formed its political organ with the establishment of the Associazione Nazionalista Italiana, the Italian Nationalist Party. Not unlike the ideological agenda expressed by Action Française in France, Italian nationalists called insistently for imperialist expansion. They called for the invasion of Libya in 1911, embraced Italy's entrance into World War I in 1915, and orchestrated D'Annunzio's seizure of Fiume in 1919.

The association of the historical costume film with Italian nationalism is very suggestive. The political rhetoric of expansionism, which called for the aggressive establishment of new colonial empires, was represented as nothing less than the enactment of a manifest destiny inaugurated by the "Italian" experience of the Roman Empire. In early May 1915, on the eve of Italy's entrance into the war, D'Annunzio delivered a series of speeches that extolled the virtues of military conquest. His call to action was expressed as a continuation of Imperial Roman tradition: "Comrades, it is no longer time for speeches, but for action, and for action after the high Roman fashion. If it is a crime to incite people to violence, I boast of now committing that crime. . . . This war, though it may seem destructive, will be the most fruitful means of creating beauty and virtue that has appeared on earth."[62]

In this context, the rhetorical reevocation of Rome was supported by its fictive reconstruction in the films. That is, at the same time that nationalist speeches referred to an ideal of the Roman past as a legitimation of their political agenda, a large set of films circulated images of Roman antiquity to larger, popular audiences. On the one hand, an argument that the early historical costume film was a simple ideological reflection of Italian imperialism clearly calls for additional analysis of the films, their textual operations, and their reading by audiences. On the other hand, even with this proviso, the contribution of the historical costume film to the establishment of basic terms for an Italian national identity cannot be overstated.

Virtually every film within the genre constructed massive sets for the historical places of their fictions. They employed huge crowd scenes for the narrative reenactment of "Italian" history: the sacking of Carthage, Hannibal's invasion of the peninsula, the mass spectacles of ancient Rome, and the nineteenth-century struggles for Italian liberation and unification. That is, at a time when a collective, national unity among its audiences didn't exist, the films insistently represented collective historical action. Audiences that had previously identified themselves in terms of their regional cultural heritage (e.g., Venetian, Piemontese, Sicilian, Neapolitan) were now presented a fictive view of themselves *in the past,* a view that provided at least the discursive invitation to erase differences among those regional heritages.

Where the political formation of the Italian state had been unable to effect a national cultural unification, both the neoclassical Roman and the more contemporary Risorgimento films elided social and cultural divisions for the diverse Italian audiences by offering them the possibility of seeing themselves as the inheritors of a supra-class, supra-regional historical unity. It is precisely in this sense that the films proposed terms for a nationalization of cultural identity. By representing a terrain in which spectators might share a common history, these films enabled that public to see themselves as simply *Italians.*

A closer look at the textual practices of individual historical costume films would certainly be rewarding. While they clearly introduce the discursive terms for an expansion of the Italian public sphere, the assimilation of disparate cultural identities into a single national past would require major ideological effort. Such an assimilation, for example, is certainly also mediated by the manner in which Italians have come to view the social role of history itself. Just how effective such ideological efforts could be during specific periods of Italian history remains an intriguingly open question. Annales school historian Jacques Le Goff has even suggested that the cultural differences between southern and northern Italy, regional and local historical sentiment, and the historical burden presented by ties to an ancient Roman heritage continue to compromise any self-conscious critical considerations of the nation's composite identity: "Thus one always returns to the idea that one of the profound reasons for this hesitation by Italians to take into account their own attitudes in relationship to the past may be the presentiment (if not the fear) of discovering at the end of the research that the contemporary Italian perceives his own past more in relationship to a region or a city than in relationship to Italy."[63] Nonetheless, having now addressed its audience (in public discussion, publicity, and criticism) as an agent within a larger social community, Italian cinematic textual production engaged in a massive historiographic reconstruction. Where its institutional practices (ticket prices, distribution patterns) articulated that audience's economic differences, the films themselves engaged in figurative and literal reconstructions of that audience's imagined communal history. In a word, they provided the audience-public with a master chronotope for its past.

From the outset of its formation as an industry, the Italian cinema mediated the ideological contradictions resulting from the country's industrialization by proposing social and cultural terms for collective identity. That is, the films made available terms of reference that large segments of the population could share for the first time. Through its textual representations of a "common" history, the Italian cinematic institution relegated to itself a privileged position within the social arena. By collapsing the distinctions between its two sides as both cultural and political agency, the cinema played a central role in what has been called the "overpoliticization" of the public sphere.[64]

More frequently than in other countries, a relatively high proportion of Italian films insert themselves into political topics: the Risorgimento, fascism, the Resistance, the mass political movements of the sixties and seventies, the mafia, and, more recently, government corruption scandals such as *tangentopoli*. In addition, representatives of Italian political institutions (state officials, party leaders, political theorists) frequently intervene in debates about the cinema's proper social function. In public discussion, cinema came to be seen, at a very early stage, as a topic that also legitimately calls for political evaluation. Thus Italian cinema is seen as an integral part of national political life in part because of the very importance ascribed to it by the country's national institutions.

In the 1930s, both film publications and public speeches by Fascist officials recall Mussolini's famed dictum that cinema was the state's *arma più forte,* literally, its strongest weapon. But even before this,

LA CINEMATOGRAFIA E L'ARMA PIÙ FORTE

Figure 3. Mussolini lays first brick of the new Istituto LUCE. Frame enlargement from LUCE newsreel (October 11, 1937). Courtesy of the Istituto LUCE.

the government had actively argued for the cinema's innate social importance through public discourse.[65] The establishment of censorship policy, for example, expressed as much concern about civic/political danger as it did fear of possible sexual/moral corruption. In the early second decade of the century, precisely when Italian cinema productions began to extend beyond the traditional length of narrative films, the Italian government under Giolitti began the ideological regulation of the film industry. In 1913 a national directive on the cinema was circulated to provincial police headquarters. The circular established a set of criteria upon which films currently being exhibited could be withdrawn from circulation. Provincial authorities were advised to block films that "render representatives of the police odious and criminals sympathetic; [or which were] ignoble excitations towards sensualism, provoked by episodes in which the vividness of the representations directly fed the most base and vulgar passions, and other films from which spring an incitement towards hatred between the social classes or, that is, an offense against the national decorum."[66] In this period, formalized Italian censorship policy differs significantly from its equivalent in the United States. In general terms, while such policies in Italy focused heavily on the representation of the state and its agencies, early institutional studies on the "dangers" of cinema in America were carried out on behalf and in the name of children and the family.

It is clear that the generality of these Giolitti guidelines created some space for interpretation and, more often, for negotiation between the industry, civic and religious groups, and the state.[67] The larger production companies had, in fact, welcomed external regulation of the cinema. They felt that government interventions that sought to ensure respectability for the industry as a whole would privilege their production of "quality" films. They would create, that is, a competitive edge over the smaller, undercapitalized companies which could not afford lavish production budgets.

As these policies were refined over time, the parameters for sexual and moral codes remained relatively ambiguous. Indeed, by the time they were enacted into national law, the number of provisos generally regarding the civic arena and specifically the state had significantly increased. Thus the 31 March 1914 Royal Decree (#532) authorized the *preemptive* censorship of films based on consideration of such issues. Up to this point, films could be pulled from circulation only after they were in distribution. The new Decree included the following expanded criteria:

> The vigilance over films intends to prevent the public presentation of:
> a) spectacles which are offensive to morale, to morality, to public decency, and to private citizens.
> b) spectacles which are contrary to the national decorum and reputation or to the reputation of the police, that is, films which can disturb international relations.
> c) spectacles which are offensive to the decorum and the prestige of the institutions, public authorities, police functionaries and agents.
> d) [films which represent] grim, repugnant, or cruel scenes, even with respect to animals; awful crimes or suicides; and, in general [which contain] perverse actions or facts which can motivate criminality, disturb the spirit and be an incentive for evil.[68]

In the pre–World War I era, these legal criteria were infrequently applied. The actual number of films removed from distribution was minimal. From this perspective, the insistent attention to the questions of national decorum and of the respectable representation of the state belies less a fear of the ideological damage that the cinema could provoke than it seeks to promote a vision of the role that the cinema *should* fulfill. The presence of censorship policy conferred legitimacy upon the cinematic institution as a cultural agency within Italian civic life. In the largest sense, the government itself attempted to ratify cinema's basic social role.

The ideological partnership between the "noble" educational mission articulated by the industry's aristocratic leadership and its discursive politicization by the state through censorship policy occurred when no other cultural agency had achieved dominance, or even centrality, within the Italian social terrain. That the overall civic landscape lacked institutions that could effectively mediate at a national level only contributed to cinema's importance. Victoria de Grazia has described this gap or weakness in Italian civil society as follows:

> Rather than suffering from a scarcity of institutions, civil society in pre-war Italy, if we use the categories of liberal sociology, might be said to have become "overpoliticized" from the failure to develop one particular kind of mediating institution: the apolitical and intraclass civic association that . . . is identified as the hallmark of a healthy liberal social order for its ability to involve citizens, regardless of class background or political belief, in common projects of self- and social betterment. From another perspective, it could be said that the economic affirmation of Italy's new industrial elites had failed to find a corresponding ideological expression in their social and cultural agencies.[69]

In the period of its formation as an industry, the cinema attempted to fill in this gap. That it would seek to provide the social function of just such a "mediating institution" would have overriding consequences on its evolution both as mass entertainment and as a cultural agency. In the case of the relationship between the industry and government censorship, there was a partially formed fusion of ideological and economic interests. More importantly, this institutionalized exchange between the cinema and the state served to formalize the process of continual discursive slippage between politics and culture. For the cinema, this slippage would have two principal qualities. First, both the cinema's textual and its intratextual practices addressed themselves to the cultural disconnections between regional identities. Second, the country's political institutions sanctioned the cinematic institution as a central agency within the national public sphere.

This slippage constituted a basic condition for the experience of cinema. It functions as one unremovable coordinate of both its critical discourse and audience participation. Throughout its history, and irrespective of the manner in which given films engaged specific political issues, the Italian cinematic institution has been continuously privileged as subject to extraordinary political reading, debate, and intervention. In a word, audiences were made aware, from quite early on, that even films which didn't explicitly engage social issues were nonetheless connected to a larger social and historical fabric.

As I have mentioned, the early industrial expansion of the Italian cinema did not keep pace with the consolidation of finance capital and industrialization in other sectors. Indeed, the politicization of Italian cinematic culture was made possible, in part, by the very disjuncture between its industrial organization and its institutional goals. That its social mission nonetheless continued to exceed its economic grasp provided the fundamental institutional framework that would be inherited by the fascist regime. This gap constituted the basic condition for the state's entrance into cinematic affairs. While the outer limits of a political cinematic discourse were sketched in during the period 1910–14, they were systematically addressed and refined in the twenties and thirties. It is true that, in the first phase of the relationship between fascism and the cinema, the state's intervention in the film industry was limited. However, as the fascist state evolved, its cultural policy began to propose specific mechanisms for the cinema's social function precisely in order to render it the most important weapon.

TWO

THE POLITICAL ECONOMY
OF ITALIAN CINEMA, 1922–1943

By promoting the development of mass media and commercial entertainment, the fascist regime was able fully to exploit
their novelty in a society where only a narrow elite had been
able to enjoy their first manifestations. Using the appeal of
the new media to exercise an increasingly powerful influence
over popular recreational habits, the regime both expanded
accessibility to them and developed its own versions for
popular consumption.

Victoria de Grazia, *The Culture of Consent:*
Mass Organization of Leisure in Fascist Italy

FASCISM MAKES CINEMATIC HISTORY

Historians traditionally mark the rise of fascism to power by a series of
dramatic political events that took place between 1922 and 1925. On
October 29, 1922, King Victor Emmanuel III formally invited Benito
Mussolini to become the country's twenty-seventh prime minister. In
December of the same year, Mussolini founded the Grand Council of
Fascism and appointed himself its permanent president. The Acerbo
election laws, passed in July 1923, effectively abolished proportional
representation within the remnants of Italian parliamentary government.[1] In the April 1924 elections, which had been preceded by unpar-
alleled Fascist terror tactics, the Fascist composite ticket was awarded
374 of 535 Parliamentary seats. Mussolini's landmark speech on January 3, 1925, is generally held as a defining moment in the suppression of

political opposition and the institutional beginning of the single-party totalitarian regime. In the speech, Mussolini boldly stated his implicit responsibility for the assassination of Socialist deputy Giacomo Matteotti in June 1924. Matteotti was killed by Fascist *squadristi* widely believed to have acted under the direction of Cesare Rossi, the head of Mussolini's press office: "I declare . . . that I, and I alone, assume the political, moral and historical responsibility for all that has happened. . . . If Fascism has been a criminal association, if all the acts of violence have been the result of a certain historical, political and moral climate, the responsibility for this is mine."

The Matteotti assassination had represented a potentially serious political liability. Yet by rhetorically accepting responsibility for *all* acts of fascist violence, Mussolini effectively attempted to establish additional political control over the most extremist strands within his own movement. At the same time, his acceptance of responsibility was largely rhetorical since fascism's remaining external opponents were unable either to indict or to sanction him for this specific crime. Led by Liberal Party Deputy Giovanni Amendola, most of the opposition deputies had withdrawn from the Parliament to protest the assassination. Not only were they unable to find support for indicting Mussolini, when a group of the opposition deputies (the Popolari) later tried to return to the Chamber, blackshirts led by Fascist Party Secretary Farinacci physically blocked their entry.[2]

By January 1926 Mussolini could issue decrees that had the full force of law. During the same period of time, one can also point to the results of a number of equally swift Fascist interventions in the cultural sphere. Almost immediately, the state began to supplant the organized recreation activities of the *dopolavoro* (literally, the "after work") that were previously run by trade unions and company clubs.[3] In 1924, it monopolized the nascent radio industry. During the 1920s, radios were not very common since the cost was beyond the means of most Italian families. By the end of the 1930s they would be a much more common household item. The establishment of the radio monopoly nonetheless indicates the importance that the state attributed to mass media. Even at this early stage in its evolution, the regime recognized how radio could be used as a tool for building consent for its policies.[4]

In June 1925, the government founded the National Fascist Institute of Culture, headed by Giovanni Gentile. Six months later it called for the establishment of an Italian Academy. In 1926, the Federazione Italiana delle Biblioteche Popolari—the sprawling network of left-leaning local libraries—was placed under direct Fascist control.[5] In the same year, a special commission on Fascist education banned 101 of the 317 history textbooks that were currently being used in Italian classrooms. And, by the end of 1926, all major non-fascist newspapers had been totally suppressed.

Yet unlike this early grasp of other culture industries, more than a decade would pass before the Fascist state would take any significant control over the production and distribution of fiction films.[6] A number of recent studies have made a great deal of this apparently anomalous relationship between the totalitarian regime and the cinema. Taking note of of the state's slow entrance into the country's cinematic affairs has served to disjoin readings of Italian cinema during fascism from fascism itself. For example, Elaine Mancini has argued that even at a much later stage in its evolution the fascist state exercised very little influence over Italian filmmaking. Mancini contends: "The first five years of the 1930's can hardly be called totalitarian or even Fascist. If anything, the film industry struggled to be free."[7] And though there are serious shortcomings to the conclusions drawn by these studies, the question itself of why the state intervened so slowly still needs to be answered.

There are three principal reasons for the timing and nature of the state's interventions, and all three are entirely coherent with the historical evolution of Italian fascism. First, the fascist consolidation of power was not as dramatic or at least as untroubled as the watershed interventions we have mentioned might seem to indicate. In his first two years as prime minister, Mussolini ran a coalition government that only implicitly excluded the participation of Socialist and Popolari parties. Indeed, until the 1924 elections, the Fascists maintained only 35 out of the 535 parliament seats. In general terms, it is fair to say that it wasn't until 1929, at least, that Mussolini was able to suppress the major internal tensions of the fascist movement and to consolidate his control over real governance in Italy. Within his own party, for example, Mussolini had to negotiate between at least four separate groups: the local fascist leaders—the Ras—and their *squadristi,* Nationalists, technocrats, and conservatives. Although Mussolini moved swiftly indeed to formalize the *squadristi*—the fascist terror squads—into his own private para-state army, the MVSN, they nonetheless remained effectively under local and regional control for quite some time. Italo Balbo, the leader of the Ferrara *squadristi,* presented Mussolini and the "conservative" fascists with particular difficulties.[8]

Even after significantly centralizing control over the Party, the process of political consolidation continued for a number of years. Adrian Lyttelton summarizes the situation:

> If, however, Mussolini after 3 January [1925] became more and more able to ignore the political opposition, this did not mean that all politics was conducted within the Fascist party. Autonomous institutions survived: and as well as the party, Mussolini had still to reckon with the views of the Crown, the Army, the Church, big business, and other interests. . . . In fact the history of 1925–9 is in large part the history of the process by which Mussolini eliminated the Fascist movement's resistance to the measures by which he achieved a stable *entente* with these institutions.[9]

In this early stage, the Fascists were not yet in a political position to take unobstructed control over cultural production, distribution, and consumption. It can be further argued that the specific political liabilities initially provoked by the Matteotti assassination in June 1924 temporarily rendered the government all the more hesitant to take a highly visible stance regarding cultural activity, especially in a sector as immediately public as the cinema. In order to distance himself from the assassination and in an effort to quash the more militant strands of the fascist movement, Mussolini forced the resignation of Press Officer Rossi, among others. In the critical two-year span after the assassination, the nascent state's relationship to the cinema had been regulated by the very same press bureau. For some time after Rossi's resignation, therefore, Mussolini avoided making any major interventions into the film industry insofar as they might also risk drawing a direct line of authority between the prime minister and Matteotti's killers.

Secondly, whereas these factors are directly political in nature, the industrial and economic conditions of Italian cinema during fascism's first decade made early involvement equally problematic. As previously mentioned, Italian film production precipitously declined throughout the entire decade of the 1920s. Even though overall attendance at the movies rose steadily in this same time frame, Italian film production decreased from approximately 150 features in 1919 to only two actual releases in 1931. A number of factors are often cited for the demise of production during the 1920s: the exorbitant taxation schedule placed on box-office receipts, the general rise in production costs (particularly the disproportionately high salaries paid to major actresses), the costly big-budget failures that attempted to recapture the earlier success of the historical epics, and the simultaneous loss of international markets along with the increasing penetration of the Italian market by foreign films. Even more important, the underlying condition for this decline was the lack of system-wide capitalization for production. Unlike the more or less continual increases in finance capital for print publication, investment in the film industry remained dependent on the individual company's ability to arrange for single film financing. The larger Italian banks were hesitant to do much more, partially due to the economic disaster of the Unione Cinematografica Italiana in 1922. They were also hesitant because control over the larger film companies had remained in the hands of the aristocratic entrepreneurs, the figures who had led the industry's initial growth in the early teens. This lack of a "modern" relationship with finance capital is well described in a 1920 editorial from the film magazine *Kines:* "In Italy we have everything, writers, directors, cameramen, actors, actresses, lights, sets, locations. To make the industry work, we miss just one genre: industrialists. . . . We don't have the necessary elements for understanding big business; we only have small shopkeepers."[10]

It would not be until the early thirties that the state would begin to arrange a more stable arrangement between the film industry and finance. Yet while the government's unwillingness to do so earlier was clearly influenced by the industry's essentially moribund condition, it also conformed to the evolution of the fascist corporativist state. That is, it corresponds to the particular form of partnership between the state and industry characteristic of Italian fascism. David Forgacs describes this partnership in terms no less than those of a political alliance:

> The Fascists did not attempt to repress these private interests or, for most of the time they were in power, to direct their activities in a "totalitarian" way. Why not? One can suggest three converging explanations. The first is that they did not want to. Fascism rested upon an alliance with private industry, whose political support and goodwill it solicited and sought to maintain. The cultural industry, like other industries, looked to the state for protection and expansion of their markets, facilitation of imports of raw materials and exports of finished products, fiscal concessions and so forth.[11]

Thus the third reason for the timing and pattern of the state's involvement with the cinema can be seen in the particular structure of the state/industry partnership. The key condition of this arrangement, and perhaps the single most significant characteristic of the industry as a whole during the 1920s, is the discrepancy between the decline in feature film production and the simultaneous increase in film attendance.

Between 1924 and 1927 alone, overall film gross box-office receipts more than doubled. And while the vertiginous decline in film production wouldn't be halted until the early 1930s, the film industry's share of the country's total spectator entertainment revenues (including theater, music halls, opera, and sporting events) steadily grew. By 1927, its box-office receipts represented over half of all such income,[12] and by 1941 an astounding 83 percent of all spectator spending went to the cinema.[13] In Rome alone, foreign films were responsible for close to 84 percent of the total box office in 1932. Ticket sales in relation to national production broke down approximately as follows: America (61 percent), Italy (16 percent), Germany (14 percent), France (6 percent), England (1.5 percent), and other (1.5 percent). To sum up the situation, from 1920 to at least 1932, more and more Italians went to the cinema and saw fewer and fewer Italian films.

One obvious consequence of this discrepancy was the industry's near total dependence upon foreign product.[14] At the same time then, it also helps to explain why the state intervened so slowly and primarily on behalf of only one sector within the industry, exhibition. Protectionist measures which might have assisted Italian films in competing with the imports were viewed by exhibitors as potentially adding to the cost of raw materials, that is, of the films which they needed to acquire for their screens. Stefano Pittaluga, the cinema's most powerful industrialist (its only mogul, to use the Hollywood term) until his untimely death in 1931, warned against the potential impact that protectionism might have: "What would be the consequences? To start with, the government would have to exacerbate the already heavy custom taxes on foreign films, and this would immediately provoke reprisals from the importing nations. Not only this, unwisely accelerated hostility with our foreign friends would cause them to once again start an open campaign against us with renewed bitterness. And in this event, we could be hard hit just as we were during the War, that is, we could find ourselves without any raw materials at all."[15]

Although industry spokesmen did lobby for some limited forms of protection—for a reduction of the import tax on negative film stock, in particular—they argued that both new tariffs and import quotas would be counterproductive since there was no real system of production to protect. Pittaluga, the single largest theater owner throughout the 1920s and therefore the unquestioned private sector spokesman for the entire industry, sent a set of recommendations to the government on the occasion of the cinema's second national congress. For

Pittaluga, such interventions "presuppose the existence of an industry which is desirous of defending itself. In our case, the industry does not exist—and on the contrary needs to be created."[16]

Since exhibitors could be fairly successful by showing a ready supply of foreign (particularly American) films, the state consistently avoided serious protectionist measures for over a decade. The net effect was not only to delay any significant vertical organization of the national industry; it also limited the state's ability to achieve *any* unmediated totalitarian control over its production until a dozen years after its seizure of political power.

The design and impact of the state's active regulation of Italian cinema can be broken down into two general periods. Between 1922 and 1931 the state followed an unevenly deployed mercantilist approach to the private film industry. Its limited interventions primarily sought to protect the financial interests of the distribution and especially the exhibition sectors. After 1931 the government became increasingly involved in shaping the industry as a whole and helped in particular to resuscitate national film production. This more active participation was supported by a key shift in the political evolution of fascism itself, the transition from the initial consolidation of power to the building of national consensus. Just how cinema should assist in building this national consensus was the center of the debate on cinema throughout the thirties.

Two primary positions dominated the ongoing debate on the best role for the cinema during this period. One position emphasized its vital importance to the reshaping of national political identity, called for direct control by the state, and envisioned an expansive "educational" deployment of propaganda. The other argued for cinema as popular culture and therefore stressed the importance of its autonomy from state ownership or control. Stressing the historical significance of the cinema as a modern form of communication, Mussolini himself seemed to support the first position and conceptualized cinema as a fundamental tool in the expansion of fascist reformation of culture. The contrasting positions are clearly evidenced in the following two citations. In a speech at the opening of the Istituto Internazionale del Cinema Educatore in Rome on November 5, 1928, Mussolini outlined the cinema's historical teleology: "Among thousands of other discoveries, there are three that signal epochs in the history of human civilization: the discovery of movable type in the middle of the fifteenth century, the discovery of the camera obscura a century later, and finally the discovery of cinematography; three fundamental points in the progress of the human spirit, three formidable instruments *for the conquest and the spread of culture*." And Alessandro Blasetti, one of the period's most important directors, suggested that state control would undermine the cinema's potential for innovation as well as its ability to develop political consensus through popular culture: "A state cinema industry must necessarily be directed towards one particular aim—propaganda. And it would fail. The products of such an industry, whether or not these received the approval of the fascist state, would be irrevocably boycotted; rejected by the market, forbidden by foreign censorship."[17]

In October 1923 the regime had begun its support of the industry by halving the tax rate on box-office income from 60 to 30 percent. It should be mentioned that, despite this reduction, the total amount of taxes generated by box-office receipts continued to be a significant source of revenue for the state. In 1925, for example, these revenues still amounted to over forty-nine million lire, for a remarkable 25 percent of the entire nation's entertainment-related tax revenues.[18] These totals were enhanced by the fact that cinema was paying a rate much higher than other forms of entertainment. Cinema industry lobbyists considered the tax particularly onerous because it wasn't calculated in relation to real costs and profit. As a flat rate applied to all ticket sales, it didn't take into account either the costs of production and rentals or the significant variations between the economics of urban and rural cinema exhibition.

While the state's major involvement in fiction film would wait until a few years later, this was not at all the case with nonfiction film. On October 11, 1925, the Council of Ministers, following instructions from Mussolini, nationalized what had been a small private organization into the Unione Cinematografica Educativa (LUCE), the state's own newsreel and documentary agency. LUCE produced and distributed all Italian newsreels and documentaries from this point until the regime's demise. The stated purpose was to educate the nation by valorizing the government's programs. Four days prior to its formal ratification by law, Mussolini himself wrote to the Council stating the new institution's mission: "As you know, I have constituted LUCE from some of the nation's major economic agencies in order to create an effective means of circulating cultural, political, scientific films, social and national propaganda: an agency for culture and 'italianità.'"[19] In addition to steadily increased budgets for its production schedule, LUCE's mandate was particularly reinforced by a law passed in 1926 (Regio Decreto-Legge no. 1000). The new legislation obliged exhibitors to show a LUCE newsreel and/or a documentary prior to every feature presentation, thereby intertwining the presence of the state with the overall experience of the cinema.[20] To cite one example, between 1928 and 1943, LUCE newsreels showed 249 events that took place at or near the Vittorio Emmanuelle, Mussolini's headquarters.

Many of the recent studies on the relationship between fascism and the cinema accurately note how infrequently the state—its uniforms, its symbols—was directly represented. However, while this is an arguably accurate assessment of commercial fiction films, the state was indeed present in the country's theaters via the mandatory projection of its newsreels and documentaries. As I will discuss later, this presence constitutes a basic component to the cinema experience during the fascist period.

The state's first significant move toward assisting feature film production was the requirement that exhibitors dedicate 10 percent of their programming to Italian films.[21] This requirement, enacted as R.D.L. (Regio Decreto-Legge) no. 1121 on June 16, 1927, was the first attempt to establish an effective limit, a quota on the importation of foreign films. There were a number of reasons, however, why this measure—ironically referred to in the press as the "Italian week"—was unable to stem the tide. First, it is not at all clear that exhibitors (especially in rural areas) complied with the requirement. Second, given that many theaters typically closed from July through September, 10 percent of the total programming dedicated to Italian films would add up to only approximately thirty days for the entire year. Third, even when exhibitors attempted to fully comply, the entire Italian industry produced far fewer films than would have been needed to cover the exhibitors' needs even for only the Italian week.[22]

R.D.L. 1121 did not provide the film industry with the basis for any real leverage against the dominant presence of foreign films within its national marketplace. Indeed, by 1936, a full nine years after this law, foreign films still took in over 80 percent of total box-office revenues.[23] At the same time, the law did mandate a series of institutional practices—both economic and ideological in their intent—that would have a major impact on Italian film culture not only during the fascist period but well afterward. It required that all imported films be dubbed entirely into Italian. Furthermore, the distribution company had to pay a rather stiff 25,000-lire surcharge for the right to dub a given film. For every Italian film it released, a distribution company would then receive three exemptions, *buoni del doppiaggio* (literally "dubbing coupons"), from the dubbing surcharge. The ratio of three to one would subsequently be adjusted to four to one. However, these savings in the costs of film distribution did not make up for the taxation on box-office receipts. Furthermore, since the industry was not yet vertically integrated (i.e., few companies in the period owned production, exhibition, and distribution arms), the law's overall impact was less economic and, as we shall see, more ideological in nature.

Italy remains one of the few countries in the world that regularly dubs (as opposed to subtitling) its imports. To this day, this institutional regulation impacts the Italian mode of production. It supports a small dubbing industry and encourages film producers to take advantage of its technical infrastructure. Indeed, very few Italian films use direct (live) sound recording, and virtually all dialogue is added in post-production. The ironic presentation of the Italian actress in Francois Truffaut's *Day for Night* (1973) actually refers to an ongoing practice of the Italian mode of film production. In the film, Valentina Cortese complains to director Truffaut that she can't be bothered with the *actual* dialogue. Saying that when she works with *Federico* all she has to do is recite numbers, she performs her scene literally without the words!

While this system of *buoni del doppiaggio* attempted to promote the economic interests of the national film industry, it also contributed to an ideological project which was central to the regime's cultural policy. The law's explicit economic intent was to provide an incentive to Italian companies to produce and distribute more national product. However, as with many of the government's initiatives up to 1931, only Stefano Pittaluga's firm, Società Anonima Stefano Pittaluga (SASP), and its production studio, Cines, were in a position to take advantage of the incentive. In 1924, Pittaluga had begun to expand his Genoa-based exhibition activities by buying and reorganizing the FERT production studios in Turin. His cycle of strongman films, centering around the characters of Maciste, Sansone, and Saetta, were the most commercially successfully Italian films of the twenties.[24] More importantly, by 1926 he had acquired exclusive Italian distribution rights to the films of Universal, Warner Bros., and First National. Thus, between his own production and the distribution of titles from these three American studios, SASP provided close to 80 percent of all the films shown in Italy in 1926.[25] In the following few years, Pittaluga remained the only producer who could effectively reinvest the *buoni del doppiaggio* in additional Italian production.

This system was ideological in design because it enacted one ongoing imperative of fascist cultural policy—the defense of a hypothetical national identity. In effect, dubbing attempted to protect the Italian public from exposure to foreign influence through language. It was one cinematic equivalent to the central goal of the Fascist Institute of National Culture. As directed by Giovanni Gentile, the institute was set up to "preserve for our intellectual life its national character according to the genius and the tradition of our race, and also to favor its expansion abroad."[26]

Exemplary of the fascist regime's desire to *purify* the national cultural landscape, one of the institute's principal activities was the defense of the Italian language. Along with a number of other agencies, it sought to protect "Italian" by banning words of foreign derivation. This was a highly publicized campaign that included newspaper contests in which the readership was asked to find the best substitutions for contaminating foreign words. Many terms in common usage, such as *bar, record* and *garage,* were considered exotic and had been virtually eliminated by the end of the thirties. The word *club* was replaced by either *circolo, centro,* or *associazione. Hotels* became *alberghi.* The *menu* was replaced by the *lista, taxi* by *tassi, chauffeur* by *autista, garage* by *rimessa, champagne* by *spumante, cheque* by *assegno,* and *boxer* by *pugile.* Tobacco products formerly known as Brittanici and Kentucky were rebranded as Fiume and Tigrina. This specific campaign against foreign influences was only one site in a larger fascist effort to reshape the Italian language. While it is true that other European countries established academies for the defense of "the" national language, in Italy the campaign was both xenophobic and linked to the regime's colonialist ambitions. As the regime expanded its interventions in Africa in the late 1930s, it also intensified its efforts at cultural autarchy through linguistic sanitation. Those efforts also included the absolute preference of the second-person-plural personal pronoun *voi*—as a sign of hierarchical respect—in place of the third-person-singular *Lei.* And, as with the ideological re-evocation of Roman antiquity in other cultural sites (cinema, uniforms, signage, etc.), this linguistic preference also attempted to link a "pure" Italian to the civilizing accomplishments of the Roman Empire. In a 1938 article in *Corriere della Sera,* Bruno Cicognani made the explicit link to the Roman tradition:

The fascist revolution intends to bring back the spirit of our race to its authentic origins, freeing it from any pollution. Then, let us bring forth this purification. Also in this, let us go back to the use of Rome, to the Christian and Roman *tu* which expresses the universal value of Rome and Christianity. Let the *voi* be a sign of respect and of hierarchical recognition. But in any other case let the *tu* be the form of communicating, writing or speaking: the grammatically, logically, and spiritually true, immediate, simple, genuine and Italian form.[27]

I have viewed most of the still extant prints, and it appears that there was a fairly widespread avoidance of such banned language in the Italian movies of the period. When such utterances do appear, especially after 1936, they are often used ironically, indicating a fascist/populist critique of bourgeois snobbism. Thus these "exoticisms" self-consciously refer to the regime's drive for linguistic purity. In Alessandro Blasetti's *La Contessa di Parma* (1937), for example, a fashion model is linguistically "corrected" by the owner of the clothing store:

The Model: I'm a mannequin in the Maison Printemps!
The Owner: Ha! Printemps! Pri-ma-ve-ra! *[Spring!]* Primavera! Can't you hear how much better it sounds? You are a *model* in the *Primavera store*.

The ideological character of the state-mandated dubbing cannot be overstated. Such was the force of the purification campaign that even in the face of extreme technical limitations, the dubbing requirement remained in place. Between 1929 and 1931, that is, until the technical infrastructure for dubbing was fully in place, the requirement led to the presentation of all foreign films without their original-language dialogue. For two years, films that could not be dubbed abroad[28] were shown with diegetic sound and music intact, but with the original dialogue muted and expressed via intertitles. Mario Quargnolo describes this anomalous situation:

On the original sound track only the music and sounds remained, while the sequences were continually interrupted—and not very aesthetically—by intertitles which translated the dialog. In this way, the original film lost its rhythm and value. . . . Among the sound films with an additional, censoriously imposed "sound track," we recall at least: *Cimarron* (1930) Wesley Ruggles, *Der blaue Engel* (1930) Josef von Sternberg, *Hallelujah!* (1929) King Vidor, *Sous les toits de Paris* (1929) René Clair, *Hell's Angels* (1930) Lewis Milestone, *Dirigible* (1930) Frank Capra. *The Show of Shows* (1929) John Adolfi, was presented with the sequence in which we see (but do not hear!) John Barrymore recite the monologue from *Richard III*.[29]

Once the technical infrastructure was in place, dubbing became a very effective vehicle for mediating between the ideological mandates of fascism and the commercial interests of the film industry. The case of *The Adventures of Marco Polo* (Archie Mayo, 1938) illustrates the balance between political and economic imperatives. The fascist censorship board initially blocked the film's importation because it felt that Gary Cooper was an inappropriate representative of the legendary Venetian explorer. After pressure was brought to bear on behalf of the film's distributor, the ideological problem was solved by changing Cooper's fictive nationality. The film's title became *Uno scozzese alla corte del Gran Khan,* "A Scotsman in the Court of the Great Khan." Any changes in the film's dialogue needed to make the narrative conform to the protagonist's new national identity could then be made in the dubbing process.[30]

This institutional collaboration between the state and the industry was deepened by the subsequent requirement not only that all foreign film be dubbed into Italian, but also that the work be performed in Italy and by Italians.[31] On the one hand, this regulation created a mini-industry with a guaranteed stream of films to work on, which was paid for (through the dubbing surcharge) by the importing company. Indeed, much of the system survives to the present day. On the other hand, not only did dubbing protect the Italian public from foreign language, it also (to a lesser degree) suppressed the usage of Italian dialects. Throughout the thirties, the state made serious efforts at erasing regional difference by attempting to create an official and unified national language. In 1931 the press was given the following instruction: "Do not publish articles, poems, or titles in dialect. The encouragement of dialect literature is in conflict with the Regime's rigidly Unitarian spiritual and political directives. Regionalism, and the dialects which constitute their principal expressions, are the residue of centuries of divisions and servitude of the old Italy."[32] Following directly from this, all English-language films were to be translated into "pure"—that is, non-accented, non-dialect—Italian.[33] The suppression of accent and dialect in the Italian cinema during the thirties provides essential background to understanding why neorealism was considered a radical break with the past. Neorealism's use of nonprofessional actors (speaking accented and dialect Italian that defined them in terms of a diverse regional identity) was therefore also a reaction against the very specific tenets of fascist cultural policy.

In 1931 the state began a series of more substantial initiatives that would soon lead to an increase in feature film production, inaugurating what has been referred to as the *rinascita* or rebirth of the Italian cinema.[34] On June 18, 1931, it enacted national legislation (R.D.L. no. 918) that authorized the state to award an amount equivalent to 10 percent of the gross box-office receipts to production companies for each Italian film they released. Almost immediately, production began to increase—from thirteen titles in 1931 to twenty-nine in 1932 and to thirty-four in 1933.[35]

While this law had an significant impact on the structure of the film industry, it did not yet constitute an attempt by the state to gain more direct control over its content. Although its statutes spelled out considerably strict criteria for what constituted an "Italian" film, the bonus was consistently awarded without reference to the film's style or content. The law stipulated three criteria for eligibility:

1. The screenplay had to be written by an Italian.
2. The majority of the crew had to be Italian.
3. The interiors and exteriors had to be shot in Italy.

This final criterion was occasionally waived when the film's narrative logic required a foreign location. Apart from the ongoing problem of a lack of serious capital investment, this may have been one of the reasons why so very few films during the period have fictions that take place outside Italy.[36]

If anything, the political component of this new system was its very economic assistance in the battle against Hollywood. Minister of Corporations Giuseppe Bottai was its chief sponsor. Bottai explicitly outlined the law's dual intent:

> With this legislation we propose to help an industry which must confront truly formidable problems in global competition. . . . The government wishes to assist the industry in one of its specific activities, that of resisting that foreign industry which brings into our market those films of entertainment, of plot twists, of fantasy and imagination which constitute a potent attraction for the public. I rarely go to the cinema but I have always noticed that the public is invariably bored when the cinema wishes to educate it. The public wants to be entertained and it is precisely on this terrain that today we wish to help the Italian industry.[37]

Despite Bottai's position, from this point forward the state would progressively deepen its involvement in and control over the film industry.

The direction of this involvement would be to create a corporate state cinema, that is, a film industry built as a commercial venture but which eventually would be owned and controlled by the state. Ironically, the model for the state's commercial venture in cinema was explicitly Hollywood. In 1932, Luigi Freddi (who two years later would direct all state intervention in the cinema) was sent to Los Angeles to study the Hollywood studio system. Upon his return, Freddi was asked by Mussolini to report his findings and to make recommendations on how the state could improve the Italian situation. Freddi would later recall: "I came back from Hollywood filled with understanding, with experiences and notes. The cinema had gotten into my blood. Upon returning to Italy, I decided to write a series of articles on the problems of the Italian cinema, which after my new experience, seemed to be in an even more desolate squalor."[38]

The major steps towards the construction of a state-owned cinema, even if influenced by the Hollywood model, soon followed, and focused on the Pittaluga holdings. At the beginning of the decade, Pittaluga's SASP was not only the largest of the film production companies, it was the only one that came close to vertical integration.[39] While Pittaluga built his position of strength by importing American films, his production studio (Cines) was supported by a chain of first-run theaters in every major Italian city. Eighty percent of SASP capital came from the Banca Commerciale Italia (BCI). With Pittaluga's death and when the worldwide economic crisis of 1929–31 destabilized Italy's major banks, the state intervened by guaranteeing BCI's capital resources. Though BCI remained a private company, in exchange for the guarantee it turned over a majority of its stock (in June 1933) to the Istituto per la Ricostruzione Industriale (IRI), the state's Institute for Industrial Reconstruction. IRI immediately sold off the weakest of the SASP divisions—the production studio Cines—to industrialist Carlo Roncoroni. SASP distribution activities were given over to LUCE (the state's newsreel agency), and in November 1935, the IRI established the Ente Nazionale Industrie Cinematografiche (ENIC, the National Agency of Cinema Industries), the first exhibition circuit directly controlled by the state. ENIC itself would come to have an ever-increasing role in all aspects of the film industry. As stipulated in its original mandate, it would be responsible for "buying, selling, production, and distribution of films, running cinemas and theaters and in general all the operations connected with the industry and commerce of cinema. It would have the ability to contract loans, to establish advances on distribution contracts, to grant subsidies, to buy interests in other companies which work in the industry and commerce of cinema."[40] Thus distribution and exhibition were effectively run as different divisions of the same company since LUCE and ENIC were both state organisms and shared the same president.[41]

On September 19, 1934, the state created the Direzione Generale per la Cinematografia (DGC, General Directorate for Cinema). The DGC was directed by Luigi Freddi—the former head of the Fascist National Party's propaganda office—and was placed under the administrative control of the Ministero per la Stampa e Propaganda (Press and Propaganda Ministry). On May 27, 1937, the Ministero per la Stampa e Propaganda became the Ministero della Cultura Popolare (Ministry of Popular Culture), through which the state intended to supervise and direct all phases of Italian cultural and intellectual life. This reorganization was significant because it centralized the state's regulation of the film industry into a single agency. It became responsible for the development of a coherent economic policy vis-à-vis the cinema, an area that had previously been within the purview of the Ministry of Corporations. Furthermore, it assumed the task of supervising the work of the censorship boards, previously the domain of the Ministry of the Interior.

The function of film censorship in fascist Italy was particularly complex, and it is surprising that it has received relatively little scholarly examination. For example, in his capacity as head of the General Directorate for the Cinema, Freddi made it clear that he did not see censorship primarily as an agency for repression by the totalitarian state. In a memorandum to Galeazzo Ciano (minister of press and propaganda, and Mussolini's son-in-law), Freddi wrote:

It is opportune to make clear above all that the commissions [censorship] should not limit themselves exclusively to repressive functions, but should instead become an instrument by which the State can apply new moral and aesthetic standards to the cinema. As such the commissions should collaborate in this effort, seeking to slow down the importation of the foreign production which is morally and artistically damaging, but particularly in order to obtain a general improvement in the quality of our national cinematographic production, rendering it able to not only hold its own in the competition with foreign productions in our own national market, but also to find an entry into international markets, and above all to contribute via its potent means of suggestion to the aims of the State.[42]

By fusing the deployment of its political and economic policy into the DGC, the state was also able to orchestrate cultural initiatives at an unprecedented level. The following were the direct result of the DGC's coordination of the cinematic institution: the expansion of the Venice Film Festival in 1934 (film was originally introduced into the Biennale in 1932 as the Mostra Internazionale d'Arte Cinematografica), the establishment of a national film school in 1935 (Centro Sperimentale per la Cinematografia), and the construction of Europe's most modern and largest production facilities in 1937 (Cinecittà).

The government's final major intervention during this period was the passage of the Alfieri Law on September 4, 1938.[43] This legislation increased the state subsidy for each Italian film from 10 to 12 percent. More importantly, it bestowed upon ENIC an absolute monopoly over the importation and distribution of foreign films in Italy. When the monopoly went into effect the following year, the Hollywood studios (Metro Goldwyn Mayer, Twentieth Century Fox, Warner Bros., and Paramount) responded by closing their distribution offices in Italy. Since the demand for films remained the same (film attendance actually continued to increase well into the war years), the impact was an immediate increase in the number of Italian films produced and distributed, from 45 in 1938 to 119 in 1942. Although American films continued to be distributed in Italy, the ratio of Italian productions to American was effectively reversed by the implementation of the ENIC monopoly. Libero Bizzari estimates that in 1938 American films represented 63 percent of the country's total box office, Italian films 13 percent. In 1940 the Italian share rose to 34 percent, the American fell off to no more than 22 percent.[44] Given the dominance of American films in Italy over the previous two decades, the state's establishment of the ENIC monopoly inaugurated virtually the only period in its history—from 1939 until the end of World War II—that the Italian cinema approached control over its own internal market.

THE IMPACT OF THE REGIME'S REGULATION(S)

From 1922 to 1931, the state's limited assistance to the film industry had no impact on the steady decline in production. The number of Italian films (over 1,000 meters in length)[45] released in each year since fascism came to government until 1931 was as follows:

1922: 144

1923: 114

1924: 66

1925: 38

1926: 27

1927: 25

1928: 31

1929: 20

1930: 8

1931: 2

After the failure of the Unione Cinematografica Italiana, the absence of an ongoing system of film finance had two additional results. First, it meant that large-budget productions capable of competing with highly capitalized American films all but disappeared. There were a number of attempts to recapture the international successes of the Italian historical epics of the previous decade in films such as *Messalina* (Enrico Guazzoni, 1923) and yet another remake of *Quo Vadis* (Gabriellino D'Annunzio and Georg Jacoby, 1924). Both films had exceptionally high budgets for the period and were similarly unsuccessful at the box office.

The lack of a system for ongoing substantial film finance was one of the economic conditions that can explain the industrial logic for the "white telephone" films of the following decade. In a word, since location shooting and large set constructions were generally too expensive for the industry, Italian narrative cinema of the thirties tended to be located in recognizable and reusable indoor settings. Second, these disastrous conditions provoked an exodus of most of the period's major directors. Mario Camerini traveled to Paris, where he worked in Paramount's Joinville studios preparing multiple-language versions of American films for release in Europe. After working in Austria and Germany, Augusto Genina made six films in France, including *Prix de beauté* in 1930.[46] Both Gennaro Righelli and Goffredo Alessandrini trained for brief periods in Hollywood. Other important figures in Italy's talent pool who had to find work abroad in the 1920s included Guido Brignone, Carmine Gallone, Emilio Ghione, Nunzio Malasomma, and Amleto Palermi.

From 1932 to 1942, the state's involvement in the film industry made possible the economic conditions for a revitalization of production. The increase in Italian titles released in these years is reflected in the following annual statistics:

1932: 18

1933: 39

1934: 32

1935: 28

1936: 40

1937: 30

1938: 45

1939: 77

1940: 83

1941: 89

1942: 119[47]

At the same time that production increased, the vast majority of films actually screened during the period continued to be imported (as we have seen), mostly from the United States. Though Italy also imported films from Germany, France, and England, all non-American titles never amounted to more than 10 to 15 percent of the total number of films seen each year. In sum, throughout the twenties and thirties, the experience of going to the cinema in Italy meant seeing principally three kinds of films: *Italian features*—in the numbers outlined above; *Hollywood narratives*—in the dominating proportions we have mentioned; and the *state's newsreels and documentaries*—shown before the screening of both the first two. As I will explore in later chapters, these three kinds of film interacted textually with one another, creating a particular historical matrix for reading culture during the period.

While feature-length Italian fiction films tended to avoid its direct representation,[48] the regime *was* omnipresent in the newsreels. In its first years of operation, LUCE produced over one hundred newsreels per year. Throughout the thirties it released an annual average of close to two hundred. On the whole, the structure and duration of fascist newsreels closely resemble those of their international counterparts such as Fox Movietone, Hearst Metrotone, British Gaumont, Pathé, and others. The visual similarity between LUCE and its counterparts was also reinforced by the practice of footage exchange between the various companies, a practice that continued until the early forties.

Like the other newsreel agencies, LUCE covered a wide range of topics, ranging from major news events from around the world to the latest fashions in popular culture, from the movements of renowned political figures and film stars to coverage of sporting events. Unlike the others, LUCE traced the evolution of fascism in great detail by reporting the accomplishments of the regime: public works projects, highway and railway construction, colonial expansion in Albania and Ethiopia, the Battle for Grain, and so forth.[49] Furthermore, the significance of the newsreel as a tool for building consensus was magnified by the still limited availability of radios and a relatively high illiteracy rate.[50] The quantity of newsreel output, coupled with the regulation that theaters show them prior to the feature presentation, gave the state its best opportunity to speak directly to the Italian public. In some sectors, newsreels were even seen as a means of dealing with Hollywood. An editorial in support of the state's agrarian policy stated: "It seems dangerous to present films which demonstrate the fascination of city life ... the brilliant comedies, the sumptuousness of certain homes, the feminine world of Hollywood with all its glamour. We need to exclude these films, which make people dream of a life quite removed from that of the peasant."[51]

Whether the state considered the cinema as a tool for education/indoctrination or as a commercial product that would entertain mass audiences, it inserted itself into the social equation in order to protect the Italian public from what it saw as the deleterious effects that contemporary cinema might have. On the one hand, this meant excising dangerous representations through censorship of film content. On the other hand, the state sought to colonize those forms of culture that, based in popular tradition, might otherwise produce anti-hegemonic effects. In her seminal work on the organization of leisure-time activities in the fascist period, Victoria de Grazia describes this second dilemma as follows: "On the level of recreational pastimes, Mussolini's dictatorship worked in a number of ways to promote a national consciousness. . . . The regime was further faced with a range of pastimes, deeply rooted in popularity and custom that threatened to retain their pre-fascist, oftentimes antifascist social and political connotations. Accordingly a systematic attempt was made to appropriate their popularity for fascist ends by absorbing their forms into nationally standardized patterns."[52]

Traditionally, theoretical discussions of the cinematic subject begin with accounts of its formation from within single texts. Such accounts, when they actually attempt to historicize that formation, tend to work backwards and outwards from the text in order to locate the subject as a real audience in its historical context. In the case of Italian cinema under fascism, however, we have an opportunity to see how an audience has already been addressed as subject prior to the main feature. Before Italian spectators entered into the symbolic order of a fictional world (offered by either American or Italian features), they had been already addressed as subjects by the state. Through its newsreels, the regime told its public that the reality of the world surrounding the cinema was, or was rapidly becoming, fascist. As I have discussed, the newsreels (and their usage as footage within the documentaries) are heavily saturated with the acts of the regime. In the newsreels themselves, this condensation of actions was infrequently tied to other acts. They were concatenated as moments that added up to a sense of overall fascist presence in the world. The primary "historical" quality of that presence constructed an overriding sense of eventfulness. Unlike the newsreel production from other nations, LUCE attempted to modify the citizen's sense of the public sphere by suggesting that, in form and function, all of contemporary fascist history was omnipresent within the cinema and, more importantly, in their shared experiences of the lived contemporary world. Paraphrasing Barbara Spackman, Claudio Fogu has put it: "The rhetorical appeal of Mussolini's juxtaposition of liberal history writing and fascist history making rested on its sudden stockpiling of 'eventfulness' rather than violence, and it pointed toward the popular culture roots of the fascist imaginary rather than the futurist rhetorics of virility." In his remarkable study of the struggle between fascism's modernist and anti-historicist impulses, Fogu goes on to say: "As the popular motto 'Fascism makes history, it does not write it' would make explicit, Mussolini's rhetorical conflation of speech and epochal eventfulness referred the idea of fascist history making to the notion of *historicness* inscribed. . . . Clearly Mussolini's popularization of history making and history writing mobilized precisely this discursive and anti-historicist notion of historicness, projecting the idea of fascism as a historic agent whose acts were not 'significant' in the eyes of history (and historians), but, rather, actively *signifying* history in the present."[53]

One important result was that LUCE enabled the state, in its representational strategies, to take the violence out of the party's past—that is, the *squadristi*—and to give the use of force a stable institutional status within the various fascist civil initiatives, especially as the regime began to prepare for its imperialist campaigns. I will come back to this representational transition in discussions of mid-thirties fictional films such as *Scipione l'africano* and *Condottieri*. For the moment, it is enough to underline that the mandatory presence of the state newsreels functioned as an intertextual prophylactic against potentially transgressive readings of the film that would follow.

Through its Opera Nazionale del Dopolavoro (OND), the national agency for leisure-time activity, the state actively encouraged cinema attendance. In 1927, it arranged for a 10 percent reduction of the sales tax on cinema ticket purchases and a 50 percent discount on fifty seats at all screenings for OND cardholders. Such practices certainly intended to build audiences of consumers in a way that favored the economics of the film industry. But they also conditioned spectatorship by collapsing traditional distinctions between private and public ontologies. The theoretically anonymous (private) identity of the film viewer—in the darkened theater—is interpolated (i.e., rendered public) in two ways. First, the very act of using the state-issued OND card connects a spectator to his/her economic status and articulates a relationship to the state as sponsor of his/her discounted entrance into the cinema. Second, once within the theater, he/she is addressed by the state both as perceived author of the newsreel text and as historical agent responsible for the eventfulness depicted in the newsreel. Since the realities depicted in the newsreels refer to spaces and times known to and experienced by the audience—that is, by Italian civil society—this second form of address additionally elides the distance between that audience's private and public standing. I contend that this elision was a fundamental characteristic of film readership under fascism and was symptomatic of the state's other attempts to transform the public sphere. This included, for example, the regime's attempts to increase birth rates through pronatalist initiatives such as the *giornata della madre e del fanciullo* and the awards given to families that produced larger numbers of children. But while these programs, conducted by the Opera Nazionale per la Protezione della Maternità e dell'Infanzia, did little to actually increase the population, they quite effectively disseminated a concept of the family as bound to the interests of the state. Fascist pronatalism militated against suffrage for women and served to keep them out of the workplace. That is, they brought the state into the most private of personal places, the bedroom.

As I have previously discussed, the preeminence of the exhibition sector both influenced the state's regulation of the film industry and paved the way for a special relationship with Hollywood. Two essential

Figure 4. Militarized women. Hearst Newsreel, vol. 10, no. 275 (May 5, 1939). "70,000 Amazons Forget Sex." Courtesy of the UCLA Film and Television Archive.

components of that relationship were ratified by the 1934 agreement signed by Will Hays and Galeazzo Ciano that limited the number of American imports to 250 titles per year. On the one hand, obtaining a guarantee from the president of the Motion Picture Producers Association that fixed a limit, any limit, on the number of foreign imports was perceived as a significant victory for fascist autarchy. On the other hand, since the actual number of films imported from Hollywood never even approached the limit of 250 per year,[54] the agreement ratifies the status quo of industry dependence on Hollywood product. Will Hays recalls meeting with Mussolini in 1936 in order to protest a planned restriction of American imports to forty-two per year:

> Nine days in Rome gave me time to see and hear plenty of evidence of constructive things that Mussolini had done for Italy. . . . First I pointed out that the total Italian receipts from motion pictures was a vast amount, with many families supported by the earnings of American motion pictures, from which same source the Italian Government also received 100,000,000 lire in taxes. . . . As to the position of American producers and distributors, I told him that the recent Italian decree was confiscatory and that we should have to move out of Italy unless some compromise was reached. . . . By now our conversation had become a joint exchange, and

at this point Il Duce asked, "What do you want?" It was as direct as that. I answered as directly: "We want to bring into Italy all the American motion pictures that the traffic will stand, and we want to take out enough money to enable us to live." . . . Mussolini said at once, "That seems fair," and picked up his telephone.[55]

In yet another regard, we can see this effective partnership at work. More often than not censorship functioned as a site of negotiation between state policy and the interests of exhibitors and distributors. This was especially the case while the Direzione Generale per la Cinematografia was administered by Luigi Freddi. Freddi often described his role as that of the mediator between the interests of the state and those of the film industry. Even though he was formally a representative of the regime, it is interesting to note that he viewed himself as *negotiator* between the state and the industry.[56] This was clearly the case with respect to the treatment of Hollywood films. As we have seen in the example of *The Adventures of Marco Polo,* the discussions centered on finding a way to resolve the ideologically problematic content of the film in order to clear the way for its entry into the country. Jean Gili describes this arrangement: "Under these conditions, once the problems of the transition to sound were overcome, the American cinema could be easily disseminated in Italy and the cases of argument with the censorship board were relatively few in proportion to the hundreds of films distributed in Italy during the thirties."[57]

Censorship did block a number of American films, but it did so primarily in cases where it was felt that the national reputation could be damaged. Because both *Scarface* (1932) and *Little Caesar* (1930) represented American gangsters as Italian in origin, neither was permitted entry. In general, however, the standards applied to American films were far more lax than those applied to Italian production. Certain subjects that were prohibited in Italian films were found acceptable in American films. In the gangster genre, for example, as long as the criminality and violence took place in America and was perpetrated by non-Italians, the state did not intervene. Since the gangster film is all but absent from Italian production during the period, the regime effectively mapped the geographical boundaries of legality and illegality. It communicated to the Italian public that crime, while deeply imbedded in the fabric of American social life, did not exist in fascist Italy.[58] Filmmaker Damiano Damiani recalled: "We discovered the films of the Roosevelt era under fascism, and one was careful not to prohibit them inasmuch as they gave a negative vision of the United States, a country of corruption, opposed to a pure Fascist Italy. . . . there was the case of *Little Caesar* which was prohibited because the protagonist was too evocative of Mussolini . . . and the Italian names given to American gangsters were also censored."[59]

A systematic study of the treatment by censorship boards and of the critical and popular reception of every American film shown during the twenties and thirties would be of great value. For example, the logic of allowing American films to show what would have been objectionable in an Italian production extended well beyond the gangster film genre. When Chaplin's *Modern Times* (1936) was initially blocked by the censorship board, Freddi defended its artistic merit and its political content. He argued that even the famous scene of the tramp with the red flag in front of the demonstrators was actually a fierce satire of socialism and therefore in concert with the ideological orientation of fascism itself. "As far as projecting the film in Italy goes, I think: 1) that it would be politically inopportune to prohibit Chaplin's film about which every one has heard, because of the work's artistic quality, and because Chaplin's arrows won't even cause a scratch; 2) that the principal target of *Modern Times* is the American world and this takes it beyond our censorial responsibilities."[60]

The dependence upon foreign fiction films in light of the imperative for autarchy opens up a major axis upon which to plot questions about Italian film under fascism. If the vast majority of Italian feature-length fiction films avoided directly representing the regime, the films nonetheless addressed the contradictions characteristic of Italian social life during the fascist period. In light of this premise, the following chapters pose three overriding questions. Given the state's hesitation to intervene in fiction film production, how did it represent itself within nonfiction productions? In what unique ways did Italian *fiction* film invoke, narrativize, and re-present the regime's ideological projects? And what role did Italian film production play in negotiating the overall cultural and ideological relationship to America and its films?

THREE

LEISURE TIME, HISTORIOGRAPHY, AND SPECTATORSHIP

Via economic preferences and corporativist assumptions, the regime denounced the private body as the site of desire, the locus of utopian visions, the ground experience. In so doing, it drew the line between fascism's political spectacle and the spectacle of commercial consumption. And though the philistine bourgeois seemed to be the preferred target of the regime's attack on hedonism, the denial of all individuals' autonomy was the base of fascism's creed. The desires of consuming shoppers in the world of goods were to be substituted with the desire for the dictator, the absorption of the individual into the body politic, the deadly consummation of one's life in the name of the nation.

Simonetta Falasca-Zamponi, *Fascist Spectacle: The Aesthetics of Power in Mussolini's Italy*

FASCIST SPORTS: HISTORICAL NARRATION AND THE NATIONAL BODY

One of the most visible aspects of the fascist regime in Italian civic life was its sponsorship and organization of both professional and amateur sports. The June 11, 1934, edition of *Il Messaggero* (one of Italy's largest daily newspapers) carried the following feature articles on its front page: "Two 35,000-ton battleships will begin construction by the end of the year," "New important experiments by Guglielmo Marconi," and "Il Duce applauds architects of the new Florence train station."

Figure 5. Heavyweight champion Primo Carnera stands before Mount Vesuvius (circa 1935). Courtesy of the Istituto LUCE.

Yet all three were dwarfed by the full-page headline and accompanying photograph: "Italy conquers the World Football Championship—The game with Czechoslovakia was won by a 2–1 score in the presence of Il Duce."

This was one example of the extraordinary importance given to sports under fascism. The Italian national football team won the gold medal at the 1928 Olympic Games and the World Cup in both 1934 and 1938. During this period, Italians set numerous speed records in car and motorcycle racing and won four world bicycle championships. Primo Carnera (*il gigante di Sequals*, "the human mountain") reigned as world heavyweight boxing champion from 1933 to 1935. Among these and many other notable achievements in sport, Italy finished a remarkable second place in the overall medal count at the 1932 Los Angeles Olympics, and came in third in Berlin in 1936.[1]

The state press, both newspapers and LUCE newsreels, gave extended coverage of these achievements. Invariably, the national accomplishments in sport were spoken of as the physical expression of fascist values. As Omar Calabrese describes it:

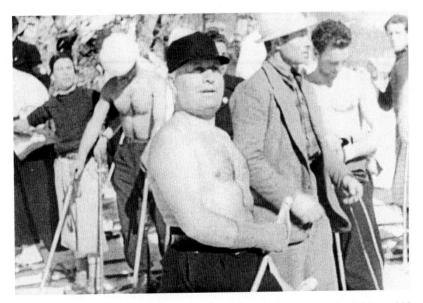

Figure 6. Il Duce, the athlete. Frame enlargement from Hearst Newsreel, vol. 14, no. 292 (circa 1942). Courtesy of the UCLA Film and Television Archive.

Fascism saw the potential of athletic success as an instrument of propaganda which could be made to square with some of the tenets of Italian supremacy: pre-eminence of physique and manliness (later of race), determination to win, order, discipline, the sacrifice involved in the practice of sport and the spirit of nationalism that goes hand in hand with sport understood as "fanaticism." . . . The myth of the athlete was to serve as an iconographic theme in the arts, figuratively merging the Roman ideal of the strong athlete and the modern and Futuristic one of speed, youth and daring.[2]

The grafting of these ideals, both fascist and futurist, onto the corpus of Italian sports achievements was fixed iconographically by recurrent representations of Mussolini as a sportsman. Throughout the entire period, Mussolini appears in many LUCE newsreels either practicing or dressed for a wide assortment of sports. Almost as often as he performs in the political role of the Duce, he was presented to the public as an accomplished fencer, equestrian, pilot, swimmer, skier, marksman, race driver, and so on. The accumulation of these appearances articulates a very precise formula. First, Italian sporting successes are evidence of fascist character. Second, the regime's character is mapped both discursively *and* physically onto the figure of Benito Mussolini.

Apart from their representation in the newsreels and printed press, the growth and success of Italian sports were supported by a civic infrastructure that the regime dramatically expanded. This expansion was part of a two-pronged campaign to organize sports and leisure activities at a national level. The hierarchical structure of the campaign was codified by the fascist Sports Charter in 1929. According to the Charter, all professional sports were to be regulated by the Italian Olympic Committee (CONI). Noncompetitive sports, leisure-time activities, and amateur associations were to be coordinated by the Opera Nazionale del Dopolavoro (the National After-work Association, OND). CONI orchestrated the state's financing of new super stadia in Rome, Bologna, Turin, and Florence, and between 1927 and 1930 it opened over a thousand new playing fields. The OND sponsored 191,773 participatory sporting events in 1933, and by 1937 it boasted an average of three million participants per year.[3]

Although the Sports Charter mandated a clear division in roles for CONI and the OND, they nonetheless shared two overriding political functions. Their activities were visible to the vast majority of the Italian population and were carried out *in the name of* the regime. As such the preeminence of sport (i.e., of fascist sport) within the public sphere and the expansion of available leisure-time activities (made available through the state) provided fascism a presence capable of crossing regional and class barriers. Taken together, the various components of this campaign corresponded to one of fascism's key ideological projects, that is, the attempt to construct a unified, supra-class national identity.

The organized performances of fascist physical culture provided a visible backdrop of common experience and shared representations for cinema audiences. The state's newsreels regularly recorded and re-presented the regime's organized sport spectacles. More importantly, such films replicated for cinema audiences their positions as members of the public that had equally participated in and witnessed such sporting events. Although such a doubled positioning did not determine the details of how the audiences interpreted specific narratives, it did implicate an overall condition of their participation as embedded within a concept of a single "national" body. In her Benjaminian analysis of aestheticized politics, Simonetta Falasca-Zamponi suggests that

> the "masses" were at the same time part of the fascist spectacle and fascism's spectatorship; they were acted upon and actors. Slogans, rallies, and images excited people's senses, though as an object of power people

were denied their senses. Benjamin's notion of aestheticized politics indicates that fascism, by resorting to symbols, rituals, and spectacle, was able to offer the "masses" a chance to express themselves and be part of a movement, even if their participation was based on a cultic experience. By beautifying politics, fascism created the auratic distance between the regime and the governed necessary to channel people's involvement in politics through faith, myths, and cults.[4]

One of the earliest and perhaps most striking points of convergence, indeed of fusion, between the state's highly public spectatorial campaigns and the period's films can be found in the strongman cycle. As I have mentioned earlier, the beginning of the cycle can be located in Bartolomeo Pagano's performance as Maciste in Giovanni Pastrone's *Cabiria* (1914). As the cycle began to flourish, especially after World War I, a new set of personalized characters followed, including Luciano Albertini as Sansonia (Samson), Giovanni Raicevich as Ercole (Hercules), Domenico Gambino as Saetta, Alfredo Boccolini as Galaor, Mario Guaita as Ausonia, Carlo Aldini as Ajax. Pagano himself appeared as Maciste in films whose narratives cover virtually the entire span of "Italian" history from classical Rome to national unification: *Maciste l'alpino* (1916), *Maciste atleta, Maciste medium, Maciste poliziotto* (1918), *Maciste innamorato* (1919), *La trilogia di Maciste* (1920), *Maciste in vacanza, Maciste salvato dalle acque, La rivincita di Maciste* (1921), *Maciste e il nipote d'America, Maciste imperatore* (1924), *Il gigante delle Dolomiti, Maciste all' inferno, Maciste contro lo sceicco, Maciste nella gabbia dei leoni* (1926).

Pagano/Maciste is distinguishable from his competitors in three significant ways. First, Sansonia, Ercole, Saetta, and Ajax generally shared in the archetypical heroic mold, typified in Hollywood by figures such as Douglas Fairbanks. Where in these cases the narrative day is saved through acrobatics and cunning, Maciste triumphed by dint of his physical strength and aggressiveness. Second, unlike the Fairbanks model, Maciste's heroism is distinctively desexualized. Although the Maciste/Pagano body is perhaps *the* central figural focus in this cycle, romantic liaisons are almost entirely absent. Third, where the other strongman actors emerged from the cultures of the circus and/or sports, Pagano came to film as a Genovese dockworker. All three characteristics were pointed out to audiences—through publicity and reviews—both before and after his films were released. These differences were especially significant given that most of the period's major stars had been recruited to the cinema from the aristocratic

Figure 7. Douglas Fairbanks in *The Thief of Bagdad* (1924). Courtesy of the Academy of Motion Picture Arts and Sciences.

worlds of theater and classical dance. Not only was his working-class background unique to the nascent Italian star system, it also provided a discursive link to the real experience shared by a major slice of the ever-growing popular audiences.

Mario Camerini's *Maciste contro lo sceicco* (1926) immediately announces his real, offscreen class background. Pagano first appears in a close-up of his forearms working to disentangle the large steel chains of a ship's anchor. The camera holds in close-up and then slowly pans back to reveal Pagano in the role of a working stevedore. This

introductory shot involves several levels of metonymy. On the most immediate level, the hands and forearms stand in for the whole body of the fictional character. The shot contributes to the construction of this specific fictional character by privileging the status of his body; it identifies him as embodiment of physical strength. Moreover, by referring backward to the kind of work Pagano did before entering the cinema, it overdetermines the ontological status of the character as existing prior to the film's fiction. It thereby invites a particular reading of the fiction as performed not by an actor but instead by Bartolomeo Pagano, the Genovese dockworker.

The narrative premise in this film holds to the general pattern in the strongman cycle. Innocence is placed in peril either by moral corruption or by xenophobically constructed *others*. In this case, the uncle of a young heiress (Cecyl Tryan) conspires to steal her inheritance. She is imprisoned aboard a merchant ship, and upon its arrival in North Africa she is sold into a sheik's harem. Maciste and a lone accomplice rescue the heiress, unravel the original conspiracy, and return the heiress safely home. As occurs frequently in the cycle, the narrative is organized less around the development of the specific plot and more toward providing performance opportunities for Maciste/Pagano to demonstrate his strength. In *Maciste contro lo sceicco,* in addition to fighting off numerous enemies, Pagano is thus given an opportunity to ride horseback, swim, break apart a rope binding his hands, climb a vertical castle wall, bend back the iron grate on one of its windows, and crash through a locked door, among other feats.

Within the filmic texts, such instances of performance invariably share at least three thematic elements with fascist physical culture:

1. Action is a morally purifying quality and therefore the preferred response to corruption, decadence, or intrigue.

2. The moral application of physical strength is selfless and almost always motivated by the need to defend an innocent party. (This lack of self-interest partially explains the absence of romantic subelements.)

3. In the majority of instances, (heroic) action is single-handed, a matter of the individual's ability to overcome superior numbers.

This last motif is repeatedly performed in *Maciste contro lo sceicco.* Just as the heiress is about to be molested by the ship's first mate, Maciste rescues her by fighting off the entire ship's company. Swimming

Figure 8. Maciste defends the innocent. Frame enlargement from *Maciste l'alpino* (1916, Giovanni Pastrone). Courtesy of the Museo Nazionale del Cinema, Torino.

to the North African shore, he fights off an entire school of sharks. And, in order to rescue her from the harem (once again, just prior to her being molested), Maciste fights through the sheik's entire army.

It might be argued that these thematic elements are common in most adventure films of the period. There are a number of reasons, however, to consider them as part of a circuit in which meaning was exchanged between the films and fascism. To begin with, the fact that Maciste's many opponents are regularly presented as foreign in origin concurs with the regime's early explanations of the need for autarchy and anticipates its explicit racism in the second half of the thirties. The successful connection between the two discourses is rendered explicit, for example, in Giovanni Pastrone's *Maciste l'alpino* (1916). In this film Pagano, as an Italian soldier in World War I, dispatches an entire company of Austrian soldiers. The film's overdetermined patriotism, especially in the wake of Italy's World War I losses, made it so popular (with the fascists and the public in general) that it was recirculated well into the twenties. Moreover, the cycle's validation of action (over failed diplomacies) fuses the spirit of Italian futurism with the fascist party's protonationalism, a cornerstone of the movement's political evolution.

At the level of cultural production, this specific overlay between textual productions and political discourses was also presented to potential audiences as a distinctive combination of modernist impulses (expressed in futurism) with the cultic evocation of traditional mythologies personified in figures such as Maciste, Ercole, and Sansone.

The use of violence as preferred response to corruption (of any type) is totally consonant with the fascist movement's first form of political expression, that is, *squadrismo*.[5] Moreover, the concentration on the athletic body (and on its strength as opposed to skill or finesse) invokes the regime's public efforts at improving the nation's body culture through its organized sports activities. In other words, the one was readable in terms articulated by the other. Thus, the equation of superior athleticism with superior morality that was presented to the audience in the films could be reenacted by that audience as exercise and sports activities that were organized by the state. The centrality in fascist culture of this dual relationship between physical activities and mass spectatorship is embedded (one is tempted to say embodied) in the figure of Mussolini himself. As Karen Pinkus suggestively describes it:

> The discourse of fascism is full of anecdotes of the perfect, consenting body: the young woman who faints when she sees il Duce in person; the infant from Ancona who is born with a mark of the fascio littorio (the fascist emblem of grains wrapped around a sword) imprinted on her skin. . . . Of course, the Duce promoted his own body in this context, the prototype for all males. Mussolini's body is promoted to such an obsessive degree that one might well say he becomes not-body, always already a representation, one step removed from corporeal presence. . . . Since the regime sought to create, in effect, a classless body, it is precisely in retrieving the gap between the presentation of the body and the lived reality of bodies that something like a fascist unconscious may be located.[6]

In addition, one can readily recognize how Mussolini's regular newsreel appearances as a sportsman recall the values of strength fictionally represented in the popular cinema by Maciste. Indeed, Brunetta has argued that the link between the films and the regime was even more specific. As Mussolini increasingly assumed the role of central character, of star, in the newsreels, he borrowed gestures directly from Pagano:

> With his bargain-basement populism and his image as righter of wrongs and protector of the weak, women and children, Maciste intertwines his destiny—in the popular imagination—with that of fascism, arriving at a sort of identification with the image of its leader to who[m] he furnishes not a few suggestions for his bare-chested performances and for an entire

Figure 9. Bartolomeo Pagano. Courtesy of the Museo Nazionale del Cinema, Torino.

series of gestures in the repertory of his appearances. Maciste is the fundamental path in the formation of the Mussolinian gesture: the image of Mussolini as a star is attributable, especially in its formative phase, in its most popular and populist attitudes, to a series of fairly clear loans.[7]

As Italian film production declined toward the end of the decade, the strongman films—as part of a recognizable cycle—also momentarily

disappear from the national screens.[8] Yet many of their thematic elements and the ideological problematics to which they refer resurface in the mid-thirties in a group of films which clearly also parallel significant transitions in the regime's political priorities. In the same time frame that Italy announces a new Empire and occupies Ethiopia, a range of epochal military costume films are released. Films such as *Cavalleria* (1936, Goffredo Alessandrini), *Pietro Micca* (1936, Aldo Vergano), *Squadrone bianco* (1936, Augusto Genina), *Scipione l'africano* (1937, Carmine Gallone), *Condottieri* (1937, Luigi Trenker), *Ettore Fieramosca* (1938, Alessandro Blasetti), *Il cavaliere senza nome* (1941, Feruccio Cerio), and *Il figlio del corsaro rosso* (1942, Marco Elter) simultaneously draw on and modify the three major thematic premises underlying the conventions of the strongman cycle. In this context, it is worthwhile noting that Pastrone/D'Annunzio's *Cabiria* (1914), the ur-text for these subsequent historical epics, was reissued in a sonorized version in 1931.

From a more long-term perspective, these films should also be placed in the context of the Italian cinema's perennial interest in historical reconstruction. They devolve from a tradition that began at the outset of Italian film production, was codified and expanded by the industry's recurrent evocations of ancient Rome in the films of the early second decade of the century, and resurfaced in significant ways during the fascist period. Indeed, over 20 percent of the Italian films produced between 1929 and 1943 reconstruct a historical setting as the basis of their particular fiction.[9]

A number of important films from the mid-thirties recall and rework the central motifs of the strongman cycle, including the protagonist versus the many opponents, the resolution of conflict through a purifying athleticism, the defense of the innocent, and the violent eradication of corruption associated with liberal-era governance, among others. The representation of the hero's body in these films continues to be a central trope in their overall textual organization. But these films also transform both the major narrational strategies for conflicts as well as the aesthetic and formal figurations for their depiction. They introduce, as it were, a master chronotope that emulates both the evolution of the regime's social policies and the shared experience of audience/publics that lived through them. From the early thirties until the end of the decade, such films are unique in the overall period of fascist rule from 1922 to 1943. These titles (in addition to the fascist "eventfulness" that was present in the state-controlled newsreels and documentaries) actually contain direct representations of the regime in uniform. They also contain, however, two significant shifts, one representational and one rhetorical/discursive. First, the foundational chronotope of the Maciste-inspired strongman mutates. Where *performed physical strength* had expressed the value of a pan-historical contemporary evocation of moral force, these newer films find strength in symmetrical *uniformed warfare*. Second, even while the films draw upon the mythic iconographies of either the never-completed Risorgimento or the accomplishments of ancient Roman civilization, violence has now been coded as a historical force that produces a new future to be lived. Where the state had excised images of violent crime, through both censorship and auto-censorship, these films found an ideologically acceptable location for violent action and placed it within the regime's intent to establish the Fascist Empire abroad. A number of films participate in this transition, including Augusto Genina's *Squadrone bianco* (1936), *L'assedio dell'Alcazar* (1940), and *Bengasi* (1942); Goffredo Alessandrini's *Giarabub* (1942) and *Luciano Serra pilota* (1938); and Roberto Rossellini's *La nave bianca* (1941), *Uomini sul fondo* (1941), and *Una pilota ritorna* (1942).[10]

As Simonetta Falasca-Zamponi has described the state's resolution of the ideological tension between types of violence: "Politically, fascism could not tolerate violence within Italy, because the regime's goal was to control the country totally. Aesthetically, conflicts could not exist within Italian borders, because homogeneity was a necessary element in the development of a beautiful fascist Italy. . . . Class struggle, which needed to be avoided in domestic politics, became the main category of interpenetration of a country's international relations. Whereas the 'masses' should not fight within Italy, Mussolini foresaw the possibility of transforming them into 'virile' warriors in the world arena."[11]

In this context, two films released in 1937 require particular attention: Luigi Trenker's *Condottieri* and Carmine Gallone's *Scipione l'africano*. Both films were exclusively distributed by the para-state agency ENIC and were given extensive runs in its chain of first-run cinemas in every major Italian city. They were widely discussed in both specialized and popular presses prior to their much-anticipated release. Articles about the films before they were actually shown to the public tended to assign equal importance to them as accomplishments in film and as significant moments in the fabric of fascist society. Mussolini's visit to the set of *Scipione,* for example, reenacts

Figure 10. Mussolini saluted on set of *Scipione l'africano* (1937), with Paolucci de Calboli and Luigi Freddi. Frame enlargement from LUCE newsreel (December 19, 1936). Courtesy of the Istituto LUCE.

his frequent inaugurating visits to recently completed public works as recorded by numerous LUCE newsreels. His appearance on the set virtually certified the film as a fascist project much like the state's other civic interventions:

> Il Duce . . . accepted the invitation from the Consortium presiding over the production of *Scipione l'africano* to make a brief visit to Sabaudia where, for a few days, two huge crowds had been assembled to take part in the reconstruction of the battle of Zama. . . . The helmets, armor, and shields sparkle, the weapons proudly slung as if not a fiction but a real battle were about to take place from one moment to the next. The presence of il Duce momentarily interrupts the preparation of the scene which is about to be shot. From the two masses a deafening shout of welcome and enthusiasm bursts forth and the vast plain resounds with the cry "Duce, Duce." [And as Mussolini leaves the set] . . . a new formidable demonstration salutes him. Romans and Carthiginians break their ranks to crowd around him, acclaiming him, loudly and repeatedly invoking his name.[12]

Both films were popular and critical successes, each winning major prizes at the 1937 Venice Film Festival. *Scipione* was awarded the

Mussolini Cup for the best Italian film. *Condottieri* won the General Cinema Directorate Cup for the film that "best depicted natural and artistic beauty." Further privileging these films as sites of exchange between the industry and fascism was the state's own large financial participation in their production. Unlike the privately financed historical epics of the 1920s, these productions were heavily subsidized by the state. Of the 71 million lire (approximately $55,000,000) that the regime invested in the film industry during 1936, one quarter went toward only these two films. The state arranged for 12,400,000 lire ($9,610,000) to finance the production of *Scipione* and 9,600,000 lire ($7,440,000) for *Condottieri*.

Most importantly, both films articulate a shift in historical narration that corresponded to the evolution of fascist politics in the mid-thirties. As we have seen, the earlier figure of the strongman appears in virtually every era of Italian history. In the previous cycle, conflicts were resolved through the performance of the character's physical/moral strength. In these instances, the primacy of performance over narrative tended to detach the characters from the specific historical episodes evoked by the films. Thus the strongman (and Maciste, in particular) appeared as a cultic, pan-historical expression of a moral force. *Condottieri* and *Scipione*, on the other hand, construct their narratives *as though* the events were the realization of unfinished histories, of historical legacies about to be actualized. The very *eventfulness* of the past in these films constitutes the premise for events that must inexorably take place in an imagined, proximate future. Since both films were heavily promoted as productions of the state, they share and underscore the regime's prioritization of programs that were either very recent or imminent. Even though these films are historical epics, they recruit particular moments of Italian history as antinostalgia. In order to project the nation into an inevitable future, they erect figural historiographies that *make way* for a new sense of national identity and purpose, one most clearly expressed by the regime's aggressive urban reconstruction at home and its imperial programs abroad. In order to achieve this fundamental historiographic transition, both films revise the three core thematic premises of the strongman cycle. Where the former achieved moral purity through physical action, these films generally aestheticize political action. Where previously the principal characters had acted in heroic defense of innocent individuals, they are now leaders committed to the greater interests of *the nation*. And finally, the athleticism of the individual strongman is replaced by the collective strength of military action. This last shift echoes the regime's rhetorical description of its civic initiatives in explicitly militarist terms: *the battles* for grain, for the lira, for demographic growth, and so forth.

Condottieri is a historical allegory for Mussolini's building of the fascist movement and is organized as a biography of the fictional military leader Giovanni dei Medici. Though set in the Renaissance, it transplants onto its narrative the Risorgimento theme of unifying Italy by expelling foreign interests. In his first confrontation with the Council of Florence, Giovanni dei Medici exclaims: "Italy! A single state from the Alps to the sea. Give me your help and I will create it!" Indeed, throughout the film, the major narrative movements intertwine the elements of personal biography with the evolution of an idealized military revolt. Giovanni dei Medici returns from exile to reclaim the birthright stolen from him during childhood by the forces of Cesare Borgia. He builds his own army by recruiting mercenaries away from an erstwhile soldier of fortune named Malatesta. He transforms the loose aggregate of fighters into ethically motivated and highly organized soldiers. After initially defeating Malatesta in a duel, Giovanni leads his new army and the local townspeople to march on Rome. Blessed by the pope and pardoned for his past misdeeds, Giovanni heroically leads one last epochal battle against his (and the nation's) enemies.

Contemporary audiences were invited to read the film as historical allegory—that is, to understand the figure of Giovanni dei Medici as a mythical precursor to Mussolini—through a remarkable series of discursive and iconic framing devices. Even before the narrative begins, the film's opening credits inform the audience that "units of the state's armed forces participated widely in the realizing of this film," in other words, the army of Giovanni dei Medici is to be understood as performed by the soldiers of the contemporary regime. The first diegetic element is a parchment scroll which pre-announces the film's status as simultaneously a textual representation of a general historical process and a discursive invitation to consider the construction of a much-awaited, new national identity: "This film is a liberal re-evocation of the time and the spirit of the Italian condottieri [military leaders], who against the ardent background of the Renaissance led, for the first time, the civil militias of the People who were rising up against the mercenaries, having as their aim the unity of the Italian nation."

This prologue establishes the film's time frame in the Renaissance but does so without locating the narrative in relationship to any specific

Figure 11. Poster for *Condottieri* (1937, Luigi Trenker). Courtesy of the Raccolta Salce/
Gian Piero Brunetta.

episode or event from that period. It suggests that the events to follow are true insofar as they belong to a past generally recognizable to the audience. It also qualifies those events as principal components in a historiography which extends beyond its own fictive time frame. That the "civil militias of the People" were led "for the first time" indicates that the uprising—both populist and nationalist in nature—would recur in the future. The film then provides figurative information that specifies this future as nothing less than the fascist revolution.

When Giovanni attempts to join Malatesta's mercenaries, they doubt his capacities as a soldier, repeatedly referring to his demeanor and attire as those of a peasant. Malatesta himself, even after Giovanni's declaration that he is the son of Caterina Sforza, the rightful heir to this domain, believes him to be a farmer. The repeated reference to his double identity as simple farmer and yet formidable solider invites a comparison to the frequent conflation of these two functions by Mussolini in the LUCE newsreels where he works both as national leader and as gentleman farmer. This somewhat general initial similarity between Giovanni and Mussolini is immediately proposed in much more specific terms. Giovanni builds his private army, naming them the *bande nere* (black gangs), a specific linkage to the uniform and name of fascist *squadristi*. The film leaves no doubt about this association insofar as Giovanni's soldiers, now dressed in black armor, recognize their *condottiere* (their leader) with the extended-arm fascist salute.

After defeating Malatesta in their personal duel, Giovanni proclaims, "Florence is ours. Long live the black gangs! To Rome!" Here, it is significant that the film offers no specific narrative explanation for the revolt. The remarkable lack of textual explanation for their movements over the film's space/time creates a historical teleology shared by fascism itself. Thus, the black shirts of the film *must* "march on Rome" as other historical agents would *inevitably* do several centuries later. As Mabel Berezin has argued, this teleology was very familiar to contemporary audiences: "The overall image of the March was that of spatial convergence. The pilgrimage of the leader . . . and the physical movement of fascist bodies across space and time set a pattern that was recognizable to the general public and difficult to ignore. Fascism used readily available cultural schemata to create a community of feeling around the memory of the March. The actions in public space—the carefully orchestrated parades and the appropriation of the public piazza—visibly proclaimed that a new social order was established."[13]

Figure 12. The Roman salute. Frame enlargement from *Condottieri*. Courtesy of the Cineteca Nazionale, Roma.

Upon their arrival in Rome, the *condottiere* and his troops rush past ineffectual Swiss guards and confront the pope. The historical confrontation is presented as a highly coded encounter between two symbolic agencies. The soldiers halt their charge toward the pope and along with Giovanni stand in awe of his presence. Without speaking a single word, the pope and Giovanni exchange glances in a series of tightly framed shot-reverse-shots. The extraordinary, almost non-narrative alternation of glances between the two is terminated when the pope slowly raises his hand to bless Giovanni and the troops. The gesture signals an end to hostilities. So abstract are the scene's narrative elements that the audience is invited to read the exchange, to recognize it, in reference to another decisive meeting in Rome between a leader of black shirts and the pope. That is, they are invited to read this meeting in relation to Mussolini's meetings with the pope prior to signing the Lateran Accords in 1929. The Accords, signed on February 11, 1929, removed the long-standing potential of church opposition to the regime's political programs. The signing itself had been preceded by three years of widely publicized negotiations between the regime and papal representatives. They contained three principal agreements: the state guaranteed the sovereignty of the Vatican and its holdings and the church recognized the fascist

Figure 13. Il Condottiere meets the pope. Frame enlargement from *Condottieri*. Courtesy of the Cineteca Nazionale, Roma.

regime as Italy's legitimate government; the agreements reconfirmed Catholicism as the sole religion of the state; and the state would reimburse the church for past damages. Apart from the extraordinary propaganda value generated by these agreements, the Accords effectively precluded any hypothetical Catholic opposition to the regime.

By intertwining its fictional representation of Giovanni dei Medici with the audience's knowledge of Benito Mussolini, the film inserts Mussolini himself into a larger historical parabola. It places him in an evolution of events that derive from ("for the first time") the general past invoked by the film. Unlike the strongman, who appears as a pan-historical expression of moral purity, the film constructs the Giovanni/Mussolini figure in terms of a populist unity with the People, the soldiers, farmers, and the land. Moreover, the figure is presented as a natural expression of a nationalist tradition that hypothetically goes back over five hundred years. In so doing, the film attempts to "historicize" the regime, conferring upon it the legitimacy that would be owed to the natural heir to the values of the Renaissance itself.

Whereas the time frame of *Condottieri*'s narrative is a generalized Renaissance, *Scipione l'africano* reconstructs a specific episode from classical Roman history, namely the second Punic War, leading, in particular, to the battle of Zama in 202 B.C. This difference in historical specificity relates to another major difference between the ideological projects of the two films. On the one hand, *Condottieri* distills certain thematic values of the Renaissance in order to characterize the initial, formative components of the fascist movement. It presents, that is, the hypothetical nationalist and populist impulses of the Renaissance as the social forces that would eventually lead to the beginning of the fascist movement. On the other hand, *Scipione* functions as a double-sided history lesson. Its narrative is organized as the unfolding of events from the history of the Roman Empire. More significantly, the film seeks to explain the continuing evolution of fascism, after its rise to power, in terms of those events. In essence, *Scipione* invokes the ancient heritage of the Roman Empire in order to inscribe a manifest destiny for contemporary Italian imperialism in Africa.

Here too, the fiction is preceded by a contextualizing prologue. Even before the narrative is under way, the prologue initiates the film's explanatory, almost didactic mode. This passage not only insists on historical detail—specific dates, numbers of soldiers, locations—it also informs the audience what is at stake in battles to follow. While the issue in the wars with Africa (in this case Carthage) is dominion over the Mediterranean Sea, it is the very existence of Rome and Italy that is at stake.

> At the end of the third century B.C., two great powers collided in competition for the prize of the Mediterranean. From the very beginning the competition between the two nations took the dramatic form of a struggle between life and death for one of the two peoples. For tens of years the two rivals let each others' blood without quarter, alternating victories and defeats. But in the end it seemed that Carthage had to win. In fact, in the year 218 B.C., Hannibal came down from the Alps at the head of 50,000 men, sowing ruin and carnage before him. Rome attempted in vain to resist his overpowering advance, and one by one, its best armies, at Ticino, at Trebbia, and at Trasimeno, were destroyed. With the road to Rome open, Hannibal encamped as the master of Italy. In a desperate attempt, Rome gathered another army, but on August 2, 216 B.C., 50,000 Romans were massacred on the plains of Cannae.

As with virtually every major trope in the film, the individual elements of the prologue refer equally to the historical "facts" of the Roman Empire in the second century B.C. and to the manner in which the contemporary regime often framed its programs and specifically its invasion of Ethiopia. Thus, the "prize of the Mediterranean" contested by the filmic Rome and Carthage can clearly be read in light of the regime's proclamation of *mare nostrum,* that is, its nascent imperialism. And the historical "life and death struggle" of the film shares the regime's contemporary justification for its expansionism as a matter of national survival.

That the history lesson promised by the prologue should also be read in relationship to Italy's current military campaign in Africa is further ensured by the very first diegetic image. This shot reveals the bodies of the fallen Roman soldiers on the Cannae battlefield. An unseen hand raises a broken Roman standard over the battlefield and an offscreen voice announces: "We shall avenge Cannae!" When mustering his troops, Scipio presents the very same standard to his army and promises that they will "avenge Cannae." At the end of the battle of Zama, the circumstances of the first battle are reversed. This time, the fallen soldiers belong to Carthage, and as the same standard is held aloft over *this* battlefield, a Roman soldier yells, "You have avenged Cannae, Hannibal is defeated."

This fulfillment of a promised revenge is identical to that which the regime circulated prior to its invasion of Ethiopia in October 1935. One of the first objectives of the war was the capture of the city of Adowa, the site of a disastrous military defeat in 1896. Announcing one of its major military objectives, the regime widely proclaimed (in radio addresses, public speeches, posters, and newsreels), "We shall avenge Adowa!" The effective association between the two wars, the two historically mandated revenges, was clearly made by the film's contemporary audiences. In 1939, the film journal *Bianco e Nero* published essays about the film written by third- and fourth-graders in Rome. The majority of the essays made the explicit connection between the history of the film and the making of fascist history in Africa.

> I liked the scene where *Scipione* announces the victory to the Romans with the words "We have vindicated Cannae." In that moment my thoughts turned to the fallen soldiers at Adowa, in the same Africa, vindicated by the Italians in the conquest of the Empire.

> At Zama the Romans won: Scipio vindicated Cannae, just like Mussolini vindicated Adowa.

> Back then they didn't fight like nowadays, but with lances, daggers, and javelins. I admired how the Romans knew how to combat gloriously. It was also nice when one solider raised the standard from Cannae and said: "Cannae has been vindicated." But Mussolini's soldiers also know how to fight with the same valor, and they too have vindicated Adowa.[14]

From the shot of the Cannae battlefield forward, the film's narrative is premised upon the promise of vindication and leads inexorably toward the final battle at Zama. In building towards this narrative/historical denouement, the film also transcribes onto *these* Romans a series of values that it had proposed and stylized in other sites of cultural production and political speech. To begin with, Scipio is distinguished from the traditional Roman political class not only by his militarism, but also by his identification with the will of the people. At the beginning of the film, Scipio proposes to protect Rome and to rid Italy of Hannibal's armies by taking the battle directly onto African soil. Fearful that Scipio will conduct the military campaign as a means of personal aggrandizement, the Roman senators initially resist his proposal. When asked if he intends to break ranks with the senate and "bring the question to the people," Scipio responds that he "will do what is best for the nation." Military strategy is thus authorized by the fusion of anti-parliamentary nationalism with an imagined democratic will. Immediately after his response, Scipio leaves the interior of the senate and is welcomed by the cheers of an awaiting crowd.

Throughout this first major scene, the film alternates between the senatorial debate inside the curia and brief conversations between individuals among the awaiting citizens. Each conversation is conducted by an "Italian" from a different region of the peninsula. By invoking this transclass, transregional concept of a composite, but now unified, national totality, these small groups are assembled into a larger body, as the constituent elements of an imagined Italian nation. This fictional formation of a nation by grouping together its original constituencies postulates Imperial Rome as the historiographic origin of the contemporary regime. It thereby provides the regime with an a posteriori "natural" destiny upon which it could construct authority for its policies and practices. Thus, when Scipio joins the crowd, he is acclaimed by a physical representation of a nation prototypically waiting to be formed. Not only is his military campaign supported by a people, it is conducted in the name of an ancient Rome that is the progenitor of Italy as a unified modern entity. As such, the film invites audiences to (re)live their imperialist present as a figurative return to their imagined historical roots in Roman antiquity.

This reading as *reliving* is activated by numerous minor chronotopes. One particularly remarkable instance takes place as Scipio, after the senatorial debate, prepares his household for the African expedition. His wife removes all of her jewelry and places the various

Figure 14. Mussolini receives wedding rings. Frame enlargement from LUCE newsreel (December 12, 1935). Inauguration of Ponentina. Courtesy of the Istituto LUCE.

pieces in a gilded box. As their son, wearing Scipio's plumed helmet, plays in the background, she offers up the gift. Whereas earlier the film had organized its narrative as the inevitable outcome of an unfolding History, this sequence establishes the terms of an idyllic Roman/fascist familial order. The family must sacrifice when the national interests are at stake. The form of that sacrifice, however, is a specific reference to a fascist practice from the 1930s. Towards the end of 1935, as the costs of the war in Ethiopia continued to strain the national economy, the regime encouraged women to give up their jewelry—in particular, their gold wedding bands[15]—to the state to support the economic needs of an expanding nation. This sequence from *Scipione l'africano* enriches the significance of the fascist practice by locating its origin as a custom that contributed to the glorification of ancient Rome.

The equation between ancient Rome and fascism in *Scipione* did not go unnoticed by the regime itself. In his preface to the schoolchildren's essays, Minister of Corporations Giuseppe Bottai commented: "The hero becomes the straw man for another hero, who claims the right of primogeniture; and in reality it is this second one who seizes our attention and dissolves the first one. Scipio, for the children, is not the Roman hero, but rather Mussolini. Scipio's actions, by virtue of their transposition, evoke the actions of Mussolini. The analogy becomes identity."[16] Such declarations constitute nothing less than *instructions for use* that the state proposed for audiences on how to "properly" read the film's representational schema. Above and beyond Bottai's direction to read the two heroic figures as a single entity, however, the film itself constructs an aesthetic parallelism between the two Romes. Throughout the film Scipio is contrasted with Hannibal, the Romans/Italians with the Carthaginians/Africans. At each major turn in the story, the film alternates between scenes of the Roman and Carthaginian camps. Where the Roman events take place in sunlight, the Carthaginians are assiduously surrounded by night and/or shadow. Where the narrative suggests that Rome is a civilizing force, Carthage stands for chaos and moral turpitude. For example, immediately after the formation of popular support for Scipio's proposed campaign, the film presents the first glimpse of the enemy forces. While the Romans/Italians altruistically offer their own resources to supply Scipio's army, the Carthaginian soldiers contemplate mutiny, complaining that their pay is long overdue. Hannibal's response to this contention (his address to the Carthaginian crowd) is the total opposite of Scipio's style of leadership. He calls for the army to assemble and then massacres the disloyal foot soldiers with his cavalry. Where the Africans are represented as raw, disorganized, and self-interested labor, the Romans are selfless citizens of the hierarchically composed nation.

That Rome brings order while Africa breeds anarchy is aesthetically represented through diametrically opposed structures of mise-en-scène. The Roman soldiers occupy screen space along rigidly symmetrical lines, and are grouped into columns, rows, and rectangles. Thus, as the narrative brings them from one location to the next (in largest terms, from Italy to Africa), Roman bodies organize the fictive space with the values of balance, discipline, and hierarchy. In contrast, Hannibal's forces are generally deployed in small, disorderly, and nonsymmetrical groupings. When the two forces meet, the depiction of battle is orchestrated not only as a contrast between divergent military strategies, but also as visual encounters between two opposing principles of spatial organization, of battles between two aesthetic regimes.

The dialogical characterizations of the two historical Romes (the classical and the modern) can be seen functioning in at least two additional ways. First, the film's presentation of Imperial Rome as

Figure 15. Two Roman armies on the set of *Scipione l'africano*. Frame enlargement from LUCE newsreel (December 19, 1936). Courtesy of the Istituto LUCE.

civilizing agent, as the establisher of order from chaos, addresses the audience's experience of contemporary Rome in relationship to the organization of space. *Scipione l'africano* participates, that is, in the regime's culture-wide project of overlaying antiquity—its symbols, icons, and visual order—upon modern Rome. Especially in the last half of the fascist period, the contemporary Italian audience's field of vision contained numerous changes to the urban landscape. Between 1932 and 1940, eleven New Towns were completed, including Mussolinia, Saubadia, Littoria, Pontinina, Guidonia, and Aprilia.[17] Within the capital city itself, the cityscape was populated by an unending stream of "modernized" antiquity. Major reclamations *(bonfiche)* removed previous architectural structures (mainly small habitations and alleyways) and widened city streets in order to reveal unobstructed views of Roman monuments such as the Largo di Torre Argentina, Colosseo, Basilica di Maxentius, Foro di Traiano, Foro Romano, and the Circo Massimo. At the same time, new urban spaces were created for new civic structures: bridges, ministries, and centers, notably including the massive sports "city," the Foro Mussolini (today known as the Foro Italico). Borden W. Painter describes the topographical overlay of Roman antiquity with "modern" fascist architecture that was achieved by the widening of the Via del Mare: "When finished, it provided another broad avenue for both vehicular and pedestrian traffic from the Victor Emmanuel to the Piazza della Bocca Verità and around the corner to the Circus Maximus. Along the way, just past the Theater of Marcellus, arose large new office buildings in the distinctly new style of Roman red brick, punctuated by windows with white marble borders and occasional upper story arcades. Buildings of these types, using ancient Roman motifs, are found all over the city."[18]

As always, the LUCE newsreels presented the modified urban settings to the entire nation. It should be said that the regime's urban renewal projects were part of an overall cultural remapping that recycled ancient Roman leitmotifs into nearly ubiquitous fascist symbology, into uniforms, statuary, road signs, graphic design, and even popular comic strips. By 1934, for example, teachers were obliged to wear the Fascist uniform, replete with insignia and Roman fasci, in the classroom. The putative date for the birth of ancient Rome was elevated to a national holiday. Newspapers and radios were instructed to create ample coverage of Roman subjects.

In addition, the regime organized major public exhibitions on "its" Roman heritage, most notably the Mostra della Rivoluzione Fascista in 1932, 1937, and 1940. Indeed, the exhibitions provide a literal point of contact between the regime and the cultural coordinates of the Gallone film. The centerpiece of the 1937 edition, the "Exhibition of Roman-ness," was organized in part by Pietro Aschieri, the set designer for *Scipione l'africano*. Aschieri's filmic sets not only recreate real locations from Roman antiquity, they also refurbish them. By restoring the ruins of ancient Rome (visible to the audience in their everyday experience of the contemporary city), the set design thereby also evokes their revival in fascist neoclassical architecture.

The filmic organization of the much-anticipated battle of Zama recapitulates another key condition of spectatorship for extracinematic mass entertainment. A number of factors privilege this scene as an event that was particularly recognizable to the audience. Much of the prerelease publicity concentrated on describing the enormity of the project to "faithfully" recreate the battle, mentioning the use of the armed forces, hundreds of elephants, thousands of extras, and so on. The raising of the Cannae battlefield standard at the beginning of the scene signals that the action to follow will fulfill the narrative and ideological promises of the thrice-invoked phrase "We shall avenge Cannae." And, finally, the battle reverses the way in which the rest of the film figures time. Earlier in the film there are many incidents that condense the passage of historical time into exemplary narrative events: for example, the prologue spans the "end of the third century B.C.," Scipio's army travels to Carthage in a single long take of ships sailing away from Italy, Hannibal returns to Carthage in a lap dissolve joining a scene from his camp in Italy with his stepping off the ship onto the African coast, and so forth. The battle scene proper, however, lasts a remarkable sixteen minutes. Here, the narrative has arrived at *the* prefigured narrative event. By literally stalling the forward progress of historical time, the scene provides an opportunity to witness the constituent events of History *in their making.* Not only does this operation recover the often-cited dictum that "Fascism makes history," it proposes that the epochal battle belongs to the same kind of history as the unfolding of fascist time. Thus where fascism, according to the traditional Christian calendar, began in 1922, the regime referred to Anno I E.F.—that is, Year One of the *era fascista.* Indeed, the film's own credits refer to its year of production as XVI E.F. instead of 1937.

Throughout the film, the war is referred to in terms analogous to a sporting match, as "rivals" fighting in a "competition" for a "prize." The battle itself assembles a mass of bodies whose actions are broken up into a series of discrete moments of athletic performance: of archery, javelin throwing, horseback riding. The tactical shifts in the disposition of the Roman soldiers (moving blocks of soldiers to avoid the charge of the elephants, for example) are perfectly homologous to the monumental collective athletics organized by the regime. At the battle's end, for example, a Roman soldier lifts the Cannae standard aloft, enunciating the fulfillment of the film's central narrative premise: "We have vindicated Cannae!" As he holds the standard overhead, his pose evokes the traditional victory stance with a trophy held high at the end of athletic competition.

More importantly, the sequence breaks with the dominant point-of-view structures that the film practices up to this point. Much of the film's fictive reality had been seen from points of view located with its fictional characters: the crowd/nation "sees" into the Roman forum, Scipio surveys his troops, Hannibal supervises the Carthaginian attacks on Rome, and so on. From the moment that Scipio pronounces, "Victory or death," the camera recedes quite literally to the sidelines. The cavalry, elephants, and soldiers cross the screen in horizontal lines, from left to right and from right to left, as though passing in front of an implied public sitting in a stadium, a public that itself is implied as the national body politic.

The sequence contains virtually no hand-to-hand combat and absolutely no head-on clashes between the armies of the type that would be seen through the point of view of a fictive participant or his/her implied stand-in. Unlike the highly narrativized grand battle sequences of archetypical films such as *The Crusades* (1935, DeMille), *Alexandr Nevskiy* (1938, Eisenstein), and *Spartacus* (1960, Kubrick), among others, here the details of the battle are broken into separate *events* (both military and sporting) that are made contiguous less by narrative and more by the act of spectating by a viewing public. Given the film's overall figurative strategy—the overlay of the modern upon the antique—this sequence therefore also functions as dialogical reenactment of mass sports spectacles shared by both temporal Romes. This is to say that, as spectacle, the sequence is both Roman and fascist. In sum, *Scipione l'africano* not only invokes Imperial Rome as historiographic justification for Italian imperialism, it also cites the regime's postulated Roman heritage as a central term for reading contemporary culture.

TRAVEL, PLEASURE, AND CLASS DIFFERENCE

The didactic effect of both *Condottieri* and *Scipione l'africano* resides primarily in their decidedly intertextual qualities. Each provides a system of rhetorical markers that explicitly invoke fascist social practice. As I have discussed, it is their didactic relationships between text and audiences that function in support of fascism's sense of historical self. In particular, these films seek to assist in the construction and circulation of a supra-regional, unified, national identity by inscribing the regime onto the pasts of the Italian Renaissance and the Roman Empire. This overt didacticism is admittedly rare for the period's films. But although most films during the period do not immediately present such ideological rhetorical structures, they nonetheless present us with critical questions about the social function of cinema in relationship to the new order sought by the regime. Quite apart from the question of propaganda, or even of whether the films merely reflected particular tenets of fascist political ideology, we must ask in what ways do these films relate to fascism? What figural and social terms do they propose even if, traditionally, they have been considered to be *just escapist entertainment?* What then are the points of contact and exchange between these terms and fascist discourse itself?

As I mentioned in chapter 1, film historian Carlo Lizzani suggests that the period's films were entirely disconnected from their contemporary social reality, referring to a "proliferation of films as non-existent, as empty, as alien to the national identity as our commercial films of those years."[19] It is interesting to note that Galeazzo Ciano, the Fascist minister of press and propaganda, shared in this general realist impulse during the fascist period. While Lizzani, after fascism, lamented the lack of such qualities in the period's films, Ciano proposed that it would be these very connections which could be the test of film as true art under fascism: "Far from wanting to imprint film production with the flavor of propaganda, I do think though that an art such as the cinema, which is often destined to cross international borders, should capture the physical and spiritual leitmotifs of the people. I think that only by taking inspiration from the operative realities of the Country, or from the glories of its history, or from its natural beauty, can it speak of our spirit and document the flowering of a powerful and new civilization."[20] Where the epochal costume film articulates the large historical terms required for a fascist conception of *italianicity,* I would like to suggest that the representation of *transportation* in many of the entertainment films during the fascist period addresses chiefly issues of class, of relations between social strata whether mobile or static. The representation of transportation serves as a point of discursive contact between many commercial films and the state's highly visible "operative realities." These representations constitute a discursive site for the negotiation of class difference under fascism.

Images of new forms of transportation (and travel) form a major intertextual trope in Italian culture from the turn of the century to the present day. From the nationalization of trains in 1905 to the construction of its first airplane in 1908, Italy shared the fascination with new modes of transportation so widely circulated in many rapidly industrializing nations. The representation of modes of transportation is a central trope in Italian cinema in the sound era. A fertile terrain of study could be opened by posing questions such as: Which modes of transportation occur most frequently in different periods of time? Which social strata have access to which kinds of vehicles? What function do these representations serve within cinema narratives? Such a study would need to include considerations of at least *the bicycle,* from Walter Ruttman's experimental *Acciaio* (1933) to Vittorio De Sica's neorealist classic *Ladri di biciclette* (1948); *the bus* (Mario Bonnard's pre-neorealist *Avanti c'è posto* [1942], which was scripted by Cesare Zavattini and starred Aldo Fabrizi); *the car* (Jean Louis Trintignant's Spider in Dino Risi's *Il sorpasso* [1962]; Terence Stamp's Ferrari in Federico Fellini's *Toby Dammit* [1968]; Alberto Sordi's taxi in his own *Il tassinaro* [1984]); and *the motorscooter* (in Nanni Moretti's *Caro diario* [1994]).

Faster and more efficient transportation took on special significance in Italy during the fascist period. "Making the trains run on time" is a highly suggestive chronotopical formula for the materialization of space and time. But it was also quite literally one of the first objectives of the new state and became a cornerstone of its economic policy. It led to the establishment of the Ministry of Communications in 1924 and to an investment of over two billion lire in order to modernize and expand the national train system.[21] Numerous new or expanded train stations were a major focus of fascist urban design, including such exemplary projects as Santa Maria Novella in Florence and Osteiense and Termini in Rome. Mabel Berezin links the state's focus on the railways to its ritualization of politics: "The geographical size of Italy also aided the proliferation of fascist ritual. The trains did more than run on time—they carried the bodies, the ritual actors, from one part of Italy to another, from one event to another. Trains are central to the story of fascist political ritual as ideology; they were a necessary infrastructure for Italian public spectacle. The small distances between Italian cities made it possible to import fascist bodies within hours."[22]

In addition, the regime embraced the exaltation of dynamism and velocity championed by Italian futurists in the teens and twenties. It made wide propaganda use of the various speed records set by Italians during the period, in auto racing, aeronautics, bicycling, and transoceanic sailing, for example.[23] Even after its enthusiasm for futurism waned towards the end of the twenties, the government continued to associate itself with these accomplishments insofar as they served to characterize the regime as *the* agency for rendering Italy more efficient, competitive, and modern. The ideological importance of these values was, once again, underscored by the newsreel presentation of the Duce as experienced aviator, sailor, and motorcycle driver.

Many of the period's films employ images of transportation—cars, bicycles, boats, buses, trams, airplanes, and especially trains—as symbolic containers of class difference. These representations are used both as markers of contradiction between social strata and as the symbolic space for their resolution. That is, while new forms of transportation enable geographical travel and temporary social dislocation or instability, they also function as a trope for eventual reestablishment of social stability. De Certeau's decoding of trains is particularly on point:

> Travelling Incarceration. Immobile inside the train, seeing immobile things slip by. What is happening? Nothing is moving inside or outside the train. The unchanging traveler is pigeonholed, numbered, and regulated in the grid of the railway car, which is a perfect actualization of the rational utopia. . . . Inside, there is the immobility of an order. Here rest and dreams reign supreme. . . . Every being is placed in its place like a piece of printer's type on a page arranged in military order. This order, an organizational system, the quietude of a certain reason, is the condition of both a railway car's and a text's movement from one place to another.[24]

Three films deserve particular attention in this regard: Mario Camerini's *Rotaie* (1929), Raffaello Matarazzo's *Treno popolare* (1933), and Camerini's *Il signor Max* (1937).

Camerini's *Rotaie* is exemplary of the transition from silent to sound film in the Italian cinema. Without digressing too far into that auteurist excavation of quality, it should be said that this is a much-overlooked and remarkable film. It was originally shot as a silent project in 1929 and was released in 1930 with nondialog diegetic sound effects added.[25] The film's representation of the modern train is the central figure around which it organizes major narrative movements. It is not only the literal means of conveyance between fictional locations, but also the figurative bridge between the changing class identities of the film's principal characters. *Rotaie* (literally, "rails") begins with a nighttime exterior dolly shot of a couple (seen from the back) walking towards a nondescript downtown hotel. The fictional couple (played by Kathe von Nagy and Maurizio D'Ancona) remains unnamed throughout the film. The narrative provides them very little background except to suggest that their relationship is dystopic insofar as it is not sanctioned by von Nagy's parents. In a word, they have no home. Once inside the hotel room, they prepare to consummate a desperate lovers' suicide pact. They contemplate a glass of poison in a series of extreme close-ups triangulated between themselves and the bubbling poison. In the first of what will become a pattern of narrative and symbolic interventions, the appearance of a train dramatically changes the direction of the narrative. The wind and vibrations from a speeding train cause the window to suddenly burst open, overturning the glass and foiling (derailing) the suicide attempt. Watching the train disappear into the city nightscape—into a horizon of neon signs of nightclubs and amusement parks—the couple realize that they are unable to pay for the room and therefore have to sneak out.

With no home to return to, the two wander the city streets. Under a driving rain, they are momentarily fascinated by highly stylized travel and tourism posters. Their attention is drawn, in particular, to a pair of 1927 art deco works by A.M. Cassandre: "Etoile du Nord" and "Nord Express." A series of point-of-view lap dissolves progressively isolates details from the "Etoile du Nord" poster. The last close-up in the series reveals a conceptual stylization of railroad tracks. Given the momentary pause in the forward direction of the narrative, in combination with the literalization of the film's title, "The Rails," this sequence announces a symbolic terrain against which one portion of narrative will be deployed. That is to say, in the context of the couple's absolute poverty and despair, the film announces an apparent ironic juxtaposition with the qualities of modernity, travel, and pleasure. The earlier nightscape neons and this vision of an abstract "other" place thus combine to prefigure a way out of their penniless, unemployed, and morally unapproved circumstances. This is, of course, the axiomatic formula of *escapism* used by the harsher critics of the period's films. But for our purposes, what becomes most interesting to investigate is the manner in which *Rotaie* provides its own social evaluation and critique of the world to which the couple will escape. Rather than simply an occasion for escapism, that is, Lizzani's "disconnectedness," the film will actually map the contemporary Italian social terrain by examining both dystopic and utopian locations.

D'Ancona recovers a cash-laden wallet dropped at a rail station café by a patron rushing to catch a departing train. Unable to return the wallet, the couple boards the next train to leave the station, without knowing its destination. The train ride not only removes the couple from the site of their misery, it also signals a temporary change in their class status. Initially boarding the train in the second-class section, the couple literally *changes class* when D'Ancona buys a ticket for a private, first-class sleeping compartment. The nongeographic nature of this transition in social identity is emphasized by the absence of a specific destination for the train. As the couple rests in their compartment, the train rushes forward, its speed conveyed by rapidly repeated shots of receding tracks, and of the train's circular gears and churning smoke stacks. When von Nagy interrupts this archetypical

Figure 16. "Where the Others Go." Frame enlargement from *Rotaie* (1929, Mario Camerini). Posters by A. M. Cassandre.

movement montage by asking, "Where are we going?" D'Ancona responds, "Where the others go." The phrase "the others" refers both literally to the other passengers and generically to others *unlike us*. The following morning, the film specifically identifies these others. As the couple takes breakfast in the first-class dining car, they "share" the meal with highly mannered aristocrats.

Fulfilling the figurative promise of the travel posters, the train arrives at an unnamed lakeside luxury resort (probably Stresa). As the Marquis Mercier (Daniele Crespi), one of their aristocratic traveling companions, watches a speedboat race (images that are borrowed directly from LUCE newsreels), the couple settles into their second hotel room of the film. This time the room is in the resort's Grand Hotel. James Hay's excellent description of their stay in this new social domain is particularly suggestive:

In *Rotaie*, as in *Grand Hotel*, the *hotel de luxe* is an extremely unstable domain wherein fortunes and lovers can be lost in games of chance; it is also very illusory—again, a sort of hall of mirrors which enables the

Figure 17. Aristocratic desire. Frame enlargement from *Rotaie*.

characters "to see themselves." Moreover, parts of the central stage of
the narrative (scenes along the road) use highly stylized camera work to
convey the fragmentation experienced in the *bel mondo*. The lifestyle of
which the Grand Hotel is emblematic is seductive—an option not unlike
the Death which they meditate. Though the lovers avoid suicide, they
do pass through an other-worldly zone—the world of jaded bourgeois
myths, of omnipotence, and of silent cinema's extraordinariness.[26]

This second section of the film begins with D'Ancona initially winning large sums of money at the gaming tables. As his gambling fever
increases, he pays little attention to von Nagy as Mercier intensifies
efforts to seduce his wife, signaling the further breakdown of even
the fragile family order described in the film's opening sequences.
The couple's initial happiness in this location is only temporary, as
the moral decadence of an unearned pleasure associated with luxury
commences their return to a new condition of despair. His gambling
fever unabated, D'Ancona begins to run out of luck. Count Mercier
covers the mounting gambling debts, but states the implicit terms of
payment by inviting von Nagy to his room. The fall almost complete,

Figure 18. Gambling fever. Frame enlargement from *Rotaie*.

D'Ancona bursts into Mercier's room (the second time an interruption into a hotel room derails a disastrous occurrence), returns the money, and rescues his wife.

For the second time, the couple leaves a hotel unable to pay their bills. Once again they have no clear prospects for the future. Yet once again the agency of the train intervenes. As they awake from spending the night on a park bench, the refreshed couple looks up to see a column of smoke rising from behind distant hedges, signaling the arrival of another train at the resort. This time, however, the train represents less the generalized "way out" of its first appearance than a vehicle for returning to a particular natural order. That is, the second train trip maps a *way back* to a social setting that the film has yet to envision. It occasions a particular set of positive values that are absent from both the dystopia of the original hotel room and from the world and class of the Grand Hotel. These different values are naturalized inasmuch as they are part of a particular location (a landscape) rather than coming solely from the actions of specific characters. The new location will delineate the positive values of the couple's real social position. To begin with, the train appears for the first time during the day. It is visually linked neither with the original urban context nor with the promises of pleasure of the resort, but with the surrounding countryside. The couple "returns" to "their" social origins by traveling in a crowded second-class compartment, which they share with a breast-feeding mother and her working family. Whereas in their escape to the resort they had shared the dining car with the aristocrats, this time they break bread with the agrarian family. Their return to the city, where they are now finally *at home,* is under more appropriate social circumstances, and the film now (re)establishes the sanctity of a more natural familial order. On the "end" of this process, we again cite de Certeau: "Everyone goes back to work at the place he has been given, in the office or the workshop. The incarceration-vacation is over. For the beautiful abstraction of the prison are substituted the compromises, opacities, and dependencies of a workplace. Hand-to-hand combat begins again with a reality that dislodges the spectator without rails or window panes. There comes to an end the Robinson Crusoe adventure of the traveling noble soul that could believe itself *intact* because it was surrounded by glass and iron."[27]

In its larger figural topography, *Rotaie* produces a socially normative map. Having (re)united them as a family, this section of the film also specifies a final social geography for the couple. As they return to the city, the film repeats the elements of the previous train-movement montage—this time in the light of day. At the end of the montage, the train's smoke stacks are transformed via a lap dissolve into the smoke stacks of a modern factory. With little background narrative explanation, D'Ancona is then seen busily working at a mammoth steam generator. He then breaks for lunch, leaving the factory along with *his* coworkers. He is joined outside the factory walls by von Nagy, who waits with lunch in hand, the film's final instance of sharing food. This last shot is the literal and figurative reverse of the film's very first shot. Where the penniless, starving couple at the film's beginning walked the city streets and were seen only from behind, they are now joined to the workplace and walk in daylight towards the camera. The formal symmetry between the two sequences emphasizes the film's containment of a potentially dysfunctional, one is tempted to say *misguided,* social mobility between classes. The momentary social destabilization, invoked by the spatial mobility that was occasioned by their access to modern transportation, is transformed into a "permanent" stabilizing of class order entirely consonant with an idyllic fascist status quo.

Figure 19. The return home. Frame enlargement from *Rotaie*.

While *Rotaie* invokes a melodramatic scenario impelled by an imbalance in familial order, it does so by setting the melodrama against
the basic terrain of social dislocation brought on by unemployment. It
dislodges the couple from an original social position in order to articulate differences between social strata, that is, between them and the
aristocracy of the Grand Hotel. It invokes questions of class so as to
suggest that they are resolvable, that they disappear precisely when the
traditional family structure is valorized by work. In a word, the film
figuratively prescribes a place for the basic family unit within the contemporary social geography that reconfirms an idealized and orderly
status quo.

Rotaie identifies the lakeside luxury resort as a site of pleasure for a
moneyed aristocracy. Raffaello Matarazzo's *Treno popolare* (1933) also
describes a site for leisure, but in this case it is for the working class.
The nonspecific locality of *Rotaie*'s luxury resort is replaced by the
Italian regional specificity of Orvieto as a tourist destination. Where
the last train in Camerini's film brings the working-class families back
to the industrial workplace, Matarazzo's film maps out a location and

activity for its after-work recreation. In fact, it literally retraces the steps of one example of leisure-time activity organized by the regime. In August 1931, the state began to offer workers and the unemployed "popular trains," that is, discounted tickets for day excursions to the Italian countryside. De Grazia underlines the importance and function assigned to this program:

> The "popular trains" also resulted from Ciano's initiative, the outcome— as he frankly admitted—of a felicitous convergence of economic calculations and political considerations. The discounts on group travel of up to fifty percent were designed to boost mass transit, thereby reducing the huge deficit of the state railroads as revenues declined during the depression; at the same time they provided the urban unemployed and poor a brief respite from the dismal depression atmosphere of the cities.
>
> Accompanied by well-devised propaganda, the "popular trains" became a new national institution, celebrated in popular ditties by a lower-class public that previously had rarely, if ever, taken train trips for diversion. Between 2 August and 20 September 1931, more than half a million travelers took advantage of the discounts.[28]

The very title of the film refers to the social reality of the popular trains. In its first sequence, a stream of families, couples, and bachelors line up to buy tickets for the discounted day excursion from Rome to Orvieto. Right from the start the film also distinguishes itself from *Rotaie* by a formal experimentation very rare in the period's commercial films. Indeed, the film has two distinct overlapping styles, each denoting a different set of thematic elements. First, the fictional narrative is often interrupted by third-person points of view more characteristic of documentary film. Thus, for example, as it introduces a loosely connected string of characters and narrative subplots, a shaky, sometimes hand-held camera overlays images of the real train station, a real crowd buying tickets and boarding the popular train. The documentary quality of these space/times shared by the fictional characters and the audience itself evokes the style of social realism and refers explicitly to the social coordinates surrounding the film, that is, to the OND's organization of leisure time. Second, the film's fictional narrative is organized as light comedy and takes up several of the thematic concerns of the famed white telephone films: small family melodramas, temptation, boudoir romance, extramarital intrigue, and so forth.

Treno popolare's formal experimentation invites a consideration of the film as a precursor of neorealism. It anticipates by more than a decade some of the post-war movement's basic aesthetic and cultural practices, including the use of nonprofessional actors, shooting in real locations and with available light, setting the narrative against a culturally specific location, and construction of a nonspectacular narrative trajectory, among other things. These practices take on added significance inasmuch as the film both participates in and contributes to the construction of Italian popular culture. The film's Nino Rota music track, for example, intones four different versions of the main theme, "Treno Popolare," a song that was widely circulated after the film's release. The close quarters of the "popular train" visually gathers together discrete members of the Italian lower classes, joining them as a public engaged in collective leisure. As the story unfolds, documentary images present examples of this public's local and popular customs, public dances, bicycle rides, weekend picnics, and so on. Indeed, the film as a whole refers to a particular form of popular activity that, as De Grazia suggests, quickly became a national institution.

By transporting a working-class urban public into contact with the Italian countryside, *Treno popolare* implicitly addresses differences between urban and rural cultures. Yet the film does not treat these as societal conflicts brought on by modernization, that is, it does not bring the city and countryside into conflict. Instead, it characterizes tensions between the two topoi as naturalized conflicts between generations. This generational conflict provides, for example, the terms of differences between the male characters of the central story. Though the film presents a series of autonomous subplots, the primary narrative is built around a competition between two "popular train" tourists—Giovanni (Marcello Spada) and Carlo (Carlo Petrangeli)—for the affections of a young secretary, Lina (Lina Gennari). Giovanni is associated with tradition, attempting to impress Lina by educating her about the historical background of the sites they visit. Bespectacled, wearing a suit and tie, he respectfully reads from guidebooks about Orvieto. Carlo, on the other hand, is antitraditionalist and travels the "popular train" primarily in search of romantic interludes. Young, athletic, and informal, he separates Lina from Giovanni by drawing her attention away from the historic monuments of Orvieto. In the end, even this generational theme is trumped by the very possibility of additional nonmarital sexual liaisons. Thus the competition between Giovanni and Carlo is resolved when Giovanni's attentions are drawn to another young girl on the return train ride. Although the film shares the narrative symmetry of *Rotaie* (departure, interlude, return), it does not invoke the question of temporary social instability. Though removed from their geographic homes in the city, all of the characters in *Treno popolare* retain their original social identities. In the station, on the train, and in Orvieto, they bring along their class-specific baggage.

The film's overall relationship to a fascist conception of social order is somewhat complex. While it documents the "popular trains" as a form of pleasure officially approved by the regime, that pleasure is described as an equal mix of tourism and temporary moral transgression. As such, the film was potentially a site for subversive readings. Although there is little to suggest that the narrative trajectory fundamentally departs from a fascist conception of the Italian family (wed to the state), the very presence of numerous unsanctioned, nonmarital relationships is very suggestive. Indeed, one could speculate that, on the one hand, the film's representations of such pleasures advertised to its audiences that the state-sponsored leisure-time activities could be an occasion to find lascivious opportunities outside the traditional patriarchal family. In addition to Carlo's seduction of Lina, the train "allows" numerous illicit affairs. One of the film's chief subplots, for example, concerns a wife's discovery that her husband's planned OND trip is simply a cover for a weekend tryst with his secretary. On the other hand, any threat to a basic familial order is limited to a fairly restricted range. Up to a point, even the suggested affairs are sanctioned by the very fact that they take place in a state-sponsored activity, that is, in full view of the state. Moreover, while invoking moral transgressivity, the film represents the liaisons as permitted inasmuch as they do not pose a threat to the social strata gathered together by the film visually and by the state throughout its after-work reforms. Ultimately, the film allows for both hegemonic and oppositional readings. More importantly, both types of readings share at least one major social coordinate specific to the audience's experience of cinema during the period. Where *Rotaie* suggests that decoding takes place along the twin axes of *luxury* and *work*, *Treno popolare* suggests that both class conflict and sexual tensions are to be located within the collective discovery of Italian cultural patrimony as collocated in the natural splendor of the countryside and the cultural legacy of "historic" sites.

In Mario Camerini's *Il signor Max* (1937), nationality and class converge on the theme of international travel. The film recounts the efforts of a newspaper vendor, Gianni (Vittorio De Sica), to rid himself of his original class identity in order to become a gentleman of high society. Here, the affectations and questionable moral character of high society are presented chiefly in terms of its infatuation with foreign (specifically American) culture. In perhaps no other film during the entire period do so many foreign usages appear, permitted in this exceptional case because they refer to the world of a decaying bourgeoisie.

Once again, the representation of transportation assumes a central role in both the film's narrative structure and its symbolic order. The first scene locates Gianni in his original social and geographic setting, a newspaper stand at a busy Roman intersection. As a hectic stream of cars, taxis, buses, and bicycles rushes by, Gianni makes final preparations for his annual month-long vacation. Whereas the tragic couple in *Rotaie* is transported to the luxury resort by equal measures of desperation and a stroke of fortune, Gianni has spent all year readying himself for his ascent into high society by taking lessons in English, tennis, golf, and bridge.

Gianni begins his trip, accompanied to the train station by his uncle Virgilio (Mario Casaleggio), a bus ticket-taker. In a direct reference to OND organized tourism, the uncle has arranged discounted tickets for the trip, planning the itinerary "train by train, city by city." Shocked that he would change reservations to first class, Uncle Virgilio reminds Gianni to at least take good pictures of the tourist sites along the way: the grottos in Postiumia, the Parthenon, Rhodes. The very next scene reveals De Sica/Gianni at the port of Naples taking pictures of the luxury cruise ship that is about to sail, instead, only for Genoa. This scene underscores the notion that his "real" desire has less to do with traveling from one classical location to another and more to do with moving from one class affiliation to another. Thus, as with *Treno popolare,* the film opens up an occasion for another misuse/misreading of the OND's intended social program.

At this point Dona Paola (Rubi Dalma) and her niece, two upper-class women who have just arrived from New York, notice that Gianni is carrying *Time* and *Esquire* magazines and mistake him for one of their own, a well-heeled world traveler. Welcomed into their traveling company, Gianni gladly exchanges the innate provincialism of his month-long tourist itinerary for a one-week trip amid high society. When Dona Paola thinks that the name on his American camera (a Max that he has borrowed from a friend) refers to Gianni, he is literally renamed as "Max." That his shift in class identity can be sustained only by a disguise, by a temporary alter ego, is reinforced in the very next scene. Gianni appears as Max for the first time the following evening at nothing less than a shipboard masquerade ball.

Figure 20. Vittorio De Sica as gentleman. Frame enlargement from *Il signor Max* (1937, Mario Camerini). Courtesy of the Cineteca di Bologna.

In his identity as Max, De Sica wears the masquerade ball's required mask, and as Gianni he sports his desired social disguise as a member of the first class.

Quickly spending all of his money, "il signor Max" returns to Rome (yet another *return*) and once again becomes Gianni the newspaper vendor. Months pass as Gianni continues to work on perfecting the skills of his alter ego. When Dona Paola's entourage pays a visit to Rome, her maid Lauretta (Assia Norris) thinks she recognizes the newspaper vendor as the sophisticated signor Max. From this point forward, much of the film is built around Gianni's attempt to maintain a double identity. He continues to court Dona Paola by trying to convince her of his sophistication. (As I will discuss later, Gianni's desire for Dona Paola occasions the film's underlying fear of the exotic.) At the same time, in order to avoid being unmasked by Lauretta, he has to exhibit the authentic characteristics of a simple, unaffected street vendor. The premise of a double identity allows the film to characterize the differences between the social strata to which each identity belongs. Dona Paola, her niece, and their companions are self-centered, arrogant snobs of high society. They travel the world in luxury liners and first-class trains and rest up in *their* Grand Hotel. Furthermore, their affectations are linked to their obsession with foreign cultures. When Dona Paola first encounters Max, she thinks he's American and they haltingly speak their first lines of dialogue in English.[29] When they discuss previous trips, Gianni awkwardly must mask the fact that he has never traveled internationally. That his experience. is limited to Italy is a source of shame that the film ultimately seeks to expiate. Dona Paola, on the other hand, refers to the "divine" Shanghai, to "my divine Orient." When Max confesses that he boarded the cruise ship to Genoa only to be with her, she characterizes his apparent romanticism with reference both to Hollywood and to the practice of dubbing:

> A delicious gesture, *alla* Clark Gable!
> What, you haven't seen the latest Gable?
> We saw it in the English version.

Since Gianni/Max is in constant alternation between the two worlds of the film, the qualities of his lower-class identity are expressed through Lauretta. She and Gianni's extended family are selfless, unpretentious, working people who save their earnings, preferring popular tourism to the gaming rooms. Their leisure time is dedicated to the unaffected and popular traditions of collective activities specific to Italian culture. Indeed, Lauretta first begins to fall in love with Gianni as he sings in a chorus at an OND social hall. In discovering Gianni's real identity, the scene functions as a symmetrical reversal of the masquerade ball on the luxury liner. Where Dona Paola spoke of "her Orient," Lauretta describes her background for Gianni in these terms: "In my city, we had friends, we danced, we had fun, we worked." Indeed, where signor Max had danced previously with Dona Paola, Gianni now dances with Lauretta. Instead of costumes and tuxedos, the participants wear their normal workday attire and uniforms, overdetermined signs of *their* social status. They drink beer in place of the expensive imported whiskeys of the cruise ship. Unlike the stilted leisure of high-class international society, the social hall is parochial, familial, and participatory.

The two represented societies are clearly in conflict. Lauretta's attraction to Gianni and his world is equaled by her disaffection with Dona Paola and hers. Although she is very sad to leave the OND concert, she is forced to return to work as Dona Paola and her niece prepare to leave for another trip. At this point, the film's focus shifts

Figure 21. De Sica as newspaper vendor. Frame enlargement from *Il signor Max*.

away from Gianni's efforts to maintain his dual identity and replaces his initial desire for Dona Paola with desire for Lauretta. It must now find a way to dismantle his disguise in order to fulfill his desire for Lauretta, that is, to sanction desire within a traditional, local, familial structure. The need to unite these two fictional characters as a couple

Figure 22. OND concert audience hears De Sica sing. Frame enlargement from *Il signor Max*. Courtesy of the Cineteca Nazionale, Roma.

is articulated not only in terms set forward by this specific narrative, but also by reference to another site of indigenous popular culture. Specifically, the promise of union between the two is doubly charged by virtue of its discursive continuity with a previous film. Norris and De Sica had starred two years earlier as the romantic leads in Camerini's *Darò un milione*. Not only was the film one of the period's largest Italian box office successes, these two actors were among the most popular and most promoted by the Italian star system.[30]

The social impact of the star system was not lost on the regime. As Stephen Gundle has pointed out:

> In the late 1930s, the regime took an interest in the appearance of stars. There was an assumption that actors should be ideal types of the Italian race, that their Italian qualities should be underlined, and that the corrupting foreign influences of previous years should be eliminated. As far as the men were concerned, there was general satisfaction with the results that had been reached. The humiliating effeminization of the Latin male for which Valentino and Novarro had been responsible was deemed to have been corrected by Nazzari and Giachetti, the two actors who were most representative of Italian virility.[31]

It is in this context—that is, the intertextual representation of gender and sexuality—that the ideological stakes become particularly charged for filmgoing audiences. In editorials, essays and, to some extent, cultural directives, the regime's spokesmen expressed a deep concern about the potentially destabilizing impact that foreign cultures, particularly American culture, could have on Italian sexuality. In a word, such exoticisms might have a corrosive effect not only on autarchically directed aesthetics, but also upon the social order. De Grazia has described what was at stake for the regime with respect to the representation of women: "Not least of all, Americanized leisure threatened to transform Italian girls, making them masculine and independent like their American counterparts . . . [and the regime responded by proposing] its own standards of female beauty: one ideal, the 'crisis woman,' was negative; the other, whom we might call 'authentic woman,' was positive. The former was a masculinized plaything, a false and alien creature, the product of Paris and Hollywood; the latter was home-grown—broodmare, mother, and mate. Fictions both, they were invented to de-eroticize females, so as not to risk sexual defeat."[32] In the terms proposed by the film, Dona Paola clearly fits this description of the "crisis woman" and Lauretta that of the "authentic woman." That Gianni's desire for Dona Paola *must be* replaced with desire for Lauretta can be seen as intertextual panic. It is a response engendered both by the regime's concern for how such "transgressive" sexuality might diminish the efficiency of its pronatalism and by its ideological imperative for the maintenance of a normative social order located within the traditional Italian family.[33]

In order to join Lauretta and rejoin his real class, Gianni must become disaffected with and disavow his desire for upward social mobility. In this sense, *Il signor Max* reverses the narrative trajectory of the earlier film. In *Darò un milione*, De Sica plays Mr. Gold, a millionaire who is disillusioned with the corruptness of his own class. Renouncing his riches, he goes in search of "one simple, honest gesture." Where Gianni/De Sica in *Il signor Max* boasts proudly of acquiring the formal attire he needs to be accepted onboard the luxury liner, Mr. Gold/De Sica in *Darò un milione* literally gives up his tuxedo in order to disguise himself as a member of the urban poor. Even with this reversal in narrative premises, both characters fall in love with the fictional character played by Assia Norris before returning to the places of their original class identity. That is to say, it is the specific narrative trajectory of both films (even though their starting points differ) *and the* contemporary Italian cinema's star system that promise a harmonious union between the two.

As with the films I have discussed previously, the conversion of the temporary social interloper is made possible through the agency of the train. Gianni rejoins Dona Paola and company as their train leaves the central Rome station. It is precisely when Lauretta confides her frustration with working for such people that he realizes his love for her. Yet when he kisses her, she responds with a forceful slap to the face. Since Gianni is stilled disguised as signor Max, desire is forestalled unless and until he sheds the trappings of the *wrong* class. In the following scene, Lauretta announces to Dona Paola (surrounded by her traveling companions and the doubled Max) that she is quitting her job. Standing together in the corridor of their first-class compartments, the group expresses their indignation over such unconscionable behavior. According to Max, however, Lauretta has "not been entirely wrong," and he too decides to leave the group. That his departure refers also to separating himself from "this class of people" is visually expressed in the subsequent shot-reverse-shot. Max first leaves the group's screen space and then walks alone down the corridor toward the second-class section of the train. In the morning, both Lauretta and Gianni board a different train, and, in a series of shots that recall the final montage in *Rotaie*, the next sequence is a set of countryside panoramas seen from the train which returns to Rome, once again to an idyllic home front.

In these films, the presence of the train refers both figuratively and (occasionally) literally to social practices operative under fascism. This is not to say that such images function merely as propaganda for the regime. They do present, however, highly structured visual tropes, a nexus of signs that resonates with the particular fascist claims of productivity, efficiency, and patriarchy. More importantly, they carve out a symbolic space in which the terms of class identity can be described for contemporary audiences. It is clear that new train routes and stations expanded the cultural coordinates of the country's public sphere. I agree with Berezin that they also constituted the practical infrastructure required to move bodies around the peninsula in order to create public rallies and mass participatory spectacles. More importantly, however, they not only facilitated the contemporary population shift from the countryside to the city, they literally brought previously separate regions and classes in sight of one another. Within this newly extended topography of the public sphere, new representations of transportation and travel construct a publicly available discursive terrain within which conflicts between these identities can be articulated and theoretically resolved.

Did such films enforce conformism to fascist political ideology? It certainly can be suggested, for example, that the very presence of the figurative binary between the exotically inspired "crisis" woman and the provincially circumscribed "authentic woman" produces the ability for spectators to construct a "reverse discourse," that is, to read against the represented grain. Indeed, a number of fascist cultural historians have suggested that not only were the state's pronatalist measures largely ineffective, they were also resisted as unwelcome intrusions into the private domains of sexuality and gender roles. That said, the cinematic circulation of images about travel—where that travel always means returning to an original, *natural* point of departure—delineates the symbolic boundaries of a single and harmonious, unified social order. As discourse, that circulation systematically proposes a preferred reading of text and social context, a reading suggested to the Italian audience/public that was embraced by the regime. When indeed the films refer explicitly to the fascist state (as in the case of the references to the OND in *Il signor Max* and *Treno popolare*), the regime is inscribed as *the* authoritative agency for the mediation of social conflicts brought about by the transition of Italy from an agricultural to an industrialized country. These particular instances do no less than negotiate for the "new" nation the terms of a *naturalized* modernity.

FOUR

ITALY AND AMERICA

Fascination and (Re)Negotiation

But what never failed to strike me most of all—and by now
I had been in almost every house—were the eyes of the two
inseparable guardian angels that looked at me from the wall
over the bed. On the one side was the black, scowling face,
with its large inhuman eyes, of the Madonna of Viggiano; on
the other a colored print of the sparkling eyes, behind gleam-
ing glasses, and the hearty grin of President Roosevelt. I never saw other pictures or images than these: not the King nor
the Duce, nor even Garibaldi; no famous Italian of any kind,
nor any one of the appropriate saints; only Roosevelt and the
Madonna of Viggiano never failed to be present. . . . To the
peasants of Lucania, Rome means very little; it is the capital
of the gentry, the center of a foreign and hostile world. . . .
Yes, New York, rather than Rome or Naples, would be the
real capital of the peasants of Lucania, if these men without
a country could have a capital at all. And it *is* their capital, in
the only way it can be for them, that is as a myth.

Carlo Levi, *Christ Stopped at Eboli*, 1947

Vuoi fare l'Americano, l'Americano, ma sei nato in Italy [*sic*].
You want to be American, but you were born in Italy.

Sophia Loren, *It Started in Naples*
(Melville Shavelson, 1960)

AUTHORIAL STATES:
MUSSOLINI AND MGM MARCH ON ROME

In the previous chapter we discussed the regime's various attempts to construct a new social order through its civic programs. We have suggested that these programs influenced film spectatorship even for the commercial cinema. This chapter explores another coordinate for reading the fascist project, specifically the presence of American culture and Hollywood cinema. Any mapping of the fascist/Italian world has to accommodate what is also outside the prescribed symbolic boundaries. But how would a nongeographical cultural map "contain" America? As we have seen, the regime was both attracted to the Hollywood institutional model and also concerned about how its texts might damage the Italian body politic. Its national film policy never completely resolved the contradiction between Hollywood as either threat or ally in the hegemonic development of national consensus. But, unlike some recent studies, I contend that the relationship went well beyond a set of unreconciled differences, of a neutral balance in which contradictory forces were merely copresent. Instead, the relationship was a dynamic *partnership* (where the ideological interests intersected) and supratextual *negotiation* (where Hollywood might create the possibility of either transgressive reading or action).

For more than a century, images of America have occupied a pivotal space within the Italian historic imaginary. The penetration of American culture into Italy began just a decade after the country's formation as a unified nation-state. It was initially brought to Italian shores in the form of news and letters from the over four million immigrants who arrived in the United States between 1880 and 1920.[1] Its preeminence within Italian society remains intact to the present day and is immediately recognizable by the dominance of American product in both Italian cinemas and television.

During the interwar years the issue of American culture took on special importance. As a term of reference within public discourse, America was second only to the Fascist regime itself. In the context of Italy's cultural map, and the heuristics for its reading, one could argue therefore that there were effectively two marches on Rome. One indicated the rise to political power of Mussolini and the Fascist party. The other was a visible cultural presence characterized by the massive circulation of American images. The latter was epitomized by MGM's opening of its own distribution office in the capital city the same year as the Fascist march on Rome. As I have discussed in chapter 2, just as Italian film production declined during the twenties, a larger percentage of the films actually viewed came from abroad. The table below clearly demonstrates that, even though local film production takes an upswing during the 1930s, Italian screens were dominated by foreign, especially American, titles:

Year	U.S.	France	England	Germany	Other	Italy
1930	220	24	19	54	30	12
1931	171	30	7	30	18	13
1932	139	16	8	47	16	26
1933	172	28	10	43	20	26
1934	172	11	20	44	11	30
1935	127	10	10	38	14	40
1936	105	12	8	54	8	32
1937	190	26	11	49	7	31
1938	161	16	16	27	5	45
1939	60	42	20	40	4	50[2]

In order to maximize their hold on the Italian marketplace, other Hollywood studios quickly followed MGM's lead. By mid-decade Twentieth Century Fox, Paramount, and Warner Bros. had also opened offices in Rome. Not only serving as distribution units, these offices also established their own publicity machines. By publishing Italian-language fan magazines, company bulletins, and posters, they sought to orchestrate interest around the films of the parent company—to provide a discursive foothold, that is, for the Hollywood star system in Italy. As they did in the United States, these publications also reinforced the attractiveness of the films by introducing the Italian public to the biographical backgrounds of the stars.[3]

The preeminence of American films needs to be seen in the context of a larger cultural dynamic at play in turn-of-the-century Italy especially as it was systematized toward the end of the 1920s. Since Italian cultural industries (newspaper and book publishing, theater, cinema) were seriously undercapitalized, they had to develop new partnerships with finance capital in order to modernize. David Forgacs summarizes this dynamic in his discussion of book publishing: "As in newspaper publishing, these factors together meant that the

Figure 23. *Topolino* (Mickey Mouse) in Italy. Advertisement in *Cinema*, February 10, 1938. Courtesy of the Cineteca del Friuli, Gemona.

costs of modernizing and expanding a firm's operations could not be met simply by increasing sales on the domestic market and reinvesting the profits. Consequently, a more ambitious publisher like Mondadori came to rely on bank loans and the state in order to expand."[4]

The case of Mondadori illustrates a number of essential components in the industrialization of culture under fascism. First, Mondadori was quick to support the regime's political initiatives, from literally printing the handbills for the March on Rome to the glorification of fascist programs in the monthly magazine *Annali d'Italia*.[5] Second, the regime mediated on behalf of Mondadori's industrial expansion. For example, Mussolini guaranteed the long-term loans with the Banca d'Italia and the Cassa di Risparmio that the company needed for its expansion. And, in an operation similar to the state's partnership with the film industry in the mid-1930s, the regime also occasionally released Mondadori from its censorship requirements. Thus, when the Ministry of Popular Culture called for the suppression of all foreign cartoon strips in 1938, the Disney cartoons—published by Mondadori—were exempted.

This last example is significant because it too brings into question the imposing presence of foreign cultural product in Italy. In addition to lack of capitalization, the culture industries did not possess sufficient product to meet the demands of new mass audiences, especially those audiences developing around the major urban centers. For this reason, the industrialization of cultural production not only meant concentration of capital and modernization of systems of distribution, it also led to an increased dependence on product from abroad. Forgacs concludes, "As modern cultural industries developed in Italy, they found themselves with a fairly limited stock of domestically-produced materials (books, films, television programmes, etc.) and had to rely on imports to build up their range and meet upswings in demand."[6]

Traces of Americana traversed virtually every sector of the public sphere in fascist Italy even at the height of the campaign for autarchy, that is, for economic and cultural self-sufficiency. On July 26, 1930, for example, *Corriere della Sera,* Italy's largest daily newspaper, ran the first of many advertisements for Coca-Cola. Similarly, Italian popular culture—its pulp literature, comic strips, and serial novels in particular—was frequented almost as much by Americana as it was by "indigenous" images. Four years before Mondadori obtained exclusive Italian rights to Disney characters (in 1936), the publishing house Nerbini had begun translating not only Mickey Mouse, but also Flash Gordon and Mandrake. As late as 1939, that is, after the Hollywood majors had been forced out of the Italian market, the fascination with America persisted even in the state-run newsreels. In that year, LUCE covered a wide range of American topics, including *The Latest Speedboat Championship in the United States* (Cinegiornale no. 1600), *The Latest Swimming Meet in California* (no. 1602), *International Polo: The United States vs. England* (no. 1607), *The Exploits of Motorcyclists and Acrobats Thrill the American Public* (no. 1620), *The Latest California Trend: Go-Cart Racing* (no. 1630), and *For You Ladies: Modern Jewels Presented on Fifth Avenue* (no. 1637).[7]

One of the most significant aspects of this culture-wide phenomenon was the fascination that American fiction held for Italian writers. Starting with Cesare Pavese, many of the period's major literary figures wrote about, discussed, and, above all, translated volume after volume of American fiction. Elio Vittorini translated novels by William Saroyan and Erskine Caldwell. In 1940, he edited for the publisher Bompiani a crucial anthology of American fiction entitled *Americana.* Alberto Moravia translated works by Theodore Dreiser, Ring Lardner, and James M. Cain. Eugionio Montale worked on Pound, Melville, Steinbeck, and Fitzgerald. Pavese himself introduced to Italy Melville's *Moby-Dick,* as well as works by Sinclair Lewis, William Faulkner, John Dos Passos, and Sherwood Anderson.

As has been widely discussed, this interest in American realist fiction, its characters and style, would become a central influence on the subsequent development of neorealism.[8] The most celebrated example was, of course, Luchino Visconti's *Ossessione* (1943), which was loosely based on James M. Cain's *The Postman Always Rings Twice.* The significance of this phenomenon during the fascist period, however, is that it simultaneously added to a popular mythology of America while also providing discursive terrain on which cultural resistance to fascism could be located. Giaime Pintor later reflected that "this America doesn't need Columbus. It is discovered inside ourselves, a land for which one holds the same hope and the same faith of the first emigrants, of anyone who, at the cost of errors and fatigue, has decided to defend human dignity."[9]

Indeed, the possibility of an oppositional decoding of culture through the translation and circulation of American texts did not go unobserved by the state. On the one hand, these novels helped the "industrial" efforts of Italian publishers to satisfy the increasing demands of their readership. On the other hand, they came into ideological conflict with fascism, insofar as they posed a substantial threat to its desire for cultural purity. They presented readers a different set of coordinates with which to decode contemporary Italian culture. In a word, they marked the presence of a desirable *other.* In response to this latter consideration, the regime steadily increased its active censorship of such literature as the decade progressed. Bompiani, for example, was prohibited from distributing *Americana* until Elio Vittorini's pro-American introductions were replaced by critical assessments written by Emilio Cecchi. And, although Visconti was able to release *Ossessione* in 1943, the translation of the Cain novel itself wasn't actually published until 1945, a full decade after its release in France. Given the historical importance of this exceptional text and, in particular, the manner in which *Ossessione* explicitly violates numerous thematic and stylistic guidelines of the fascist regime (its representation of sexuality and crime within the national borders), the circumstances surrounding the film's release require additional study. There is some anecdotal information that may explain how the film was released and, more importantly, how it avoided serious censorship cuts before that release. By this time, Mussolini regularly viewed every Italian film before it could receive a green light from the Direzione Generale per la Cinematografia

Figure 24. Vittorio Mussolini in Hollywood (with Our Gang). Frame enlargement from Hearst Newsreel, vol. 9, no. 204 (September 27, 1937). Courtesy of the UCLA Film and Television Archive.

(DGC). Mussolini was so appalled by *Ossessione* when he viewed it at his Via Torlonia residence that he stormed out of the projection room without saying a word. This apparently made it possible for the pro-industry DGC (headed by Luigi Freddi) to justify the film's unhampered release insofar as it could be said that Mussolini saw the film and voiced no objections.

The contradiction between the heavy presence of American culture and the fascist drive for autarchy constitutes a basic axis along which to plot conditions of readership in the interwar years. The presence of American fictions on Italy's cinema screens was continuously and vigorously debated throughout the period. Even while the Italian film industry was depending so heavily on the importation of American films, its representatives often registered disapproval in cinema magazines. In 1930, screenwriter Guglielmo Giannini wrote:

> After the American army, the American firemen, the American military academy, the American air force, that is, after *The Big Parade*, *The Fire Brigade*, *West Point*, *The Legion of the Condemned* and other American things, we have the American college with *Prep and Pep*. Later we are going to have the American nursery school. We will pay resounding millions in order to happily suffer "made in America" Kultur as the perfect idiots

we all are in this Europe which has been reduced to the level of an intellectual colony of the elected people which exacts from us, the electorate,
gigantic tributes.[10]

Above and beyond the economic dependence on foreign imports, this
tension between fascination with and resistance to the myth of America can be seen at work within three separate kinds of film texts. First,
not only do LUCE newsreels return regularly to American topics, the
fascist regime recognized America's importance—as a matter of foreign policy—through a number of state-sponsored documentaries.
Second, a specific range of attitudes vis-à-vis American culture is articulated in its fictional representation by Italian entertainment films.
Third, the films of Mario Camerini during the 1930s—as a body of
work—constitute a point of supratextual exchange, of negotiation and
competition, between Italy and Hollywood.

PARTNERSHIP AND COMPETITION WITH HOLLYWOOD

With an autographed picture of Mussolini on its cover, the May 5,
1928, issue of the *Saturday Evening Post* presented the first install-
ment of the Duce's autobiography. Notwithstanding pockets of antifascist opposition, the regime received considerable good press in the
United States, at least until its passage of anti-Semitic laws in 1938
and its entrance into the Pact of Steel with Germany in 1939.[11] Despite occasional press caricatures of his bombastic style, Mussolini
was regularly portrayed as a reasonable national leader whose great
social experiments were motivated by a much admired anticommunist
sentiment. Cast in the image of a down-to-earth problem solver, as
a man of action, his "courageous statesmanship" provoked frequent
comparisons to Theodore Roosevelt. Indeed, it was reported that
Mussolini embraced such comparisons. In 1927 journalist Irving S.
Cobb recounted the following exchange in *Cosmopolitan* magazine:
"'Do you know, your Excellency, what a great many Americans call
you? They call you the Italian Roosevelt.' By this he was obviously
gratified. 'For that,' he said, 'I am very glad and proud. Roosevelt I
greatly admired.' He clenched his fists. 'Roosevelt had strength—had
the will to do what he thought should be done. He had greatness.'"[12]
Realizing the political value of vocal international support, the regime
capitalized on this type of favorable coverage of Mussolini. It organized profascist propaganda campaigns in the United States, focusing

its efforts in particular on Italian American social clubs, newspapers, movie houses, and radio programs.

A primary example of such efforts was the 1932 production of a feature-length documentary entitled *Mussolini Speaks*. As one of many initiatives dedicated to celebrating the tenth anniversary of the fascist rise to power, this documentary was intended primarily for consumption abroad. It was designed to present foreign audiences with an unfiltered view of the regime's accomplishments in order to mobilize international political support. In fact, responses to the film are valuable indications of the wide-ranging popularity enjoyed by the regime in the United States. A remarkable 1933 letter from the Buck Jones Rangers Club, for example, was addressed directly to the Duce: "As national chairman of the Buck Jones Rangers Club, an international organization composed of over five million boys and girls, I have the great pleasure of recommending the picture *Mussolini Speaks* to the members. As *Mussolini Speaks* shows in detail the great work you are doing in training the youths of Italy and interesting boys and girls in sports and cultural development, I feel that this picture is going to be a great inspiration to them."[13]

The organization of youth culture was of particular importance to the regime, and in April 1926 it was consolidated under a national agency, the Opera Nazionale Balilla (ONB). The ONB was responsible for coordinating both civil education and sports/athletics activities for Italian youth. "Balilla," the term used to signify fascist youth, was widely circulated in the period. Its use culminated in the naming of a 1930 FIAT compact model as a reciprocal symbol of the dynamism of both Italian youth and the Italian automotive industry under fascism. (A separate study of the representation of youth culture in Hollywood and Italian cinemas would undoubtedly also illuminate the similarities and differences between the sociologies of the two countries.) We have already discussed some of the ways in which the state appropriated aspects of Italian history in order to justify its contemporary practices; the treatment of youth within fascist culture erected a vision of an idealized future, a next generation, for the regime.

As with many of its propaganda efforts abroad, the regime focused its publicity campaign for *Mussolini Speaks* particularly on Italian immigrant communities. In the United States, the film itself was released primarily in Italian American theaters and was highly publicized in Italian-language newspapers. An extraordinary aspect of the overall campaign was a nationwide contest organized in conjunction

Figure 25. Balilla. Poster for 1930 FIAT.

with the screening of the film. After watching the film, the audience was asked to write a 250-word answer to the question "What is the basis for the success obtained by Mussolini?" The twenty-four winning respondents received an all-expenses-paid two-week stay in Italy and were granted a personal audience with the Duce. The winners traveled aboard the famed Italian luxury liner *Rex,* which also carried a gift-wrapped copy of the film to be presented to Mussolini himself upon arrival.

Mussolini Speaks is significant for a number of additional reasons. First, insofar as it is a compilation of materials from the regime's

LUCE newsreels, it constitutes a privileged condensation of the state's view of itself in 1932. The distillation of separate events into a single overarching celebration of ten years of fascist governance allowed the state to propose its own unmediated historiography of contemporary Italy. Second, insofar as the film was coproduced by Columbia Pictures, it also points to the deeply embedded relationship between the two cultures and the limited partnership between Hollywood cinema and the Italian state. In point of fact, the film's English narration was provided by Lowell Thomas and the visual compilation was edited together by Edgar G. Ulmer.[14] Some accounts indicate that Jack Cohn supervised the film and although the specificity of the guidelines from Rome remains unclear, it is significant to note that Columbia's publicity campaign highlights the film's historiographic claim, that is, that it contains facts that make up a part of history.[15] According to the studio's own newsletter: "*Mussolini Speaks* presents an exclusive and authentic film autobiography of the Italian Dictator with the *actual events* in his colorful career serving as the incidents of the story. The camera first introduces us to Mussolini's birthplace and then carries us through highlights that are now *part of history*, such as Mussolini's valiant war career."[16]

The emphasis placed upon the film's authenticity extends beyond Columbia's desire to support the Italian government's propaganda efforts. As I have discussed previously, the regime's application of censorship to foreign films was particularly acute in cases where Italians or immigrants of Italian origin were portrayed negatively. For example, the regime blocked the importation of *Scarface* (1932) exactly for these reasons. DGC director Luigi Freddi maintained that the distributors showed "good common sense" by not trying to import the film. Freddi himself had seen the film in a private screening in London. Despite the fact that he described *Scarface* as the foundational film in this very popular genre, he gave the following reason for its undesirability in Italy: "But apart from the character of the film, which is a real crime school, one cannot forget that all of the criminals, who support the overall structure of this terrifying topic, even if they live in American environments, were scrupulously and deliberately classified as Italians."[17] Moreover, the film aroused serious resentment among many Italian Americans in the United States, who engaged in a ferocious denunciatory letter-writing campaign.[18] Coming soon after the uproar over *Scarface*, *Mussolini Speaks* should be viewed in the context of a collaborative effort between Hollywood and the regime to combat such negative representations by presenting an idealized image of that community's original homeland.

Despite the implicitly political nature of the film's publicity, *Mussolini Speaks* opens with a series of rhetorical gestures that attempt to depoliticize its subject. The film begins with radio and newsreel commentator Lowell Thomas directly addressing the audience from the geography-less neutral space of a nondescript darkened studio. His physical presence locates/identifies a known interlocutor for the audience, thereby attempting to distinguish the film from even a hypothetical status as official government propaganda. At least initially, it is Thomas's well-known third-person address (not the Italian state's) that speaks for the film. His opening comments inform the audience that the subject of the film is a mix of biography and history which seeks to educate less about the politician and more about the man:

> For many years, the eyes of the world have turned to Italy, to witness the rise of a new man. We can admire his political actions, but what interests us is the man . . . who turned himself into a leader, who forges history . . . it's the man of action, furnished with a rare gift, personal magnetism. How did this man of the people get so far? Was his youth particularly rich or marked by exceptional schooling? How could he overthrow the government of his country and thereby become the prime minister of the Italian kingdom? And what has he done for Italy? How does he govern? In sum, what man is this Mussolini? Let us see for ourselves.

Although these comments are not literal quotations from Italian sources, they clearly embrace the dictum that fascism *makes* history. The questions provide an explicit rhetorical framework within which the film constructs three major concepts for the identity of Mussolini. And, as the last line of the prologue invites, these concepts will appear as part of a collective process of discovery in which Lowell Thomas and the audience will "see for ourselves."

As the prologue itself announces, the first step in this process of discovery is to humanize the figure of the dictator Mussolini. Thus the first diegetic image in *Mussolini Speaks* presents his birthplace, the village of Predappio near the Romagnola city of Forlì. The narration then links Mussolini to a series of images typical of agrarian Italy at the time. As we see peasants harvesting crops by hand, herding sheep, and washing clothes in a stream, Lowell Thomas says that "these are the images which Mussolini saw as a child and from which he gained his profound understanding of working peoples." That Mussolini's formation as a man began in an agrarian-based work ethic is to be read in both geographic and genetic terms. The terrain of his origin is linked less to an idyllic pastoral countryside than to work activities that take place in it. "This country is harsh, the people are unpolished, simple, hard working." And, according to narrator Thomas, Mussolini's father was a "blacksmith, a strong worker." His mother cuddled him only infrequently because "she had too much work to do." The introduction of personal biographic elements, in particular the valorization of work, repeats throughout the remainder of the film. The first images of Mussolini once he becomes prime minister, for example, echo these initial attributions. As he busily pores over state documents, the narrator informs us: "Mussolini's first declaration was 'And now to work.' He is an indefatigable man. He works incessantly."

As the film begins to fuse Mussolini's personal biography with the history of contemporary Italy, this second major figurative operation is speedily overlaid on the first. After locating Mussolini's origins, the film then presents a series of juxtapositions in which the evolution of Italian society is figured in terms of Mussolini's personal growth. From Predappio, the young Mussolini travels to Milan, "where his true genius began to be revealed." His move to Milan, illustrated by archetypical images of city trams, is a personal reenactment of one of the major social transformations in Italian civil society during the period, the massive immigrations from the countryside to the new work centers of the industrial cities. Mussolini then "decides, along with a million young men," to offer his life for his country by enlisting as a "common soldier" at the beginning of World War I. Rather than describing this decision in relation to the development of world events, the voice-over says that the outbreak of war signaled "the beginning of Mussolini's spiritual evolution." Indeed, as the film presents a classical montage of images from the war—artillery barrages, trench warfare, marching troops—it omits any geographical or political detail about the battles depicted. At the same time, it provides remarkable detail regarding Mussolini himself. As these war images pass by, the audience is told, for example, that after Mussolini was wounded, "forty-two pieces of shrapnel were removed." In a word, the film transfers its condensed history of World War I onto the personal experiences of Mussolini, figuratively onto his body. As with many other instances within contemporary Italian culture, Mussolini's body is presented as an auratic site of history in the making. It simultaneously holds the scars of Italy's recent past (the experience of World War I) and the physical force to dynamize its future (fascist political programs). By the end of this sequence, this figurative fusion becomes virtually explicit. As Mussolini's "glorious regiment" returns from the front "in triumph," signaling the end of the war, Lowell Thomas announces that "it was at this moment that fascism had its beginning."

The third component to the construction of the Mussolini identity resides in his elevation to the status of great statesman. To accomplish this, the film first dissociates Mussolini from the more radical fascist elements. Thus the film presents the March on Rome as an orderly transfer of power depicted as a regimental procession of black shirts to the capital. The orderliness of the March, as presented in *Mussolini Speaks*, recalls the significance of the aesthetization of political action that would, for example, turn up in epochal fiction films such as *Scipione l'africano*. The narrator additionally deemphasizes the terroristic aspects of fascist militancy by explaining that "Giovanezza," the fascist anthem, "is a melody, a song of joy." Indeed, as groups of *squadristi* file through the streets of Rome, the soundtrack plays the music of the anthem but entirely suppresses its lyrics. The words to the song, in fact, were particularly militaristic and included verses such as:

Del pugnale il fiero lampo
The proud lightning of the dagger
della bomba il gran fragore,
The great thunder of the bomb
tutti avanti, tutti al campo
Everyone forward, everyone to the battlefield
là si vince oppur si muore
There we win or we die
Sono Ardito fiero e forte
I am a proud and strong Ardito (assault soldier)
non mi trema in petto il cuore,
My heart doesn't pound in my chest
sorridendo vo'alla morte
I go to my death smiling
pria d'andare al disonor
Before I go to dishonor[19]

The substitution of an organized, disciplined, and even "joyous" group for the image of fascist terror squads effectively demilitarizes the iconography surrounding the movement's leader. Having dissociated him from fascism's violent past, the film is now able to transport Mussolini into the world of international diplomacy as a dignified and reassuring representative of the Italian state. The March on Rome is immediately followed by another "momentous" occasion. "One of the most important events in the history of modern diplomacy was American Secretary of State Stimson's visit to Mussolini. They discussed the collaboration between Italy and America. Il Duce amply helped disarmament. Mussolini defines war as atrocious. 'All those who have been in war,' he says, 'know how atrocious it is.'"

The narrator's emphasis on the themes of collaboration and peace between the two nations is underscored by the stately visual composition of the encounter. Stimson and Mussolini sit across from one another, discussing these topics as political equals on the international scene. Mussolini's status as international statesman continues to be elevated in the following sequences. After the colloquium with Stimson, he meets on a yacht with British Foreign Minister Chamberlain. And, after the Lateran pact with Cardinal Gaspari is signed, the process reaches its apotheosis when the narrator invokes no less an authority than the history of Catholicism: "In the secular history of the Catholic church, the Roman pontiffs have seen and studied many men who, with their will power and the force of their intellect, became leaders of millions of men; from Charlemagne to Richelieu, from Napoleon to Bismarck, and now Benito Mussolini."

The remainder of the film seeks to answer the other principal question posed in the prologue: "What has he done for Italy?" It does so by interspersing micromontages of fascist initiatives with excerpts from Mussolini's speech in Naples on the tenth anniversary of the 1922 March on Rome. As Mussolini reminds the Neapolitan crowd that fascism is the force "building" a new Italy, a series of images display roads, bridges, railways, and hydroelectric plants under construction. When he invokes the regime as the engineer of social welfare, the film cuts away from the site of his speech, revealing images of new apartment buildings, schools, and hospitals.[20] Mussolini mentions the importance of Italian agriculture, and the film couples the mechanized draining of the Pontine marshes with footage of the Duce himself manually harvesting wheat.

The alternation between points of view, that is, between the Neapolitan assembly listening to the Duce and the cinematic audience witnessing the accomplishments of fascism, creates a particularly complex rhetorical structure. To begin with, the speech itself is overdetermined as the epochal center of the film. It takes place only after the figure of Mussolini has been elevated to international importance, an exaltation of relevance to the prevalently Italian American audiences the film addresses. In fact, the alternation between newsreel images of Italy and Mussolini's speech continues for the remainder of the film. This structure is terminated only when Lowell Thomas offers his closing comments. This alternation literalizes the film's title. Mussolini speaks as audiences listen and bear witness. Furthermore, in direct address to the audience, the narrator draws attention to the almost conversational character of this rhetorical structure by literally invoking the title and issuing instructions to the audience: "Attention now, Mussolini speaks."

The triangulation of points of view in this section of *Mussolini Speaks* forges a discursive link between Italian Americans and Italian fascism. While Mussolini literally addresses the crowd in Naples, the film as a whole interpellates the Italian immigrant community as its subject. That is to say, insofar as the Italian public in Naples can see Mussolini only as he speaks from the stage, the film presents a view of the evidence of what he has accomplished. Since any theoretical public for this view is not anchored in a specific vantage point within the film, the repeated transitions from Naples to the rest of fascist Italy thus imply a much larger public, inviting it to stand in for the public in the film.

Constructed in this way, the film's mode of address itself contains the overall ideological project, that is, to simultaneously present an accurate picture of contemporary Italy and to garner the political support of Italians abroad. It stipulates Mussolini as author of Italy's great accomplishments. And, by fusing the history of these events with his personality, the film establishes Mussolini as authority for the expatriates' reading. The film proposes that authority not only for the specific moments within the documentary, but for the events in a world that includes the film's international audiences, into which they have now been rhetorically drawn, to which they now belong.

Up to this point, I have discussed two large textual and institutional domains of the relationship between the United States and Italy. In the previous section, I described how documentaries such as *Mussolini Speaks* represent a particular use of the cinema in order to regulate readings of the regime's relationship to the United States.[21] By addressing Italian Americans as Italians, it constitutes them as part of an original Italian public. In chapter 2, I outlined how the state's partnership with the film industry was forged, in part, by the commercial need to accommodate American films on Italian screens. The regime did this through a range of institutional responses including the development of a censorship policy that allowed depiction of problematic subjects in Hollywood films so long as they figured as part of a non-Italian social reality. Crime did exist during fascist time but it did not exist within the regime's social borders. Indeed, two exceptional fiction films specifically identify New York as the epicenter of modern moral turpitude. Carmine Gallone's *Harlem* and Guglielmo Gianini's *Grattacieli* (both 1943) are exceptional because they were the only Italian fiction films of the entire period that were actually set in America. Italian heavyweight boxing champion Primo Carnera even makes a cameo in *Harlem,* warning the film's main character to be wary of the moral decay characteristic of contemporary America. At the same time, it is important to see these rare films as textual expressions of the regime's ambivalent view of the modern city. As I have mentioned, the state expended great energies on urban redesign. But the conspicuously dark vision of urban crime and corruption presented by these films clearly also participates in the fascist concern about the relative instability of concentrated metropolitan centers. Ghirardo describes the state's fear in the following way: "Once in power, Mussolini propagandized against the phenomenon of urbanism, the spectacular growth of the cities, and the depopulation of the countryside. Political reasons underlay this position, for the crowded urban areas held a potentially radical working class, dangerous if unified. In consequence, Fascist propaganda extolled the virtues of rural living, healthy physical labor on the land, and a renewed morality, and ultimately set in motion an unsuccessful campaign to stem the flow of population from the country to the city."[22]

The Italian cinema under fascism spoke about the diffusion of American culture at yet another level. Through its own fiction films, the Italian cinematic institution engaged Hollywood in supratextual dialogue. It referred to generic, iconographic, and stylistic conventions of Hollywood film in order to re-elaborate them for an Italian audience. This is to say that the films themselves functioned as heuristics for a proper (fascist) reading of America and Americana. Such shared references constitute what David Forgacs has termed the "relays of information," which serve to construct a sense of nationhood without geographical borders:

> However, if the media have helped to bring nations into being and to define their boundaries, it is also important to recognize that nations are not the only communities they have shaped in this way. Newspapers and broadcasting may be local or regional as well as national, and most

national newspapers and news channels give information about events in other countries. Moreover, national communities are often also the recipients of other nations' media. In other words, the geographical limits of the media and the imagined geographical limits of the nation do not necessarily coincide.[23]

Thus supratextual exchange can be seen as a telling site for the construction of national identity through cinema in particular and cultural values in general. It suggests that we can map components of that identity without dependence on purely geographic coordinates.

This dialogue between cinematic institutions is particularly evident in the many films during fascism that contain explicit representations of Americans and Italian Americans. In geographies *other than* the United States, Italian Americans appear as fictional characters in films such as *Due cuori felici* (1932, Baldassare Negroni), *La cantante dell'opera* (1932, Nunzio Malasomma), *Non c'è bisogno di soldi* (1933, Amleto Palermi), *L'albero di Adamo* (1936, Mario Bonnard), *Joe il rosso* and *L'anonima Roylott* (1936, Raffaello Matarazzo), *Fuochi d'artificio* (1938, Gennaro Righelli), *Chi sei tu* (1939, Negroni), *Due milioni per un sorriso* (1939, Carlo Borghesio and Mario Soldati), *Grattacieli* (1943, Guglielmo Giannini), and *Harlem* (1943, Carmine Gallone). Baldassare Negroni's *Due cuori felici* is one of the earliest examples of Italian feature-length fiction films that borrow genre conventions from Hollywood filmmaking while also speaking about America. It is a musical comedy in early Lubitsch style in which Vittorio De Sica plays an American automobile magnate, Mr. Brown. By reworking some of the genre's rhetorical conventions, *Due cuori felici* capitalizes on the popular successes that the American musical comedy had with Italian audiences. At the same time, it also grafts onto the genre an Italian actor widely recognizable to these same audiences for his performances in specifically Italian vehicles. Already on his way to becoming the period's most popular male actor, De Sica was a featured artist in Mario Mattoli's theatrical company Za Bum prior to starring in Mario Camerini's box office hit *Gli uomini che mascalzoni* (1932).[24]

The incongruity between the nationality of the fictional character and the nationality of the actor manifested, for example, by De Sica's use of an American accent creates a basic structure of irony in such films. Irony is produced by the audience's recognition of the film's conflation of real geography with the symbolic map of the fiction. In other words, Vittorio De Sica not only plays the fictionalized American character, the film foregrounds his presence within the fiction as a performance of national difference. This rhetorical operation allows the audience to pursue two distinct layers of identification. On the one hand, the audience is invited into the text, as any audience is, through the forms of address articulated by the musical comedy form. On the other hand, the ironic overlay opens up the possibility for an Italian audience to identify and take pleasure in discrete elements of the doubled De Sica character, to enjoy his very cultural differences. Although this might not produce the effect of an oppositional reading, the film proposes to Italian audiences how one might pleasurably negotiate with American culture.

Due cuori felici provides a view of certain supposed American character traits as exactly those mannerisms, attitudes, and gestures that differ from the Italian-ness of the real-life actor. As a fictional character, Mr. Brown is ignorant of Italy and its customs. De Sica is introduced to the audience as this Mr. Brown at the very beginning of the film, not only by his accent, but also when this *Neapolitan* actor misrecognizes Lake Garda for the Bay of Naples! As an American industrialist, the character is a locus of satire for the putative cold efficiency, speed, automation, and overemphasis on the importance of money attributed to the culture from which he comes. While Americans may have more money, we have our authentic local culture, its cinema, and its stars. Thus through De Sica's performance of the fictional character, the film by deflection valorizes his status as Italian actor. The cold efficiency of the fictional industrialist is replaced by the wit and charm of the supra-class, supra-regional *Italian* persona embodied by one of *Italy's* stars. The actor is equally able, for example, to frequent the world of high society nightclubs as to socialize in the city's working-class taverns. As the film works to unravel the many mistaken identities and misunderstandings that are common in the musical comedy genre, De Sica's extrafilmic status as an Italian surfaces. Indeed, as the film progresses, his feigned American accent wanes. De Sica finally realizes that he has fallen in love with Italy and its people when he discovers their true identity in a local tavern. Here, the collective singing of popular songs is contrasted to the jazz of the upper-class nightclubs. In this scene, the discursive gap between his two identities is momentarily closed inasmuch as, when De Sica breaks into a song, the film re-evokes his prior image of singer/performer from his variety-show days in the twenties and, more recently, his membership in the Za Bum company.

In general terms, the ironic structure embedded in Italian films with American themes negotiates a certain ambivalence toward the pervasiveness of American culture. It addresses Italian audiences, that is, both in terms of a culture-wide fascination with the myth of America while also recognizing that audience's own cultural specificity. In certain cases, it can even function as a response to the representation of Italian nationality in Hollywood films. Two films by Raffaello Matarazzo in 1936 employ this structure, for example, in order to correct such representations as articulated by the American gangster film.

The first film, *L'anonima Roylott*[25] (alternatively titled *The Vultures of the City*), is a compendium of characters, virtually all of whom are implicated in at least one kind of organized crime, including labor-union corruption, extortion, patent infringement, and embezzlement. In every case, however, the film introduces each of these felonious characters at the top of their first screen appearance by their American names: the Roylott brothers, Mr. Harris, Mr. Evans, and so on. That the film scrupulously maintains the association between criminal behavior and American nationality is seen even in its usage of the archetypical lap dissolve montages of newspaper headlines. As in the Hollywood gangster genre, this formal convention serves to indicate passage of time and major developments in the narrative. In this case, however, the front pages of the film's fictionalized American dailies contain two types of stories, corresponding in figurative terms to two different nationalities. Whereas the articles dealing with crime news contain the American names of the specific characters and are written in English, all of the remaining articles—the local news—are in Italian.

The second film, *Joe il rosso*,[26] is yet another form of corrective to the *Little Caesar* and *Scarface* syndrome. Where *L'anonima Roylott* borrows from the conventions of the crime-film genre, this film is a musical comedy that attempts to redeem the figure of the Italian American gangster. In the role he had previously made famous on the stage, Armando Falconi plays Joe Mark, the cigar-smoking, swaggering, Italian American bootlegger who returns home to answer his niece's call for help. *Joe il rosso* initially invokes the iconography of the gangster film. It opens with a nighttime car chase in which Joe and his gang, pursued by the police, make their getaway in a hail of machine-gun bullets. The film then initiates a satire of the genre itself when Joe, in heavily accented broken Italian, breaks into song celebrating the successful escape. Through a travel montage of cars, planes, ocean liners, trains, and finally sea-planes, Joe arrives just in time to help his niece, who has been implicated in the theft of a Murillo painting.

Not only does the satire of the gangster genre separate Falconi from any real association with gangsterism, he actually solves the crime of the theft, thereby rescuing his niece. Furthermore, the film avoids any association between even this single theft and contemporary Italian society by locating the scene of the crime in a generalized representation of southern France. When Joe the bootlegger takes on the role of the working detective, he sends his gang (now his "associates") to check with all the known fences in "Bordeaux" and "Marseilles." Finally, both films, by repeatedly indicating that criminality and corruption exist only on foreign soil, function as a textual corollary to the state's censorship policy, which attempted to suppress all representations of Italian criminality.

A major site for supratextual dialogue between fascist Italy and Hollywood is the body of Mario Camerini's work during the interwar years. His films reveal both a fascination with Hollywood and an interesting strategy for competing with it. This is not to say that Camerini's films break in a significant way with the basic structures of textual production of classical narrative cinema. Rather, he attempted to create an international style of performance within the classical narrative form. The purpose of this style was to deploy a supratextual recognizability for the actors in his films, to differentiate them from the Hollywood stars with whom Italian audiences were very familiar. Camerini was one of the period's most prolific directors. Between 1923 and 1943, he directed an extraordinary twenty-seven feature films, all of which were box-office successes. This level of output is especially notable if we recall the precipitous decline in Italian productions until the mid-thirties. In a very concrete way, therefore, it is fair to say that Camerini's work—as a unified example of nonexperimental, entertainment cinema—occupies a place of central importance for Italian cinema audiences during the fascist period.

Camerini has said that his first memories of going to movies were of seeing American films whose titles he could not recall[27]—as if to say that what remained was more his recollection of Hollywood iconography and style. Camerini enters into film production at a moment that crystallized both the demise of Italian national production and the dominance of the American cinema. His first feature film as director, *Jolly-Clown da circo,* was made in 1923, the year that saw the formal dissolution of L'Unione Cinematografica Italiana as well as the opening of MGM offices in Rome. Camerini's filmography as a whole is an extraordinary litany of creative exchange between Italy and Hollywood, of remakes and adaptations spanning six decades beginning with *La riva dei bruti*—Camerini's 1930 version of William Wellman's *Dangerous Paradise*—and continuing right up to *Once Upon a Crime*—Eugene Levy's 1992 remake of Camerini's *Crimen* (1960).[28] In the general context, which saw the Italian cinema's industrial and creative practices forced to take into account the dominant presence of Hollywood films, Camerini's position is particularly interesting. He was placed in direct contact with Hollywood filmmaking practices as they were to address European audiences. In the late twenties, for example, he worked at Paramount's Joinville studios, where multiple-language versions of American films were prepared for European release.

One of the central thematic preoccupations in his films was an interrogation of social identity. Virtually all of Camerini's films deal with a central character who is either misrecognized within or temporarily dislodged from his/her original social milieu. Though in most cases the characters are returned to their original places, they do so in a cultural terrain that is populated by Americans, American films, and what Geoffrey Nowell-Smith calls the ethos of Hollywood.

> The focus of the films of the 1930s is prevailingly domestic, the background bourgeois and petty-bourgeois. There is no sense of a mobilized society: on the contrary life is refreshingly normal. Virtue is rewarded by happiness. The ethos is Hollywoodian—since it was Hollywood that had to be beaten at its own game—but without the manifestations of populism and democratism that erupt in Hollywood films of the same period.
>
> Here and there however, there are eruptions of something that could not be successfully contained. The absence of any admitted possibility of social transformation turns the films inward. Comedy occasionally becomes hysterical; dramas are allowed unhappy ends.[29]

Camerini's films both imbibe and differ from that ethos. One of the clearest examples of an Italian film that simulates Hollywood film style of the thirties while also approaching uncontainable elements can be found in his *Darò un milione* (1935). In the film's finale, an exuberant group of tramps spends the gift of cash from Mr. Gold to enjoy rides on all the circus attractions, which previously had been reserved to paying customers. The scene is an epilogue to the successful return of the film's main character (Mr. Gold, played by Vittorio De Sica) to his original class status. The celebration of entertainment by his former underprivileged associates in this scene anticipates by six years the epilogue in Preston Sturges's *Sullivan's Travels* (1941). On the one hand, the prisoners in the Sturges film laugh redemptively at the church-room movie presentation of Mickey Mouse—thereby sanctioning a positive, socially transcendent role for Hollywood entertainment film. On the other hand, Camerini's tramps play out a certain populist rejection of the rules that govern moneyed society. The basic narrative premise had been that Mr. Gold/De Sica would offer one million dollars to anyone who could perform a single act of sincerity without reference to social status. The tramps jubilantly use the money (given to them by De Sica), which the film had repeatedly described as the cause of mistrust between classes. In both films the main characters give money to transients. De Sica gives all of his cash to the transients he had temporarily befriended in *Darò un milione,* and Joel McCrae hands out five-dollar bills to the homeless in *Sullivan's Travels* in an attempt to improve their lives. By spending it collectively, selfishly, and in order only to have fun, the Italian troupe recovers the validity and usefulness of pure capital as consumption. Under these terms, the film's epilogue is a final rejection of its own original devaluation of the importance of money. Since its use can have only a temporary, nontranscendent social effect, the scene also serves as an ironic reminder of the material differences between classes.

Darò un milione is a remarkable site of contact between the two cinemas. One clear indication of its affinity to the interests and cultural projects of contemporary Hollywood is the fact that the rights were rather quickly picked up by Twentieth Century Fox for an American remake. Fox viewed the property as a potentially very serious project. Following the circulation of rumors that the new version would star Gary Cooper, both Tyrone Power and Don Ameche were proposed for the De Sica/Mr. Gold role. An article from the *Los Angeles Examiner* also gives a sense of why the film so interested Hollywood. "Several weeks ago Darryl Zanuck read a review that intrigued him on a picture made in Italy. He sent for a print and became so enthused he bought the entire production. It's an Italian 'Mr. Deeds Goes to Town' with comedy and clever dialogue. . . . There are underground whispers Twentieth Century Fox will try to borrow Gary Cooper for the star role."[30]

That it was thought of as an Italian *Mr. Deeds* might appear, on the surface, as a basic misrecognition, since it inverts the narrative premise of the Frank Capra film. Whereas Capra's Cooper/Deeds ascends the social ladder by suddenly inheriting twenty million dollars, Camerini's De Sica/Gold steps down among poor vagrants quite prepared to do without his own wealth. Both films, however, do perform a similar ideological operation that was common to many Hollywood and Camerini films of the period. The protagonists are initially separated from their original class status and are ultimately returned to that same class. After discovering real values, the axiom that money cannot buy happiness, for example, the characters return to the worlds where they belong. The very inevitability of the return to origins in these films suggests that membership in a paraticular social stratum flows naturally from a permanently stable social hierarachy. Thus, for example, class differences are transparently represented as matters of individual, fictional characters. Differences between characters then are treated as incidental qualities that flow from a social ontology, which is often also nongendered and nonregional.

While this operation is generally shared by Walter Lang's 1938 remake, *I'll Give a Million,* there are a number of interesting differences. After initially placing the drama in the south of France, Camerini presents an imaginary world that contains virtually no referents to specific national or regional identity. Walter Lang's version, by overdetermining its fictive reality as a Hollywood vision of a real France, essentially renders the theme of national identity opaque. In fact, the undeflected transnational (probably American) role played by De Sica was identified in the first American treatment (written by Niven Busch) as "Nick Richtoven," a Belgian millionaire. By the time Lang's film actually began production, and after several changes, the lead character had become Tony Newlander, an American industrialist. Within the film proper, the importance of one's national identity is evident from the very beginning. Once the millionaire, the *Newlander,* has exchanged clothes with the suicide-attempting tramp (Peter Lorre), he too befriends a circus girl (Marjorie Weaver in the role played by Assia Norris in the original), but this time their mutual affinity is solidified by her pronouncement "I'm an American too!" His relief at finding a compatriot is underscored by Weaver's unmistakable southern drawl.

The difference between opaque and transparent treatments of national identity also surfaces in two versions of another film: Mario Camerini's *Batticuore* (1939) and the remake by Sam Wood, *Heartbeat* (1946). In *Batticuore,* Camerini brings the theme of artifice (of fictive identity) to the surface by, among other strategies, naming an entirely invented fictional country, Stivonia. In Sam Wood's 1946 version with Ginger Rogers, stock footage of the Eiffel Tower and the Arc de Triomphe as well as the presence of French actor Jean-Pierre Aumont (in the role originally played by John Lodge) both anchor the film in a fictional representation of a very real place, Paris. This contrast between a fictionalizing abstraction of nationality, on the one hand, and geographic specificity on the other reveals two very different institutional strategies embedded in films which otherwise appear very similar.

Both *I'll Give a Million* and *Heartbeat* can be seen as part of a long Hollywood tradition which attempts to "Americanize" representations of *the foreign*. The insertion, without much disguise, of famous American actors into a fictional reconstruction of a real place renders *the other* recognizable while simultaneously promising the pleasures routinely offered by the Hollywood star system. In the first film, traces of this strategy include: the entire cast's forced French accents, Peter Lorre (in the role originally played in the Italian version by Cesare Zoppetti) as a very *French* tramp, and the nonstop interpellation of "monsieur" by fictional characters who speak English. In the second, it is epitomized by a key exchange between Jean-Pierre Aumont and Ginger Rogers. Rogers attempts to clarify her real identity by explaining why she was temporarily forced to become a thief. But Aumont is uninterested, and in order to make sure that she understands his lack of desire, yells "good night" to her in English, German, Italian, and French. Rogers responds by referring to her identity outside of the fiction (i.e., as a prominent figure in American popular culture) by forcefully mispronouncing "good night" in each of the three foreign languages.

For Camerini, the abstraction of fictional premises helps to generalize, to render more international, the nature of the thematic conflicts in his films. Where Warner Baxter will play Tony Newlander as a highly productive American capitalist (in *I'll Give a Million*), De Sica had played Mr. Gold (in *Darò un milione*) as a disaffected but very debonair aristocrat. Where Newlander is disillusioned because of specific betrayals at the hands of his friends, his ex-wife, and even his butler, Mr. Gold is, more existentially, bored by his own aristocratic lifestyle. Indeed, at the very beginning of the film, he confesses to the first tramp he befriends that the reason he desires to renounce his class status is that he suffers from a "spiritual crisis."

Both films provide for a conventional happy ending. In *I'll Give a Million*, Baxter/Newlander donates half of the million dollars he had originally offered to the city (for all the trouble his lark has caused) and half to the tramps, on the condition that Weaver/Jean marry him.

In contrast to Camerini's populist reverie at the circus, the more conventional American version actually ends with a wedding ceremony.
Thus Baxter/Newlander's return to his original social status is supported by his entry into a traditional familial order. In *Darò un milione*, De Sica/Gold simply tells the captain of his yacht to sail off to
an undetermined destination (reminiscent of the vague destination for
the couple in Camerini's *Rotaie*, "where the others go"). This happy
ending explicitly has no specific place in the film's fictional geography.
Where Walter Lang's film shows a coexistence between the rich and
the poor—even as they sit uncomfortably side by side during the wedding ceremony—Camerini's film makes no explicit accommodation
for any re-regulation of class relations. In a word, Lang's film functions also as a civics lesson that is relevant to a depicted class society.
Camerini's *Darò un milione* is a much more generalized examination
of both manners and values. It stipulates neither a geographic setting
nor a relationship to a specific familial order as the backdrop for its
narrative resolution. And, in the general context of the pervasiveness
of the American cinema, it is this very abstraction that serves to vie for
an equal status in international cinema. The fictional characters played
by Vittorio De Sica and Assia Norris could come from any place, any
society. It might be argued, therefore, that the film's generality, the abstraction allowed in the delineation and performance of character (the
openness or innate democracy often used to describe American cinema
of the classic period), increases Camerini's potential to address a wider
audience and that, in effect, *Darò un milione* is a much more effective
Hollywood film than its American counterpart. Finally, *Darò un milione* addresses yet another significant question of exchange between
the two cinemas. Since De Sica plays an American (Mr. Gold) but is
self-evidently not a Mr. Gold, his portrayal of an American is refracted
by the Italian audience's awareness *both* of De Sica's previous roles and
also of Hollywood stars. In other words, the audience is invited to read
the De Sica persona in terms of its knowledge of Americans through its
contact with the Gary Coopers, Clark Gables, Jimmy Stewarts, Tyrone
Powers, Joel McCraes, and others.

In *Centomila dollari* (1940), Camerini attempts to address this issue by grafting the representation of an archetypical American onto
the nascent Italian star system. In this case, Amadeo Nazzari plays
the character of a rich American industrialist traveling through Europe on business. An Italian actor in the role of a visiting American
industrialist recalls Vittorio De Sica's much-acclaimed performance

as Mr. Brown in Baldassare Negroni's *Due cuori felici* (1932). In this film, however, the main character (Mr. Woods/Nazzari) doesn't fade into a geography-less, nation-less fictive land, as De Sica does in *Darò un milione*. Instead, there are continuous referents to his American identity throughout. Nazzari is a container of hypothetical American character traits, a man of action who works too much and who can do without much of a sentimental life. In the terms provided by the film, the more he is successful, the further he wanders from real happiness as offered specifically by marriage.

Early on in the film, there is a remarkable synthesis of an apparently anti-American sentiment. Nazzari/Woods has offered to pay his fiancée (played by Assia Norris) $100,000—the sum referred to in the film's title—if she would only dine with him prior to their wedding ceremony. The outlandish offer provokes her relatives to make the following consideration about all Americans:

> La faccia tosta di questi americani! È incredibile!
> *The nerve of these Americans! It's incredible!*
> Si credono padroni del mondo perché hanno quattro soldi.
> *They think they own the world just because they have some money.*
> Farabutto, farabutto.
> *What a scoundrel.*
> Mi ha offerto del denaro!
> *He actually offered me money!*
> Naturalmente, per loro non c'è che denaro.
> *Naturally, for them that's all there is.*
> La dignità e l'onore non contano niente.
> *Dignity and honor don't count for anything.*
> Americanate! Tutto si compra in America.
> *American things! Everything is for sale in America.*

Once Norris's relatives learn the offering price, however, they reverse course and ultimately find a way to justify what had been previously read as an unpardonable American insult. The horrified chorus of anti-American sentiment is quickly turned into ironic criticism of the wedding party's opportunism and provincialism. Yet what has been set into motion is perhaps a little more complex and harder to contain.

The initial playful criticism of American values was a priori irrelevant to the Nazzari character/persona. Just as De Sica is self-evidently not a *Mr. Gold,* neither can Nazzari become a neutral vessel for the fictional expression of an American national identity. The film

Figure 26. Amadeo Nazzari, proto-hero/star. Frame enlargement from
Luciano Serra pilota (1938, Goffredo Alessandrini). Courtesy of the
Cineteca di Bologna, Fondo Mario Natale.

additionally rules out any such equation by linking Nazzari to his
specific place in the Italian star system—as one of the period's main
romantic and heroic leads. When a storm threatens his business
flight to Brussels, Mr. Woods, the businessman, moves quickly to
the cockpit in order to pilot the plane to safety. The film thereby specifically re-evokes Nazzari's famed role in *Luciano Serra pilota* from
two years earlier. It is this backward reference to Amadeo Nazzari as
Italian cinema star (above and beyond his status as a fictional character specific to this film) that provides for Italian audiences the ability
to cleanse him of his American traits. Once divested of this initial cultural contamination, he breaks with his scheduled business meeting,
and returns to Assia Norris, normality, and *marriage* Italian style.

Centomila dollari erects a fictional Mr. Woods—as an American—precisely so that he can be denied by a very real Nazzari—as a prototypical Italian. In other words, the film's multiple identifications and its ironic presentation of uncontainable misidentifications create a supratextual discourse wherein the cultural coordinates of both Italian and Hollywood cinema can be negotiated. Camerini has invoked the audience's memory of *both* cinemas in order to construct an extrafilmic domain which can deliver to these audiences the pleasures (recognition, expectation, and identification) of a particular form of the star system. In the Camerini filmography, the transnational status of that system allowed his films to speak in terms familiar to Italian audiences during the latter half of the fascist regime and to compete with the Hollywood cinema for their attention.

It might be argued that the transnational character of the star system as it operates in Camerini's films is discordant with the ideological imperatives of Italian fascism. As we have seen in a range of historical costume films and the state's own non-fiction productions, both the past and the present accomplishments of the Italian nation are often directly linked to a fascist order. On the one hand, the historical epics invoke the contemporary fascist state as the evolutionary inheritor of a grandeur that once was. On the other hand, the newsreels and documentaries present the regime as uniquely responsible for the country's contemporary progress, as singular author of what is and what will be. The multinational quality to performance and meaning in Camerini's films offers no such direct connection. Moreover, there is little evidence to suggest that his filmography participates in the fascist regime's drive to purify Italian culture. Camerini's films, as with many entertainment films during the fascist period, do not explicitly articulate fascist ideology. However, in at least four very significant ways, they function in support of it.

First, Camerini's films compete economically with Hollywood films for a higher percentage of box-office receipts within the Italian market. They thereby conform to at least the economic component of the regime's desire for self-sufficiency. On the intranational level, his films also negotiate the tension between parochialism that might have been the natural outcome of the state's drive toward autarchy and competition for international status vis-à-vis the Hollywood cinema. Although his films make use of both a traditional form of fictional narration and genre conventions that are typified by the classical Hollywood cinema, the evolution of an international style of performance attempts to broaden the appeal of the Italian product.[31] Second, the Camerini filmography contains no direct negative representation of the regime, its symbology, or its officials. In addition, we can deduce few, if any, rhetorical positions within this body of work that point to the possibility of a critical reading of the fascist social order. Third, the specific form of narrativization of class difference provided audiences with a discursive framework that was entirely complementary to the regime's extensive attempts to construct national consensus. That is to say, the often-repeated movement of fictional characters away from and always back to their original social status proposes a model of social mobility that initially invokes class differences only to dissolve them into a *stable, natural* configuration of differences between individuals. The symmetry of such itineraries not only effaces the structural or historical conditions of difference between social strata, it emphasizes the desirability of remaining within the confines of one's original social placement. We recall, for example, the vague "spiritual" conditions that initially motivate De Sica/Mr. Gold in *Darò un milione* to abandon his own class. After setting forth these terms, both De Sica and the transients—his temporary class-mates—find happiness only by returning to their original social strata. It should be pointed out that this trajectory is unlike several instances in American genre cinema. In the gangster film, for example, social mobility as such is not called into question. Here the locus of ideological regulation has much more to do with the legitimacy of the means used to move up the social ladder. Fourth, and most importantly for our project, the body of Camerini's work proposes figural terms with which Italian audiences could recontextualize their experience of Hollywood cinema in a manner that was indeed consonant with fascism's concerns about the polluting effect that cinema might have upon the new fascist public. Indeed, this cross-reading of Hollywood films through the filter of Camerini's films produced one specific new form of pleasure offered by the Italian commercial cinema.

Above and beyond their economic fortunes, or even their ideological treatment of class issues, Mario Camerini's films also need to be placed alongside the overall experience of cinema in Italy between 1922 and 1943. At the outset of this project, I argued that this experience was characterized by processes of exchange and mediation between two dominant authorial agencies: fascism itself and the Hollywood cinema. I additionally suggested that these processes provided the basis for how films were read by Italian audiences during this fascist period. This linkage between authorial agencies and readership is made possible only if we stipulate a mechanism whereby subjects recognize in cinema texts the traces of authorship that they also recognize (as members of a non-cinema public) as discourses and practices visible to them outside of the cinema. Paul Willemen describes this mechanism in the following way: "The reader constructs the author as the other of the image he or she recognizes or accepts as his or hers in relation to the text. . . . It is in this sense that inscribed subject-positions are never hermetically sealed into a text, but are always positions in ideologies. Texts can resist readings (offer resistances), they can't determine them. They can hinder the productivity of the plurality of discourses at play within them, they can emphasize certain discourses as opposed to others (through repetition or other 'foregrounding' devices)."[32]

As we have shown in our discussion of the regime's institutional regulation of the cinema industry, its reenactment of sports spectatorship, its obligatory exhibition of nonfiction films, and its negotiated relationship to the American cinema, the two principal *authors* during the period were in fact the fascist state and Hollywood cinema. It is these two identities that the Italian "reader constructs . . . as the other of the image he or she recognizes or accepts as his or hers in relation to the text." In other words, these two agencies constitute the most common enunciated traces of authorship in this Italian audience's field of vision both inside and outside the text.

That Camerini's films compete for the attention of this audience is significant because they participate as components of the Italian state's overall organization of mass culture. To be very clear about this, the state neither produced Camerini's films nor did it seek to monopolize control over Italian film production in general. However, through the extension of its own visibility in the public sphere, it did seek to establish general terms of readership for that cinema. Moreover, through its regulation of the Italian film industry and its limited partnership with the Hollywood film industry, the regime sought to constitute authorities upon which reading could take place. During this period, the state was unable to completely block the importation and exhibition of undesirable images, the American gangster film, for example. Although this is explainable in terms of the economic benefit that such films guaranteed to Italian film exhibitors, the regime went to great lengths to overdetermine these films (as opposed to the musical for example) as reflective of American decadence. Thus Italian audiences were encouraged to read issues of criminality—otherwise absent from Italian screens—as symptomatic of the American failure to resolve contradictions characteristic of modern urban life.

FIVE

THE FASCIST CODEX

The spectacle presents itself simultaneously as all of society, as part of society, and as instrument of unification. As a part of society it is specifically the sector which concentrates all gazing and all consciousness. Due to the very fact that this sector is separate, it is the common ground of the deceived gaze and of false consciousness, and the unification it achieves is nothing but an official language of generalized separation.

Guy Debord, *La société du spectacle*

FASCIST HEURISTICS: MAJOR CODES OF READERSHIP

Throughout the twenty years of fascist rule, Italian audiences primarily saw mainstream Italian and American feature films in combination with LUCE newsreels. The timing and nature of the state's intervention in the Italian film industry reflected the evolution of fascist political economy. During its first nine years, the state neither monopolized the industry nor did it set up a unified hierarchical system of control over cinema production. Its most significant foray into the cinema was the establishment of the Istituto LUCE in 1925. But apart from this single and significant exception, the state generally followed a mercantilist, almost laissez-faire approach toward financing and regulation. Between 1922 and 1931, as the regime resolved its own internal political contradictions and progressively extended its control over government, it did little to modify the structure of cinema institutions that it had inherited from the Giolitti-era government. In this first period, where the state did intervene in support of the film industry, it did so modestly and almost exclusively in favor of the exhibition sector.

When Mussolini marched on Rome, the loss of foreign market share and the vertiginous decline in local film production were already fully under way. The new government left virtually intact, and infrequently applied, the censorship provisions established by Giolitti in 1913. Delayed by the controversy caused by the assassination of Matteotti, the state was slow to deploy a unified cultural policy toward the cinema. Yet despite the lack of active governmental support, cinema attendance continued to rise. And in addition to its success as popular entertainment, Italian cinema had already contributed significant frameworks of knowledge for a fascist conception of national identity. Its recruitment of well-known literary figures and the invocation of grand moments of the new nation's previous history claimed primacy for that construction.

In the regime's second decade, the extension of its authority over civil society was reflected in an increasingly activist role in the promotion and regulation of cinema culture. In 1931, reduced taxation on box-office revenues (and a series of postproduction awards to films that met the government's definition of truly Italian filmmaking) helped to revitalize the production sector of the industry. While a dozen locally produced titles were released in 1931, the number rose to a remarkable 119 by the end of 1942. In broader terms, during the second half of the *ventennio nero,* the state implemented a series of institutional reforms in order to build a fascist film culture. In 1934, it established a single state agency for the regulation of distribution, dubbing, and censorship, namely the General Directorate for Cinema (DGC) under the Ministry of Popular Culture. The DGC's accomplishments included the establishment of the Venice Film Festival in 1934, inauguration of the national film school (Centro Sperimentale di Cinematografie) in 1935, and the completion of Europe's largest production facilities (Cinecittà) in 1937. By the end of 1938, the Alfieri protectionist laws undermined the previously unfettered distribution of Hollywood films within the national market. With the departure of the major American studios, the state had finally realized the autarchic goal of a vertically integrated national cinema system.

Nevertheless, by far the most significant institutional measure in the creation of that system was the deployment of dubbing practices. Until 1938, the state did little to address the exhibition sector's dependency upon foreign films. By 1933, however, all imported titles had to be dubbed in Italy, and this dubbing requirement afforded the state an effective mechanism with which to shape key features of cinema content. Applied more often than traditional censorship methods, dubbing policies followed the "purist" impulse articulated by the National Institute of Fascist Culture, led by Giovanni Gentile. It allowed the state to "protect" a hypothetically "standard" Italian language from contamination by words of foreign derivation. Moreover, by proposing a unitary national language through the suppression of Italy's many dialects, dubbing serviced the regime's ideological ambitions for a composite supra-regional, supra-class national identity.

Even as fascist political practice evolved between 1922 and 1943, the state never fully resolved the philosophical contradictions between competing schools of thought regarding the ideal role of a fascist culture. Left largely unsettled were the tensions between culture as entertainment and the didactic use of cultural production in the service of state propaganda, between modernism and traditional cultural practices, and between a pluralist mass culture and state-inspired vanguardism. The most visible of these tensions was the disparity between fascist cultural autarchy and the dominating presence of American films. For the cinema audiences, the Italian map of imagined spaces and characters was overlaid by extremely attractive Hollywoodian landscapes. On the one hand, I have argued that the relationship between the fascist state and Hollywood cinema constituted a limited, global partnership. American films were essential to the economic viability of the industry's exhibition sector until very late in the period. American films provided the regime with the ability to locate dystopic social phenomena within a fictive map of urban decadence contained within American borders. And, most importantly, the systems of representation of the classical Hollywood feature were not fundamentally transgressive to an imagined fascist social order. Thus, for example, the chronotope of the *inevitable return* to "authentic" class locations is almost as common in American films of the twenties and thirties as we have seen in the Italian films produced during the interwar years.

On the other hand, Hollywood did present a threat on several other levels. The dominance of American product, given the lack of Italian protectionist measures, meant that the national cinema had virtually no opportunity to become vertically integrated. Hollywood's arguably richer range of representations of women and its more modern depiction of sexuality were of great concern to the regime. If these were left unchallenged, Italian audiences might desire and embrace distinctly unfascist role models. In a word, the regime feared that these exotic images might be more popular and could provide more satisfied desire for viewing audiences than its own national cinema. In the context of its decidedly mixed industrial policy, the state and the cinema therefore competed both economically and intertextually with Hollywood as a friendly *other*.

At the start of this project, I posed questions about the convergences and divergences between a fascist rhetoric of social organization and the figural strategies within the period's cinema. My argument has been that the points of contact, denial, and exchange between these two sites of discourse construct authorities both for textual reading by audiences and for the development of consensus by the state. Thus the audience's familiarity with the state's civic initiatives, that is, its quotidian contact with the very visible signs of fascist governance, was a central condition of readership of the period's films. This is not to claim that real audiences read all Italian films as the state may have desired. No state apparatus can guarantee the success of its own hegemonic codes. Even though the regime's actions were discursively coded in terms that were entirely intelligible to cinema audiences, no system of encoding (even within a totalitarian context) can prevent impromptu, irreverent, purposeful, or accidental misreadings. In the realm of social engineering, for example, the state's pronatalist laws were not entirely embraced by the public. In addition to its bonuses to particularly fecund families, the state also taxed bachelors. However, as David Horn points out, the net results fell short of reaching the state's goals for increased birthrates: "In order to discourage late marriage and bachelorhood (and their degenerative effects), the regime instituted a progressive tax on unmarried men between the ages of 25 and 65, 'for the sole fact of their status,' which took effect on 1 January 1927. . . . But though the tax was not economically insignificant, it had little observable effect. It neither lowered the average age at marriage nor increased the marriage rate."[1] Moreover, convincing arguments have been made that the state's intrusion into reproductive issues engendered the opposite effect. De Grazia has pointed out that, once the state began to legislate familial matters, once private matters were rendered of interest to the nation, Italian women were just as likely to use such interferences as a site social of contestation.[2]

Yet despite the limited success of individual social programs, one of the principal characteristics of Italian fascism remains its extraordinarily visible occupation of the public sphere. Indeed, it is the very tension between the heuristics proposed by fascism and oppositional, or at least discordant, readings that colors the most complete historical account of the experience of cinema in the interwar years. Based on the textual analyses in chapters 3 and 4, I can now offer some general conclusions about the basic coordinates for the experience of cinema in the fascist era. I propose that much of that experience was characterized by *at least* four major overlapping heuristic codes, a general codex that exists at the intersection between the state's public appearances and the positions of cinematic readership.

First, the social order of Italian national life *is always only a fascist order.* The totalizing claim of responsibility and therefore of authority in almost every aspect of civic life is the unequivocal metadiscursive bracket of the regime's newsreels. LUCE newsreels give privileged coverage to the state's own initiatives and projects. When they covered activities and events not directly sponsored by the state, uniformed representatives are nonetheless almost always present as witnesses. These witnesses stand in for the audience, whose point of view on the depicted events is thereby relayed through a literal fascist presence. This practice is significantly different from the paradigms of presentation found in newsreels produced in the same period by companies like Hearst Metrotone, Fox, and Pathé. Even when such newsreels speak in favor of a specific government policy, they do so either by attempting to efface a nameable political perspective or by clearly foregrounding their ideological orientation as that of a nonpolitical private company.

As I outlined in chapter 1, Italian cinema history, from its origins, was characterized by continuous slippage between its cultural and political status. The regime's extensive claim for social authority in the interwar years represents a specific historical shift in that slippage. The fascist state injected itself into that continuum as the exclusive agency for the construction of civil society and did so not only through its management of political power, but through its virtual omnipresence in the public square. If I might use a term more frequently applied to describe modern consumer society, it could be said that Fascism branded itself as producer of an idealized social organization. The regime designed its own symbology, dress codes, salutations, and linguistic preferences. It named or renamed both its New Towns and its renewed urban centers, their buildings and streets. Claudia Lazzaro summarizes the overall effect: "Emblematic images taken from Roman antiquity and reproduced in innumerable contexts, scales, and materials made the past a living heritage. Through constant repetition, these images became widely intelligible and created a collective visual imagery which substituted for a common language and culture. The proliferation of the fasces [for example] extended to all aspects of material culture: official stamps, medals, and stationery, and domestic lamps, desk accessories, jewelry, toys, and furniture."[3]

In the context of the nonstate fiction films, witnessing fascism as the author of the Italian social order takes a different, more implied form. That is, many commercial texts reenact forms of audience participation common to collective activities organized by the state. In cases such as the historical costume film, the orchestration of point of view often invokes the assemblage of citizens in the state-sponsored athletics. Thus, the cinematic spectator witnesses the unfolding of events from a vantage point that is rhetorically identical to the position from which it observed fascist sports spectacles. In films where the representation of travel is a major trope, the audience's reading of specific cinematic narratives is informed by its direct participation in state-organized leisure-time practices. The overall map of these two sets of discursive coordinates (located in the nonfiction and the fiction films) indicate for this Italian audience/public that the world from which they have come into the cinema and the world to which they will soon return is unavoidably linked to the totalitarian regime.

Second, *the Italian past is Roman, the present and future are fascist.* Having charged audiences with the responsibilities of citizenship, that is, having linked the cinema audience to its membership in a civilly defined public, the cinema under fascism consolidated the political space occupied by cinema in the public sphere. Building upon the institutional practices inaugurated before the Fascist takeover, the civic component to the experience of filmgoing was multiplied by the addition of a peculiarly fascist historiography. Thus the fictional presentation of contemporary history was to be read as a descendant from a classical past. As seen most evidently in the costume epics, fascism was figured as the inevitable incarnation of a national character originally expressed through Imperial Rome and subsequently refined by the experience of the Renaissance.

Fascist historiography also pointed to the future. Within months after the March on Rome, the new government moved to establish its authority over dates. It quickly replaced the traditional (socialist) celebration of Labor Day on May 1 with April 21 as the holiday that simultaneously signaled the foundation of Rome and a new, fascist labor day. Time itself was branded in 1926 by the establishment of the fascist calendar, which superimposed the dates of the *era fascista* upon the traditional Christian calendar. While the official calendar marked past events (establishing national holidays in commemoration of both Roman and fascist moments), fascist cultural spectacles and exhibitions produced a sense of eventfulness that was predictive of future accomplishments. In this context, the state's evocation of efficiency—of timeliness—not only expresses an idealized quality of fascist character, it also projects the regime's imminence. In a word, fascism is the momentous historic agency that *will continue* to mold Italian civil society in the future. The clearest example of fascism's predilection for making rather than writing about history is found in the body of the state's nonfiction films. Here the cumulative concatenation of events produced by the state points to prior accomplishments in anticipation of even greater authority. In the fictional films, the frequent representations of new modes of transportation not only resemble the futurist fascination with velocity, they indicate at least one site in which fascist society tilts toward modernism even within the commercial cinema.

Third, fascist cultural programs imagine a *contemporary geography that naturalizes the contradictions between rural and urban topographies*. The state's massive land reclamation projects enabled the establishment of its New Towns, that is, of population centers based on agricultural rather than industrial production. On the one hand, it has often been argued that fascist population policy was resolutely antiurbanist. For example, while noting the limited efficacy of the state's attempts to police and limit internal migration from the countryside to the city during the interwar years, Carl Ipsen also describes the underlying political motivation for such policies: "Nonetheless, anti-urbanism served a political purpose. It helped to prevent the creation of large and potentially revolutionary urban mobs by threatening many workers (both employed and unemployed) with repatriation to their home *comuni* should they draw attention to themselves. It was also consistent with Mussolini's general revolt against urban culture, a significant aspect of his attempt to create a new Fascist civilization based on the 'rural' masses."[4]

On the other hand, it is equally important to recognize that the regime believed it *could* in fact control demographic mobility by efficient management of spaces, that is, that population trends could be engineered through both pronatalism and better geographic distributions. Thus the fascist state undertook to give literal directions for population growth. As Ipsen points out, "This position found expression in institutions and programs which discouraged migration abroad and to the cities, seeking instead to direct these currents to new rural population centers within Italy and eventually also in the Italian colonies."[5] Despite its massive economic and cultural investment in urban renewal, fascist cultural policy seeks a balance between conservative ruralism and futurist visions of metropolitan life.

This global balance is frequently achieved textually through the trope of the inevitable return to origins. Yet, unlike Hollywood cinema of this period, very few Italian productions figure the escape from the evils of cosmopolitan life as anything but transitory. Characters may leave the city, but they always come back. The fascist cultural map does indeed recognize that such urban evils exist, but it locates them outside of *its* cities. Thus social dislocation and alienation exist, but only precede a return to a naturalized home front. The ideal fascist city largely excludes itself as site of moral decay, overpopulation, dehumanized workdays, crime, and traffic. Urban crime does take place within the Italian commercial cinema but is located either in the United States or in entirely fictionalized European countries. The fast life of the grand hotel is presented as leading to moral decay, but such diversions tend principally to be situated in resorts, onboard luxury liners, or *somewhere along the way.*

Fourth, *Italian fascism addresses its audience/public as an undifferentiated national body.* As we have seen in the example of the Mario Camerini filmography, differences between social strata are based upon personal, psychological issues of identity and are subsequently effaced by the very narrative trajectory of each film.[6] In the broadest terms, the Italian commercial cinema figured its audience as a classless, regionless, and largely sexless collective body. And, although the state infrequently intervened into controlling issues of content in entertainment films such as these, where it did so the intercession was for the purpose of cleansing them of cultural references that might prove troublesome to the constitution of national consensus.

These interventions, carried out in large part by the regime's censorship boards and through the mechanism of dubbing, were particularly evident with respect to the use of language. Linguistic references to other nationalities, that is, words from non-Italian languages, were all but expunged. At the same time, linguistic references to regional differences *within* Italy were largely suppressed. This suppression is especially significant with respect to the differences between northern and southern Italy. It is arguable whether a class component is automatically carried by distinctions between, for example, Lombardy and Piedmont, two of Italy's most highly industrialized regions. However, it is clear that the cultural references to the differences between a northern Italian region and *any* southern region unavoidably also refer to the north's historic political and economic domination of the south, a domination that was uninterrupted by fascism. As I will discuss later, this is one significant way in which neorealism's use of regional dialect, for example, would come to incorporate within its "style" a distinctively unfascist political discourse.

In sum, effacing the discursive markers of difference between audiences also meant that these differences remained invisible to those cinematic audiences when they were addressed as members of the Italian civic public. It has been argued that the dissipation of such markers is a general characteristic of a society's entrance into modernity. Michael Warner describes the general social effect of this process in the following way:

> In the bourgeois public sphere, which was brought into being by publication in this sense, a principle of negativity was axiomatic: the validity of what you say in public bears a negative relation to your person. What you say will carry force not because of who you are but despite who you are. Implicit in this principle is a utopian universality that would allow people to transcend the given realities of their bodies and their status. . . . The bourgeois public sphere has been structured from the outset by a logic of abstraction that provides a privilege for unmarked identities: the male, the white, the middle class, the normal.[7]

Yet what is critical to an understanding of the specific formation of the public sphere under fascism (as opposed to the broader context of Italy in the multidecade experience of modernization) is that it begins by eliding these identities only to name two larger ones. Thus, acceptable or legitimate public discourse is made possible first by removing these markers and second by adding those of *the nonregional national* and *the fascist*. In broadly Foucauldian terms, establishing the limits of readership has a direct relationship to the acquisition and application of political power. In a word, the issue of which policies and practices can and cannot be challenged is often a matter of how the terms for social discourse are framed, of what can and cannot be read. The overall *arrangement* of the cinema during the fascist period conditioned cinematic readership. It limited and directed participation in social activity. As opposed to the collective identification characteristic of liberal democratic states, as a loosely affiliated set of differentiated individuals, participation in the specifically fascist public sphere was mass-oriented and consolidated under the name and discourse of a unitary national identity.

DISSOLUTION OF FASCIST ORDER, ANTIFASCISM, AND/OR NEOREALISM

What becomes of the national unitary identity sought after by fascist cultural and social policies? In film scholarship there has been a long-standing debate over the extent to which the postfascist cinema represents a complete cultural and/or political break. The battle lines are drawn between a somewhat romanticist association with antifascist resistance and a broader historical framing that focuses on a longer *longue durée*. For the former, the historical break is absolute. For the latter, the break has been much exaggerated.[8]

The answer is more complex than either of these formulations. Both sides of the debate tend to identify the postwar period entirely with neorealist cinema. This conflation creates two historiographic problems. First, periodizing Italian cinema history in terms of neorealism requires a precise account of the specific aesthetic paradigm that informs neorealist films. And yet, to this day, there is little agreement about what exactly constitutes the core realist aesthetic of neorealist film as opposed to a generally realist commercial cinema, which participates in one or more aspects of neorealistic film practices. Second, naming this the *period of neorealism* ignores the overall composition of Italian film production within which such films only ever constituted a small percentage. It is estimated, for example, that between 1945 and 1953 only 30 percent of Italian film production could generously be considered neorealistic.[9] Second, the postwar part of the historical bracketing loses sight not only of prewar films that either resemble or anticipate neorealism itself—*Sperduti nel buio* (1941, Nino Martoglio), *Uomini sul fondo* (1941, Francesco De Robertis), *Avanti c'è posto* (1942, Mario Bonnard), *Campo dei fiori* (1943, Bonnard), *1860* (1934, Alessandro Blasetti), *Quattro passi tra le nuvole* (1942, Blasetti), and *Treno popolare* (1933, Raffaello Matarazzo), among others—but also of those "classic" neorealist titles completed before the end of hostilities in May 1945, for example, *Ossessione* (1943) and *Roma città aperta* (1945).

Excessively stringent aesthetic requirements for a truly neorealist text lead some scholars to a draconian reduction in the total number of titles that could be included in the canon. Noting both stylistic and political inconsistencies, Ennio Di Nolfo, for example, argues that only six films qualify—*Roma città aperta, Sciuscià, Paisà, Ladri di biciclette, La terra trema,* and *Germania, anno zero.* He further reduces the number by questioning the status of *La terra trema,* which "is a formal and substantial model for a cinema of denunciation, and represents neorealism tinged by Communist propaganda and dominated by a Zhdanovian aesthetic—it was partially financed by the Italian Communist Party. Today both the film's inspiration and its neorealist designation seem debatable."[10] But both purely aesthetic and exclusively political evaluations miss or underestimate the significant institutional and social changes that characterized cinema production and consumption between the fall of the Fascist government in July 1943 and the first elections of the new republic in April 1948. Framed in this way, there was a five-year period of transition in the country's political and cultural history within which the Italian cinema was composed of both traditional, genre-based, commercial cinema and a generally oppositional approach to previous cinematic traditions. Thus, some neorealist films were certainly made before World War II and certain neorealist influences would continue to be felt well into the late forties. Even though neorealist titles remained in the statistical minority in comparison to the commercial cinema, a significant body of films nonetheless carved out a distinctively social approach to the cinema as a whole, a shared status which was largely unknown to cinema audiences during the interwar years. Here, we agree with Angelo Restivo and Frederick Jameson:

> What Bazin saw as essential to neorealism was its status as reportage, which in turn was connected to the fact that the *meaning* of the post-fascist nation was still in the process of being fixed. It is because of this that the products of the first flush of neorealism might be considered "vanishing mediators," in the sense that Jameson has developed the term. For Jameson, the vanishing metaphor mediator is that which emerges in moments of historical transition, in the moment when the historical situation is radically "open," and which vanishes as soon as the new order establishes itself and necessarily then erases any notion of contingency, i.e., that it could have turned out any other way.[11]

The question before us now is how to characterize the factors that defined this transitional period and the moments of radical openness that it occasioned. In a word, what becomes of the two dominant authorial agencies, the fascist state and Hollywood cinema.

On July 25, 1943, Mussolini was forced from office and arrested. Forty-five days later, on September 3, interim head of government

Badoglio signed a secret armistice with the Allies. In that brief span of time, important changes to the Italian cinema were already under way. When the armistice was made public on September 8, massive antifascist demonstrations took place in most of Italy's major cities. Demonstrators set fire to numerous offices and tore down the symbols and insignia of the fascist regime. Istituto LUCE cameramen, who had previously recorded the ubiquitous signs of the fascist order, reversed their former role by filming these oppositional reactions to fascism and its symbology. In fact, during these forty-five days, the seven newsreels that LUCE actually released contained no reference whatsoever to the regime. They now included topics such as women in the workforce, mining coal from the sea, new medical discoveries, a model airplane championship in Florence, a message from the pope to the world, and the rebuilding of Spain's merchant shipping fleet.[12] The fascist uniform had entirely disappeared and with it the role of witness to the making of fascist history. The dismantling of this state apparatus continued when most of the equipment and a good portion of the staff were transferred to Venice. During the time of Mussolini's republic of Salò, the downward spiral continued. Production activities were severely decreased due to the lack of raw stock and laboratory facilities. Thus one major mechanism for what we have called fascist authorship virtually vanished from public view well before the end of World War II.

During the remaining war years, many of the figures who had regulated cinema during the regime remained in place. But final authority for institutional decisions was squarely in the hands of the Allies. From the outset, an interim Film Board took up two basic policy positions. It sought to dismantle fascist cinema legislation and simultaneously to pave the way for renewed importation of films from Hollywood. At a meeting of the Board in June 1944, shortly after the Allies had entered Rome, Rear Admiral Ellery Stone, chief of the Allied Commission for Italy, expressed a remarkably unequivocal condemnation of the country's previous cinema: "All of the legislation created by fascism must be dissolved. . . . The so-called Italian cinema was invented by the fascists. It must therefore be suppressed. All of the instruments which gave life to this invention must also be suppressed. All of them, including Cinecittà. There has never been a film industry in Italy, there have never been film industrialists. Who are these industrialists? Speculators and adventurers, that's who they are. In any case, Italy is an agricultural country. What need does it have for a film industry?"[13]

Indeed, Cinecittà was turned into a refugee camp and would not open up again until 1947. By 1945, the long-term intent of Admiral Stone's speech would have the force of law. On October 5, all of the major fascist film laws were repealed. The new legislation (Deputy Legislative Decree no. 678) would have two immediate effects. First, exhibitors were no longer required to show LUCE newsreels and documentaries before every feature film. Second, the decree dismantled the Ente Nazionale Industrie Cinematografiche (ENIC) and therefore the state's monopoly over film distribution. In so doing, it also revoked any quotas on film imports. In this friendlier economic environment, six American studios opened or reopened offices in Rome, including MGM, Paramount, 20th Century Fox, Warner Bros., RKO, and Universal. By block booking the backlog of films that it hadn't been able to export during the monopoly years (1939–45), Hollywood reestablished its dominion over Italian screens, this time at even higher levels. During the entire fascist period, the highest number of American features films distributed in Italy was 221 in 1930. With the implementation of the Alfieri protectionist laws in 1939, the number had dropped to 58. But with the return of the majors under this new system, over 188 American titles were distributed in 1946. In 1947 the record of 221 under fascism was superseded by the importation of 287 American films. In 1948, the number grew to 344. When, in 1949, 95 Italian films were released, the Hollywood film industry established an all-time record of 369 imported titles and earned 73 percent of all box-office receipts.[14]

This dominant return of Hollywoodian authorship is clearly part of another form of cultural dumping. Throughout the war and in the years that immediately followed, the Italian public was introduced to a flood of consumer goods that entirely overturned the social designs of fascist autarchy. As Stephen Gundle has put it, American (and to a lesser extend British) soldiers brought with them the material signs of a different social order: "Such items as DDT, chocolate, chewing gum, nylon stockings, dollar bills, and V-discs were symbols of a new way of life that fed popular fantasies and contributed to the changes in customs that marked life in urban areas and in the more developed regions."[15] American products, both films and consumer goods, were to be marked by equal amounts of fascination and, later, opposition for many years to come.

Finally, what becomes of the major heuristic codes that surrounded Italian cinema during fascism? With the entry into war, the dissolution

Figure 27. Silvana Mangano and Vittorio Gassman dance the boogie-woogie. Frame enlargement from *Riso amaro* (1948, Giuseppe De Santis). Courtesy of the Cineteca Nazionale, Roma.

of the fascist government, the growth of the partisan movement, and the arrival of Allied forces in Italy, each of the four core principles are either partially dismantled or entirely replaced. The emergence of new culture-wide coordinates for reading, almost as much as the artistic achievements of individual texts, contribute to the sense of a new experience and explain the societal force of a historical break. The *always also* fascist order comes to be undermined by the wide evocation of social and sexual instability, and by the specific cultural differences among social strata and among the peninsula's regional identities. Visual iconographies and thematic concerns that the state had sought to repress begin to emerge with intensity and frequency. In response to only one occasion of this shift, for example, Vittorio Mussolini is reported to have proclaimed at a screening of *Ossessione,* "This is not Italy!" before storming out of the theater.[16]

Along generational lines, for example, we need only note the abrupt appearance of troubled youths in many representations of destabilized or entirely absent family structures. We see this in a variety of films including Vittorio De Sica's *I bambini ci guardono* (1944) and

Sciuscià (1946), Pietro Germi's *Gioventù perduta* (1947), and Luigi Commencini's *Proibito rubare* (1948). Adultery and other forms of illicit sexuality show up in films such as Luchino Visconti's *Ossessione* (1943) and *La terra trema* (1948), Roberto Rossellini's *Roma città aperta* (1945) and *Paisà* (1946), Marcello Pagliero's *Desiderio/Rinascita* (1945), and Dullio Coletti's *L'adultera* (1946). In a word, shortly after its demise, the regime's often-invoked fusion between the family and the state unraveled.

Even apart from its evident deformation by the experience of the war, Italian civil society began to represent signs of dystopia almost immediately after the dissolution of fascist governance. Representations of criminal activities had been discouraged, expunged through censorship or transferred onto foreign soil throughout the interwar years. Crime now overflowed the country's urban centers and rural landscapes, as seen in films such as De Sica's *Ladri di biciclette* (1948), Aldo Vergano's *Il sole sorge ancora* (1946), Luigi Zampa's *L'onorevole Angelina* (1947) and *Anni difficili* (1948), and Giuseppe De Santis's *Riso amaro* (1948), in addition to most of the titles listed above. Representations of unemployment and labor unrest also begin to appear at unprecedented levels. In addition to the recurrent generalized theme of poverty during and immediately after the war, the specific question of labor is now investigated less in terms of the limits to social mobility and more in terms of basic survival. We see this shift again in *Sciuscià, Ossessione, La terra trema, Ladri di biciclette, Riso amaro,* and also in films such as De Santis's *Caccia tragica* (1947) and Borghesio's *L'eroe della strada* (1948).

De Sica's *Sciuscià/Ragazzi* (1946) is a remarkable instance of antifascist cinema. On the one hand, it is tempting to identify the film as expressing the generalized neorealist impulse to record the everyday social realities of Italy in the immediate postwar period. The familyless children live in abject poverty and are imprisoned for trafficking in the black market of goods (chocolate, blankets) introduced to Italy by American soldiers in Rome. Their day-to-day existence is a litany of urban dystopias as they move from one site of homelessness to another, sleeping in an elevator, a barn, a temporary shelter, and finally a reformatory. The very title of the film is a linguistic byproduct of the war experience. *Sciuscià* is an Italianization of the English "shoeshine." It literally refers to the work the children perform in order to carve out a meager living. But it also refers figuratively to the cultural confusion (in the previous era, this bilingualism would have been considered linguistic contamination) brought about by the new social authority of the American military presence.

On the other hand, even before the narrative proper begins, the film locates the causes of that dystopia in a specific relationship to fascism. The prenarrative titles appear superimposed over a stable long shot of the interior of the prison into which the young boys will eventually be brought. The architectural design of this space, in particular its rounded arches, is extraordinarily similar in volume and structure to that of the neoclassical façade of the Palazzo della Civiltà, one of the first buildings constructed for the Esposizione Universale di Roma (EUR), a new fascist city within Rome that was intended to celebrate the twentieth anniversary of the March on Rome. That the prison is a still-active remnant of the earlier regime is additionally fixed by the character of its director. His overtly authoritarian treatment of the prison's young wards—accused variously of crimes including black marketeering, fraud, armed robbery, patricide, car theft, and homelessness itself—clearly expresses a critique of fascist social policies. The director laments, for example, the rise in crime of 60 percent in comparison to 1936. And when inspecting the kitchen, he reflexively (albeit with a note of embarrassment) returns the fascist salute to the prison's cook.

Interestingly, *Sciuscià* also contains metatextual traces of the changes to the fascist cultural scene. The film's climactic prison break takes place during the projection of a newsreel. But instead of an edition of LUCE, this film-within-a-film is an institutionally unbranded product simply entitled "Notizie del mondo libero" (News from the Free World). That the contemporary reality of the children in this audience is chaotic is underscored by their misreading of the news. As the projected images depict dramatic naval battles in the Pacific, one of the children is instead taken by what he perceives as an underlying idyllic beauty: "Pasquale, il mare!"

The second major fascist heuristic code is the historiographical model that locates modern Italy as a nation-state derived from the conceptual unity with its Roman past. The totalizing centrality of this code is now often replaced by metonymic representations of a nation made up of regional *pasts,* that is, of histories that extend south to north, east to west, and to the islands. As, for example, in Rosselini's *Paisà* (1946), Italy is now constituted by epistemological *pieces* that do not emanate from a geographical history centered in Rome and by Romans. Indeed, the organizing principle of the film's narrative, its

I PERSONAGGI E GLI AVVENIMENTI DI QUESTO FILM SONO PURAMENTE IMMAGINARI.

Figure 28. (Fascist) prison interior. Frame enlargement from *Sciuscià* (1946, Vittorio De Sica). Courtesy of the Cineteca Nazionale, Roma.

internal textual history, is a geographic movement from place to place over time which is determined by a distinctively un-Roman causality, namely, the advance of Allied forces.

Given the virtual disappearance of LUCE newsreels and historical costume films in this period of transition, the significance of the new historiography proposed by Rossellini's *Paisà* is particularly compelling. Like *Sciuscià*, the title of the film linguistically prefigures the text as a new vision of the nation. The word *paisà* derives from *paese*, which means both country and town, that is, both the larger nation and the localities which constitute it. *Paisan*, the title of the English-language version of the film, refers either to citizens of the same village or more generally to countrymen. This coexistence of local pieces and the national whole provides the epistemological framework within which the film seeks to put the country back together. Thus the film's six episodes not only follow the general time frame of Italy's liberation, they are also the conceptual map coordinates for a country *in the process of becoming.*[17]

The unfolding of events in this new geography radically departs from the *twin* fascist historical model in which current events derive from the

Figure 29. Fascist architecture: Palazzo della Civiltà, Esposizione Universale di Roma (EUR). Courtesy of Il Manifesto, Cosima Scavolini.

almost mythological Roman past in order to project a specifically fascist future. Moreover, the eventfulness of fascist time is replaced by the uncertainties, the instability and openness, of the postfascist era. Each episode is preceded by a specific date. The first section, for example, begins with images of bombs as they fall into the sea off the coast of Sicily. The moment is precisely dated by voice-over narration: "July 10, 1943." Each episode is also introduced by newsreel footage of the war that is once again conspicuously unbranded. The progression of episodes thus starts with the Allied landing in Sicily and moves northward to Naples, Rome, Florence, a remote monastery in the Apennines, and finally the Po River valley. But these sites couldn't be more different from the itineraries and locales visited by the OND-sponsored tours represented in *Treno popolare,* the pleasure cruises of *Il signor Max,* and the luxury resort of *Rotaie.*[18] The sunny shores, picturesque landscapes, and famed monuments are replaced by darkness and the rubble of bombed cityscapes. Indeed, each site is an occasion for miscommunication and/or cultural misunderstanding. In the Sicilian episode, for example, an American soldier (yet another Joe) attempts feebly to communicate with the non-English-speaking Sicilian Carmela: "Are you a fascist? I'll bet you're a fascist." "Me Joe, boy. You Carmela, girl."

When Joe illuminates family photographs with a lighter, he is tragically shot by German snipers, just as it appears the two have begun to understand each other. Apart from the melodramatic undercurrent of this and other episodes, the overall phenomenological unfolding of events—as opposed to fascist imminence—and the Babylonian linguistic confusion between characters—as opposed to theoretically neutral and national Italian proposed by fascist language policies—invite Italian audiences to participate with the film's figural reconstruction of the nation. Giuliana Muscio has suggested that this invitation to a different form of readership was generally characteristic of the entire neorealist project: "By seeing themselves and their dramas represented on screen, audiences experienced their contribution to the reconstruction of the country from a moral, cultural as well as material point of view. The film theater thus becomes the site of a civil, political and moral regeneration."[19]

The last two of the four fascist heuristics regard the relationship between urban and rural topographies and the manner in which fascist cultural practices tend to address their public as an undifferentiated national body. The mutations to these codes are closely interwoven. In many of the films that followed the experience of fascism, the overall topographical relationship between center and periphery is radically reoriented. For example, Visconti's *Ossessione* and *La terra trema,* films that have much more in common with postfascist society than they do with the major cultural orientation of films during the interwar years, are not only located in specific *peripheral* regions, their very language (the dialects they speak) had to be translated and dubbed in order to be intelligible to other Italian publics. The Italian national body public comes now to be addressed by the invocation of class and regional difference through language. In addition to the cases we have already mentioned, numerous films—even non-neorealist genre titles—now freely speak Italian dialects, in recognition of Italy's uniquely regional composition. Moreover, the trope of inevitable narrative return to the point of social origin (usually in the city) becomes much less certain. One need only think of how this previously closed circuit is either left ambiguously open or entirely bypassed in the endings of films such as *Sciuscià, Paisà, La terra trema,* and *Riso amaro.*

To cite one case of how the Italian public is addressed differently, we can consider Giuseppe De Santis's *Riso amaro* (1948), whose overall rhetorical structure is stunningly distinct from that of, for example, *Mussolini Speaks.* In the latter, the audience/public witnesses the

Figure 30. Radio Torino. Frame enlargement from *Riso amaro*. Courtesy of the Cineteca Nazionale, Roma.

making of contemporary Italy as it listens to the speech by the head of state. In the De Santis film, the public is invited to see itself as active participants in that making. The film opens with a close-up of a narrator who speaks directly to the cinema audience. The first lines are "This is Radio Torino. Today we want to open a special program to our listeners." He then describes the film's basic narrative premise, that is, the experiences of *mondine,* women rice-pickers. This fictive representation of a radio journalist corresponds to a devolution of the fascist centralization of culture. Between 1945 and 1946, regional radio stations momentarily replaced the Rome-centric system that had been established by the fascists. The fascist radio system, the Ente Italiano per le Audizioni Radiofoniche (EIAR), was retitled Radio Audizioni Italia (RAI), the institutional name that today still refers to all state-run radio and television. Radio Torino was only one example of regional entities that fought to maintain their autonomy and cultural distinctiveness.

As the narrator/journalist informs the audience, the *mondine* "come from every part of Italy. It's a mobilization of women from all ages and trades. They are mostly peasants and workers, but also shop girls, seamstresses, and typists." And again, the women speak a rich range of distinct Italian dialects. But the characters are not just regionally defined laborers; they are active interpreters and consumers of new cultural forms. They sing traditional rhyming verses to *clandestinely* defy the prohibition against speaking while on the job. But they also dance the boogie-woogie, chew American gum, and avidly read *photoromanzi,* popular publications that are a hybrid of the stylistic conventions of film melodrama, romance novels, and the form of the extended comic strip. The film's visual style is a particularly rich mixture of Soviet social realism—in its heroic representation of the bond between work and nature—and the American film noir—in its subtheme of a jewelry heist and subsequent intrigue. But it's the *photoromanzo* adaptation of noirish style that provides the key to understanding the film's characters and events. The film's central female lead actually insists that "everything in these magazines is true, you know." Not only do various such publications turn up in numerous scenes, the main focus is on *Grand Hotel,* whose first edition appeared the year before *Riso amaro* and whose circulation quickly rose to over one million copies per week. Thus the film provides a particularly evocative picture of how new Italian culture might address locally specific questions about labor (the rights of the *mondine*) in the context of the country's fascination with Americana and Hollywood. In a word, *Riso amaro*'s fiction literalizes a new and complex form of cultural readership.

In addition to these new thematic and stylistic phenomena, the surrounding heuristics of the fascist social order are disrupted by the emergence of new forms of media consumption and distribution. And in turn, these new practices provide the foundation for oppositional reading in the nexus between culture and politics. One of the clearest examples was the rise of clandestine listening during the war years. Notwithstanding the possibility of arrest and punishment by the fascist government, Italian audiences increasingly tuned in to the antifascist transmissions of communist stations and the BBC's Radio Londra. The social effect of this phenomenon was to increase the viability of oppositional reading to fascist culture. As David Forgacs has described, "Clandestine listening suggested that radio audiences wanted not just one source of information but a plurality of stations and the freedom to choose between them. Broadcasters in the liberated zones, too, experienced not only a freedom to transmit anti-fascist messages, but also a new conception of who their listeners were and of their relationship with them."[20]

The cinema also created a temporary but significant alternative to the previous mainstream. Throughout the period of transition, cinema exhibition continued to grow. By 1949 there were 3,000 more theaters than before the war.[21] Yet the dominance of American films and the increasingly hostile position taken up by the Christian Democrats toward neorealism decreased the number of screens available to nontraditional films. Thus, toward the end of 1945, cine-clubs and *circoli di cinema* began to appear. Such venues were not only alternative venues for films that could not be placed in the major circuits of distribution. They also attempted to alter the manner in which cinema was to be experienced. The evening program of a *circolo di cinema,* for example, also typically included pre- and post-film moderated discussions, debates on the films' social significance. Indeed, the historical legacy of the *circoli* and the early cine-clubs still informs the practices of many Italian film festivals to this day.

Few films in the transitional period contain extended, explicit representations of the fascist regime. Systematic filmic investigations of fascist aesthetics would not appear with any frequency until some decades after the end of the war.[22] That said, a significant number of films participate in the dissolution of the fascist order through their evocation of markers of social difference. Indeed, it is precisely this evocation of difference that would later make neorealist filmmaking so influential with postcolonial cinemas in India and Asia. Moreover, clandestine listening and alternative avenues for film exhibition created the possibility for a new kind of filmgoing experience. Thus, in addition to the consumption of Hollywoodian cinema, it also became possible to search for voices and information that had been largely suppressed by fascist authorship. Though fascinated with Hollywood, Italian audiences now also engaged in oppositional readership of culture in general.

EPILOGUE

Resistance and the Return of the Local

The multi-institutional dynamics between political discourse and cinema that were consolidated during the twenty years of fascist governance have left a trail and continue to influence contemporary Italian cinema. At a micro level, for example, dubbing is still the law of the land. But, more importantly, the institutional traces of the fascist experience also point to the possibility of cultural resistance. The case of Massenzio poses intriguing questions about political accounts of cinema culture, the state-sponsored organization of leisure activities, the inescapable relationship between the Italian and American cinemas, and culture-wide struggles for the establishment of "authoritative" readings of cinema texts. Moreover, it turns on phenomena within film culture that originate from the consolidation of the film industry in the period 1910–14 and the subsequent Italian experience of cinema under fascism. The Massenzio experiment specifically addresses one of the common effects of the four central codes of fascist culture, namely, the regime's attempt to close down or at least to redirect the slippage between culture and politics.

In 1977, the Municipality of Rome's Cultural Council inaugurated a massive series of summer events designed to revitalize the city's sluggish menu of civic activities. The *estate romana* (literally, the Roman Summer) included musical concerts, mass public dances, theatrical and street performances, art exhibitions, and fashion shows. The cornerstone of the series was its open-air film and television retrospectives.

Nicknamed "Massenzio" for the fourth-century Roman emperor Maxentius, the film and television component recalls a series of considerations on Italian film culture that lie at the core of our project. The popular attention and critical responses to Massenzio reveal some of the crucial intersections between the filmgoing experience, cultural practice, and political power in Italy. The *estate romana* responded to the annual vacation exodus of Romans from Rome. It attempted to fill the void created by a summertime flight that had traditionally left many of the city's private and public cultural venues—cinemas, theaters, museums, and nightclubs—all but dormant from mid-June to mid-September. The project's overall structure also aimed beyond a simple quantitative addition to the city's inventory of cultural activities. An integral part of the Massenzio project became the contemporary utilization of Rome's cultural heritage.

The *estate romana,* and particularly Massenzio, was the brainchild of Renato Nicolini, the Communist director of Rome's Cultural Council from 1976 to 1984. Faced with a general scarcity of resources and specifically the limited number of "appropriate" locations in which to hold the planned events, Nicolini made modern use of Rome's architectural patrimony. Thus, from 1977 until 1984, when city government passed from Italian Communist Party to Christian Democrat administration, the activities were situated in or around Imperial Roman structures, officially designated as national monuments. The films in the Massenzio series, for example, were presented in the Basilica di Massenzio, the Colosseum, and finally the Circus Maximus. All of these sites fall within the boundaries of the city's *centro storico,* its historical center. In 1985, the new political administration displaced the Massenzio project to Rome's outer periphery, presenting it instead in the shadows of the fascist-designed office complexes of L'EUR.

The Massenzio initiatives, their administration, their geographic placement within the city, and the cultural policy that produced them were fiercely contested. The debate had been often played out along narrowly drawn political lines, with the Italian Communist Party (PCI) hesitantly accepting the program's successes and the Christian Democratic Party (DC) attempting to provoke and then to capitalize on its putative failures.[1] Yet this hegemonically circumscribed struggle for political power had also extended beyond determined political affiliations. Nicolini had, in fact, encountered a certain resistance from within his own party, the PCI. The question of Massenzio was also articulated within a larger context as a contest for ideological authority over cultural policy in general. It turned on terms no less expansive than fundamentally divergent visions of culture and history.

Until its domestication in 1985, Massenzio was criticized in two primary ways. First, placing the activities in national monuments generated concern over possible physical damage to the sites. Projecting films within the Circus Maximus, for example, was seen as an environmental hazard to a precious archeological space. In conservative quarters, this commingling of contemporary popular entertainment and the city's revered classical heritage constituted nothing short of cultural desecration. For the Ministero dei Beni Culturali e Ambientali, the government ministry charged with the preservation of national monuments, the Massenzio activities were culturally improper, a violation of such sites. Since the Ministero also viewed its charge as the general protection of the Italian *past,* it feared not only a potential physical degradation, but also that Massenzio, as a cultural project, might destabilize these monuments as iconic referents to history itself. From their perspective, the Colosseum should recall the achievements of classical Rome rather than present popular entertainment from contemporary Hollywood. The terms of this debate recall the contestation over the appropriate place for Hollywood culture within the framework of fascist autarchy.

The second major criticism generally did not engage the matter of whether or not it was appropriate to fuse contemporary leisure activities with history, that is, to place the events in historical settings. Instead, Massenzio was criticized for creating culture that evaporated into mere popular consumption, a culture of the ephemeral *(cultura dell'effimero)* that left no significant ongoing traces upon Italian social life. The most often cited problems concentrated, generally, on weak organizational planning and, specifically, on the absence of a unified program structure, of catalogues, conferences, and seminars. Indeed, unlike fascist cultural policy, Massenzio built no monumental artifacts. As such, the series was seen as creating an inexpensive postmodern version of *panem et circenses.*[2] What is crucial to underscore is that Massenzio was insistently besieged from *both* the left and right of the Italian political spectrum. Whereas, in the first instance, the initiative was criticized as an almost antihistorical sacrilege, in the second it was seen as frivolously ahistorical.

From either perspective, however, the attention paid to the *estate romana* film series indicates the continuous importance of the status bestowed upon cinema within Italian social life. In a limited sense, by using alternative sites, Massenzio had attempted to dramatically expand access to cinema. That is, above and beyond the scarcity of cultural venues, it also responded to a set of specific conditions that significantly limit both the number and types of films available to the public. As was the case during the *ventennio nero,* the popular and critical demand for cinema far outruns the Italian cinema industry's ability to supply it. Standard fare, offered through Italian theatrical distribution, still concentrates almost exclusively on a safe selection of contemporary American large-budget films. At the same time, the alternative venues provided by a rich circuit of revival houses and cinema clubs has declined in direct proportion to the rise of home video ownership and the private television networks operated by Silvio Berlusconi. As such, Massenzio and its festival counterparts in other Italian cities attempt to respond to what has become a pressing cultural demand to go beyond standard fare, to see what cannot otherwise be seen. As a single instance of directed intervention into the limits of Italian cinematic culture, Massenzio is far from unique. There are, after all, more publicly funded film festivals in Italy than in any other country in the world.[3] Like its festival and conference counterparts, Massenzio must also be understood within a broader picture of the Italian cultural landscape. That is, to explain the huge numbers of festivals and conferences, to locate the origins of that demand or need for more cinema, we need to recall the privileged position given to the cinema both before and during fascism.

Massenzio's historical locations produced a series of extraordinary viewing conditions for the Roman audiences. For example, one highlight of the 1982 edition was the retrospective of American film noirs projected onto a gigantic makeshift screen at one side of the Colosseum. Casual passersby were stunned by the gargantuan images from Jacques Tourneur's *Out of the Past* (1947) that filled the evening sky. No less striking was the 1983 full-orchestra, multiscreen performance of Abel Gance's *Napoleon* (1927) in the Circus Maximus. During the screening, portions of the stands developed into partisan cheering sections. In a way, this collective participation with the film as spectacle re-evoked certain elements of the Circus Maximus's original, ancient function.

Perhaps the *estate romana*'s most striking encounter between popular culture and the archaeological remains of the Roman past was the 1984 Massenzio presentation of William Wyler's *Ben Hur* (1959). The audience responded vociferously to the film in a series of shouted sarcasms, catcalls, boos, and food fights of near-riot proportions. Selecting this film to open the 1984 series would not have seemed a particularly inappropriate or provocative decision, given especially the Italian film audience's extended familiarity with the historical epic genre. As I have described earlier, the cinematic representation of history, and the literal and figurative reconstruction of historical positions for spectacle, appear almost continually over the course of Italian cinema history.[4]

It was provocative, however, to project *Ben Hur* in the Circus Maximus. Along with the Colosseum, the Circus Maximus had been the first and predominant public space for ancient Roman mass spectacle: circuses, chariot races, gladiatorial combat. In fact, the very term *circus* came to represent a conflation of two meanings: space and place, where the circularity of a defined space (a given setting) established it as a place for spectacle.[5]

Given their central locations, each of these monuments is normally seen by a large sector of the Roman public—the pool from which the Massenzio film audiences were drawn—almost every day. It has been argued that their value as symbolic referent to a distant history (the Colosseum = ancient Rome) has been partially secondarized, that is, taken for granted. In other words, constant visual contact may tend to relegate their historical significance to the background of that audience's memory. At the same time, however, viewing films from within these ancient monuments creates a rich and sometimes provocative historiographic interplay. *Out of the Past* and *Napoleon* are cultural objects familiar to audiences in the context of cinema as a specifically twentieth-century art form. Viewing these films from within the Massenzio locations calls attention, at the very least, to the unusual nature of the event. By calling attention to the exotic juxtaposition of two different historical frameworks (Colosseum ≠ drive-in), these viewing circumstances tend to unravel that process of secondarization. Ironically, the very historiographic inappropriateness of a twentieth-century art form (motion pictures) experienced in ancient sites returns the historical significance of those sites to the surface, that is, to the foreground of contemporary memory.

The presentation of the 1959 *Ben Hur* in this ancient site for spectacle played an important part in its reception and contributed to the manner in which the film was read. That is, the Circus Maximus mediated between the film and traditional patterns of audience participation and identification. Major portions of the film take place in

Imperial Rome and make reference to the Circus Maximus; the set for the film's famed chariot race was built on a model of the Circus itself. Thus, when shown inside the Circus Maximus, the world of the filmic diegesis literally circumscribed itself as containing the place for its own reception. In a word, the Massenzio audience was able to participate in a narrative reconstruction of a historical setting (Roman antiquity) from within that *same* place in 1984.

As Stephen Heath has suggested, one of the fundamental functions of classical narrative cinema is the manner in which a film contains an ideal viewing of its own fiction, the way in which it converts something that is seen into a scene: "The drama of vision in the film returns the drama of vision of the film: the spectator will be bound to the film as spectacle on the basis of a narrative organization of look and point of view that moves space into place through the image-flow; the character, figure of the look, is a kind of perspective within the perspective system, regulating the world, orienting space, providing directions— and for the spectator."[6] For the Massenzio audience looking at *Ben Hur* projected on a screen in the middle of the Circus Maximus, the visual field of the space being moved "into place" literally surrounds the screen. Thus, the scenes, that "narrative organization of look and point of view," refer back to the original seen, the Circus Maximus.

This complication of fictive and real spaces is significantly different from traditional self-reflexive strategies: films within films, direct address, subversions of the unity between image and sound track, and so on. Whereas in these cases attention is drawn to the process of constructing filmic texts, the case of *Ben Hur* draws attention to the historical significance of the place of its reception. The audience, after all, viewed the film's reconstruction of history from within archaeological remains of Imperial Rome. Indeed, this concatenation of historical fictive and contemporary real spaces produced an extraordinary additional condition of spectatorship. It produced the extrafilmic discursive context in which the audience engaged the film. Just as many industry figures and film critics in 1924 had decried the virtual monopolization of Rome's sound-stage resources by Fred Niblo's 1925 MGM production of *Ben Hur*,[7] the Massenzio audience inveighed against the film's representation of Imperial Rome. In addition, its very vocal dialogue not only addressed the film's vision of history, it self-consciously contested nothing less than its status as cultural object.

Before the opening credits, the prologue to *Ben Hur* clearly overdetermines its status as a reenacted history. The very first image etches the Roman lettering "ANNO DOMINI" over a period map of Judea. The first sequence, an elliptical representation of the events leading up to the birth of Christ, is contextualized by voice-over narration: "In the year of our Lord, in the seventh year in the reign of Augustus Caesar, an Imperial decree ordered every Judean each to return to his place of birth, to be counted and taxed. . . . Even while they obeyed the will of Caesar, the people clung proudly to their ancient heritage, always remembering the promise of their prophets, that one day a redeemer would be born among them to bring them salvation and perfect freedom."

The end of this first sequence is bracketed by a second date, ANNO XXXVI, etched this time over a symbol of the crucifix. The actual locations of these dates and of the crucifix within the diegesis are never established. Similarly, the narrator is never connected to one of the film's fictional characters. Standing somewhere outside the world of the fiction, the dates and the narrator do not only indicate the time frame of the story. They locate, as well and more importantly, the ontological source for the story's narration. That is, the film's narrative moments are organized by an authoritative and yet never identified chronicle, written long before the film was made. The events that follow the film's prologue, that is, thirty-six years after the birth of Christ, are thus presented as the reenactment, the unfolding of history itself. This ensemble of factors—the scene, the seen, the public, this place—explicitly explodes back that slippage that fascism and fascistic culture sought to suture for over two decades. Indeed, the Circus Maximus had been the site for numerous state exhibitions during the thirties. In 1937, it housed the Mostra della rivoluzione fascista, a series of well-attended exhibits that celebrated both the regime's current programs and its Roman heritage. One of the exhibits, which commemorated the two thousandth anniversary of the birth of the Roman Emperor Augustus, was flanked by a large statue of Mussolini himself. Marla Stone has described this doubled historical valence in the show's opening: "The inaugural events festishized the founding days of Fascism: uniformed officials and Fascist heroes processed the banners and pennants from the first Fascio di combatimento (Fascist fighting squads of 1919–21) to the entrance like relics. . . . The contemporaneous inaugurations wrapped the Mostra della rivoluzione fascista in a cloak of ancient, historically predestined empire. 'Italians will resee,' one reviewer wrote, 'when visiting its rooms, a magnificent summary of the glorious and epic deeds that have given the Patria its new Empire.'"[8]

In the film's narrative, after the birth of Christ, the first event in that history is the arrival of Roman troop reinforcements in Judea. As a column of soldiers passes by Joseph's carpentry shop, a client inquires, "You're not watching the Romans, Joseph?" With Joseph's reply, "We have seen Romans before," the audience erupted into a dialect chorus of Rome's soccer team war cry: "Forza Roma! Forza Lupi! So' finiti i tempi cupi!" ("Go Rome! Go Wolves! The dark times are over!"). On the one hand, the arrival of Roman soldiers, within the narrative terms of the film, is treated as a continuation of Judea's political subjugation. On the other hand, the audience's prideful fan-like salutation welcomed the triumphant passage of the oppressor Roman soldiers. That is, their salute expressed a popular resistance to *Ben Hur*'s view of history.

Agreeing with Joseph, the client resigns himself to the inevitable, though clearly undesired, Roman presence in Judea: "Yes, and we will see them again." At this point, the Massenzio audience disparagingly addressed itself to Joseph, once again, in the Romanesco dialect: "A Peppi! Stamo tutti quanti qui!" ("Hey, Joey! We're all right over here!"). By addressing its sarcasms directly to Joseph, the crowd intentionally disregarded *Ben Hur*'s status as fictional film. They inscribed themselves into a contemporary discursive relationship with the film, interpellating its fictional characters as if they were participants in a social, extrafilmic conversation. Moreover, by vociferously asserting a historical correction to accounts offered by the film's fictional characters, identifying themselves as the real Romans being spoken of, the audience engaged the film in nothing less than an open political debate. The popular derision and historical opposition continued throughout the entire screening. By the end of the film, the audience had also taken issue with the personage of Charlton Heston, seeking to replace his status as fictional character with that of Heston as Hollywood star. Within the body of the film, Heston plays Judah Ben-Hur, prince of Judea. He is banished to slavery on a Roman galleon by Messala, military governor of Judea and former childhood friend. With the dissolution of the childhood bond, the film clearly represents Judah as the heroic savior of an oppressed people and Messala as the immoral agent of Roman imperialism. In the film's much-acclaimed climactic chariot race, however, the Massenzio audience rooted for Messala. Addressing itself not to Judah Ben-Hur, but to Charlton Heston, the crowd shouted a torrent of Romanesco expressions ultimately equivalent to "Yankee Go Home!"

This extraordinary level of political interaction with the cinema is derived from the audience's decades of experience with the organization of the country's film culture. When visible to the public, the relays of knowledge between Italy's diverse identities activate that critical slippage between explicitly cultural and political terms of reference. The question of that slippage, that is, the precondition for debate, repositioning, and rereading, is particularly relevant today. Indeed, much critical discourse currently addresses the troubling hyperconcentration of media control by Silvio Berlusconi's extensive media empire and by his government's regulatory control over state-owned media. The case of Massenzio is a particularly compelling benchmark because it is a model of cultural organization which self-consciously calls into question univocal reading of Italian culture. It represents a resistant and possibly destabilizing term of authorship whereby the audience/public speaks its own constituent parts. By expressing the very differences encoded in the localities of gender, class, and regionalism, it suggests an alternative strategy that is found not in textual production or in critical inquiry alone, but in both.

Notes

INTRODUCTION

1. Leopoldo Zurlo, *Memorie inutili: la censura teatrale nel ventennio* (Roma: Edizioni dell'Ateneo, 1952); Adriano Aprà and Patrizia Pistagnesi, eds., *The Fabulous Thirties: Italian Cinema 1929–1944* (Milano: Gruppo Editoriale Electa, 1979).

2. Benedict Anderson, *Imagined Communities: Reflections on the Origin and Spread of Nationalism* (London: Verso, 1983). Though his work is regularly cited in contemporary studies on national cultures (and especially in media scholarship), a growing body of thought has been particularly critical of Anderson's narrow definition of the nation-state. See John D. Kelly and Martha Kaplan, *Represented Communities: Fiji and World Decolonization* (Chicago: University of Chicago Press, 2001).

3. Vittorio Martinelli, *Il cinema muto italiano: i film degli anni venti, 1923–1931* (Roma: Edizioni Bianco e Nero, 1981), 405–6. Some discussion remains on exactly how many films were actually produced in the years 1918–32. No account, however, places the total higher than four films produced in 1931.

4. In a 2002 article Ennio Di Nolfo suggests that the break between neorealism and fascist cinemas was not as complete as one might expect. For Di Nolfo, this cultural break has been exaggerated by American critics, owing in part to their limited knowledge of the Italian industry. Di Nolfo, "Intimations of Neorealism in the Fascist *Ventennio*," in *Re-viewing Fascism: Italian Cinema, 1922–1943*, ed. Jacqueline Reich and Piero Garofalo, 83–104 (Bloomington: Indiana University Press, 2002).

5. Claudio Fogu has suggested that this transition was less a matter of the obliteration of the early formulations than, more accurately, an institutional codification of core values: "The modernist impulse of the fascist historic

imaginary did not subside in the second decade of the fascist regime. On the contrary, it was institutionalized into a proper historic culture that redirected the fascist historic imaginary away from 'history belonging to the present' and toward 'history belonging to the future.'" Fogu, *The Fascist Imaginary: Politics of History in Fascist Italy* (Toronto: University of Toronto Press, 2003), 17.

6. Two insightful micro-studies of fascist autarchy can be found in Bruno Regni, "Autarchia di materiali, autarchia di forme," and Luigi Veronelli, "La cucina autarchica," in *L'economia italiana tra le due guerre,* 460–65 and 238–41 (Milano: IPSOA, 1984).

7. Andrew Higson, "The Concept of National Cinema," in *Film and Nationalism,* ed. Alan Williams, 52–67 (New Brunswick, NJ: Rutgers University Press, 2002).

8. Michael Holquist, ed., *The Dialogic Imagination: Four Essays by Mikhail Bakhtin* (Austin: University of Texas Press, 1992); Michel de Certeau, *The Practice of Everyday Life* (Berkeley and Los Angeles: University of California Press, 1984).

9. Janet Staiger, *Interpreting Films: Studies in the Historical Reception of American Cinema* (Princeton, NJ: Princeton University Press, 1992), 9. Staiger is quoting Jonathan Culler.

10. Staiger, 72. The passage from Morley comes from David Morley, *The "Nationwide" Audience: Structure and Decoding* (London: British Film Institute, 1980), 15.

11. The most often cited text-activated theories of textual openness are found in the work of Roland Barthes. See in particular *S/Z* (Paris: Éditions du Seuil, 1970) and *The Pleasure of the Text* (Paris: Éditions du Seuil, 1973).

12. Margherita Sarfatti, "Art and Fascism," in *La civiltà fascista,* ed. Giuseppe Luigi Piomba (Roma: 1928).

13. Stuart Hall, "Encoding/Decoding," in *Culture, Language, Media: Working Papers in Cultural Studies 1972–1979,* ed. Stuart Hall, Dorothy Hobson, Andrew Lowe, and Paul Willis (Birmingham, UK: Centre for Contemporary Cultural Studies, 1980).

14. See specifically Robert Morley, "Texts, Readers, Subjects," in *Culture, Language, Media,* 163–76. In a larger context, Bakhtin's concept of heteroglossia radically expands the structures of possible readerships to include factors such as gender, sexual orientation, race, and generational and regional differences. See Bakhtin, *The Dialogic Imagination.*

15. Hall, "Encoding/Decoding," 134.

16. Robin Pickering-Iazzi, ed., *Mothers of Invention: Women, Italian Fascism, and Culture* (Minneapolis: University of Minnesota Press, 1995), xx.

17. The reference to the *public sphere* depends largely on the conceptual definition provided by Jürgen Habermas. Thus the public sphere contains the sounds and images that are available to a historically definable population and which, because they are familiar to that population, provide the recognizable components of social discourse. See Jürgen Habermas, *The Structural Transformation of the Public Sphere: An Inquiry into a Category of Bourgeois Society* (Cambridge, MA: MIT Press, 1989), and Craig Calhoun, ed., *Habermas and the Public Sphere* (Cambridge, MA: MIT Press, 1992).

18. For a number of reasons it is important to note that we focus on the regime's *attempts* to build national consciousness. First, the concept of a unified and stable national identity is somewhat problematic inasmuch as such identities are composite in their construction and always also include oppositional or at least discordant voices. Second, the Italian context specifically requires additional historical consideration of the role of the Catholic church in the ideological construction of *the national.*

19. See Gilbert Allardyce, "What Fascism Is Not: Thoughts on the Deflation of a Concept," *American Historical Review* 84, no. 2, April 1979; A. F. K. Organski, "Fascism and Modernization," in *The Nature of Fascism,* ed. S. J. Woolf (New York: Random House, 1968); and Roland Sarti, "La modernizzazione fascista in Italia: conservatrice o rivoluzionaria?" in *Il regime fascista,* ed. A. Aquarone and M. Vernassa (Bologna: Il Mulino, 1974).

20. James Hay, *Popular Film Culture in Fascist Italy: The Passing of the Rex* (Bloomington: Indiana University Press, 1987), 6.

21. Louis Althusser, *Lenin and Philosophy and Other Essays* (New York: Monthly Review Press, 1971).

22. As we will see later, the historical costume epic was a mainstay of film genre production from the earliest period of Italian film history. The key, however, is that this genre's conventions were modified in order to address audiences with terms specific to the ideological needs of a fascist historiography.

CHAPTER ONE. AMNESIA AND HISTORICAL MEMORY

1. One notable exception is the series of articles by Libero Solaroli: "La legione straniera degli intellettuali italiani," *Cinema Nuovo,* 1 January 1953, no. 2; "I mille di Garibaldi: Protagonisti del primo film storico italiano," *Cinema Nuovo,* 1 February 1953, no. 3; "Independent Productions," *Cinema Nuovo,* 1 March 1953, no. 6; "La terza cines indossa la camicia nera," *Cinema Nuovo,* 1 April 1953, no. 8; "Lo sciopero di Visconti," *Cinema Nuovo,* 1 July 1953, no. 14.

2. Pierre Leprohon, *The Italian Cinema* (New York: Praeger Publishers, 1972), translated from *Le cinéma italien* (Paris: Éditions Seghers, 1966). Among the predominantly Italian sources that Leprohon cites are Carlo Lizzani, *Il cinema italiano* (Firenze: Parenti, 1961); Vinicio Marinucci, *Tendenze del cinema italiano* (Roma: Unitalia Film, 1959); Roberto Paolella, *Storia del cinema muto* (Napoli: Giannini, 1956); and Brunello Rondi, *Cinema e realtà* (Roma: Edizione Cinque Lune, 1957).

3. Leprohon, 72.

4. Lizzani, *Il cinema italiano,* 69.

5. Giuseppe Ferrara, *Il nuovo cinema italiano* (Firenze: Le Monier, 1964), 4.

6. *Bianco e Nero* was the backbone of conservative Italian film criticism from 1937 to 1981. *Cinema Nuovo,* which had a generalized left-wing orientation, began publication in 1952 and is still active.

7. Once again, Solaroli's series of *Cinema Nuovo* articles are an exception. They are, in fact, principally dedicated to neorealism's deeply imbedded heritage in the prior decade.

8. The hesitance of film scholarship to delve into the fascist arena is part of a larger cultural negation of the fascist past. Post–World War II historical studies of the period were conducted almost exclusively in partisan political terms until the early seventies. The 1974 publication of Renzo De Felice's six-volume study of fascism represented a major breakthrough in decontaminating the subject. De Felice's monumental history was one of the key steps that would open the way for a revisionist reexamination of the period in cultural studies. Renzo De Felice, *Mussolini il duce: gli anni del consenso, 1929–1936* (Torino: Giulio Einauldi Editore, 1974).

9. An initial survey of which films still existed and where they were located was conducted in 1975. See Jean A. Gili and Adriano Aprà, "Elenco di reperibilità film italiani 1929–1944," in *Nuovi materiali sul cinema italiano, 1929–1943*, vol. II (quaderno informativo numero 72; Roma: Mostra Internazionale del Nuovo Cinema, 1976). In recent years, numerous copies of Italian films from this period have been located in non-Italian archives, notably at the National Film and Television Archive in London and at the Cinémathèque Royale in Brussels. On the whole, the five major Italian archives have not sought to repatriate these films.

10. Gian Piero Brunetta, *Storia del cinema italiano, 1895–1945* (Roma: Editori Riuniti, 1979); Aldo Bernardini, *Cinema muto italiano: arte, divismo e mercato* (Bari: Editori Laterza, 1981). Though both studies were published at the close of the decade, their research projects, film viewing, and document analysis began in earnest in 1970. Brunetta's earlier publications anticipated the fully formed two-volume history of Italian cinema. See, in particular, *Cinema italiano tra le due guerre: fascismo e politica cinematografica* (Milano: Mursia Editore, 1975).

11. Francesco Casetti, Alberto Farassino, Aldo Grasso, and Tatti Sanguinetti, "Neorealismo e cinema italiano degli anni '30"; Sergio Grmek Germani, "Blasetti dal periodo fascista al neorealismo"; Jean A. Gili, "L'utilizzazione degli ambienti naturali nel cinema italiano dal 1930 al 1944"; and Vito Zagarrio, "Primato degli intelletuali e neorealismo," in *Il neorealismo cinematografico italiano*, ed. Lino Miccichè (Venezia: Marsilio Editori, 1975).

12. All translations are mine. Lino Miccichè, "Il cadavere nell'armadio," in *Cinema italiano sotto il fascismo*, ed. Riccardo Redi (Venezia: Marsilio Editori, 1979), 14. The reference to "not one single film" alludes to Cesare Zavattini's polemical essay "Poesia, solo affare del cinema italiano," *Film d'Oggi*, no. 10, 25 August 1945. The larger context of the citation is as follows: "I maintain that . . . twenty years of cinema [the fascist era] protected like no other, much freer than one might believe . . . produced not one single film. I mean one, three thousand meters that is, from within three million meters of stock that was exposed." The reference to "not one frame" is a quotation from Carlo Lizzani's *Il cinema italiano* (Firenze: Parenti, 1961): "Today, not one frame from the hundreds and hundreds of films produced from 1938 to 1943 can be cried over or remembered."

13. Above and beyond the group of Italian film historians who concentrated on the cinema of the twenties and thirties, the liberation from determinist film criticism was characteristic of an entire new generation of scholars, including Lucilla Albano, Francesco Casetti, Alberto Farassino, Sergio Grmek

Germani, Enrico Ghezzi, Marco Giusti, Enrico Magrelli, Andrea Martini, Emmanuela Martini, Giuliana Muscio, Roberto Turigliato, Giovanni Spagnoletti, and Vito Zagarrio.

14. Tobias Jones, *The Dark Heart of Italy: Travels through Time and Space across Italy* (London: Faber and Faber, 2003), 40. A more rigorous historical approach to postwar Italy can be found in Paul Ginsborg, *A History of Contemporary Italy: Society and Politics, 1943–1988* (London: Penguin Books, 1990), and Ginsborg's *Italy and Its Discontents: Family, Civil Society, State, 1980–2001* (New York: Palgrave, 2003).

15. Adriano Aprà and Patrizia Pistagnesi, "The Unknown Italian Cinema," in *The Fabulous Thirties: Italian Cinema 1929–1944,* ed. Adriano Aprà and Patrizia Pistagnesi (Milano: Gruppo Editoriale Electa, 1979), 24.

16. The retrospective took place at the Museum of Modern Art in New York in 1979 and later toured to the Pacific Film Archive in Berkeley. It was curated chiefly by Adriano Aprà and Patrizia Pistagnesi, both of whom had worked as organizers of the Pesaro initiatives five years before.

17. *The Fabulous Thirties,* 73–113.

18. More recently there have been a number of very fine contributions in this area by American scholars, including James Hay, *Popular Film Culture in Fascist Italy: The Passing of the Rex* (Bloomington: University of Indiana Press, 1987); Marcia Landy, *Fascism in Film: The Italian Commercial Cinema, 1931–1943* (Princeton, NJ: Princeton University Press, 1986); and Elaine Mancini, *Struggles of the Italian Film Industry during Fascism, 1930–1935* (Ann Arbor: UMI Research Press, 1985). By and large these studies bypass the political conditions that characterized cultural study in Italy.

19. Vittorio Martinelli lists only twenty-seven fiction films for the year 1927. See the filmography in Vittorio Martinelli, *Il cinema muto italiano: I film degli anni venti, 1923–1931* (Roma: Edizioni Bianco e Nero, 1981). The imbalance between box-office receipts and the number of films actually produced indicates the traditional strength of film exhibition in Italy as well as the dominance of foreign films within Italian circuits of distribution.

20. As prime minister, Giovanni Giolitti was responsible for a number of modest liberal reforms in the second decade of the century, including the partial expansion of suffrage. Turn-of-the-century Italian liberalism was viewed by the fascists, however, as responsible for the country's major military defeats during the period. Furthermore, its inability to either suppress or incorporate the nascent, extremist Italian nationalism that immediately followed World War I is widely pointed to as a key condition for the rise of fascism.

21. For a generally reliable list of Italian films produced between 1904 and 1915, see the filmography in Maria Adriana Prolo, *Storia del cinema muto italiano* (Milano: Poligono, 1951).

22. Relatively little research has been done on the evolution of early film distribution in Italy. It is safe to say, however, that national distribution chains didn't develop until much later in the period. In many cases, the early production companies produced films for their own local theaters. In others, the films were either sold outright to specific theaters or leased to regionally based distribution agencies.

23. Exhibitors were forced to present a "mixed" program of Italian and foreign films. Until the subsequent radical increase in national film production, this meant a dependence on the importation of French films.

24. Film production companies had been established in Italy as early as 1905. In May of that year, for example, the Società Italiana per il Cinematofono was founded in Genoa.

25. Given especially Pastrone's contributions, the evolution of Itala calls for a separate study. For a general discussion of these "corporate" transitions, see Aldo Bernardini, "Industrializzazione e classi sociali nel primo cinema italiano," *Risorgimento*, vol. 2, no. 3 (1981): 147–64.

26. Aldo Bernardini, "Il primo boom del cinema italiano (1911–1920)," in *Bianconero rosso e verde: immagini del cinema italiano 1910–1980,* ed. Davide Turconi and Antonio Sacchi, 13–27 (Pavia: La Casa Usher, 1983).

27. Each of the other original companies dramatically increased their output in this time frame. See Prolo, *Storia del cinema muto italiano,* 117–84.

28. *Lux,* 5 March 1911 (Special Issue on *Inferno*).

29. Kenneth MacGowan lists it as five reels long. Up to this point, films were generally 250 to 300 meters in length, i.e., one reel. He also refers to it as the first feature film to be "road-shown" in American theaters. MacGowan, *Behind the Screen: The History and Techniques of the Motion Picture* (New York: Dell Publishing Co., 1965).

30. In addition to specific cases in both the United States and Sweden, we can note, for example, Albert Capellani's *Les Misérables* (1912, Société Cinématographique des Auteurs et Gens de Lettres, 3,450 meters).

31. Bernardini, "Il primo boom del cinema italiano," 17.

32. See Silvio Lanaro, *L'Italia nuova: identità e sviluppo 1861–1988* (Torino: Einauldi Editore, 1988).

33. Salvatore Saladino, *Italy from Unification to 1919: Growth and Decay of a Liberal Regime* (New York: Thomas Y. Cromwell Co., 1970), 94–133.

34. Sileno Salvagnini, "Luoghi dello spettacolo e immaginario urbano tra Otto e Novecento," in *La meccanica del visibile: Il cinema delle origini in Europa,* ed. Antonio Costa (Firenze: La Casa Usher, 1983).

35. "L'età Giolittiana: 1899–1914," in *Storia d'Italia contemporanea,* vol. II, ed. Renzo Renzi, 43–54.

36. Nationalization of the trains meant that the new combines of steel works and heavy-machine manufacture were guaranteed a monopoly over the internal market. They became virtually the sole providers of both rails and locomotives to the state. For an overview of the process of industrialization in Italy, see, at least, the following sources: Rosario Romeo, *Risorgimento e capitalismo* (Bari: Laterza, 1959); A. Caracciolo, ed., *La formazione dell'Italia industriale* (Bari: Laterza, 1973); and Shepard B. Clough, *The Economic History of Modern Italy* (New York: Columbia University Press, 1964).

37. Nicos Poulantzas, *Fascism and Dictatorship,* trans. Judith White (London: Verso Editions, 1970). Poulantzas sees the infusion of foreign capital as a principal linkage between Italy and Germany within "the imperialist chain." From this perspective, he posits the process of industrialization as within the evolution of the political economy of advanced capitalism. Indeed, a number

of mixed banks, founded in the 1890s with German capital, invested heavily in Italy's industrial expansion. The most widely cited example is the 1894 establishment of the Banca Commerciale in Milan.

38. For a discussion of the Motion Picture Patents Company's protectionist measures with respect to the importation of foreign films, see "Regaining the American Market," in Kristin Thompson, *Exporting Entertainment* (London: BFI Publishing, 1985), 1–27. Similar protectionism did not occur in Italy until after the First World War.

39. In 1938, the fascist state organized a semiprivate, state-sponsored monopoly over film distribution. Soon after, the major American studios closed their Italian branches and gave up on the Italian market.

40. Salvatore Saladino, *Italy: From Unification to 1919: Growth and Decay of a Liberal Regime* (New York: Thomas Y. Crowell Co., 1970), 26–131.

41. David Forgacs and Geoffrey Nowell-Smith, eds., *Antonio Gramsci: Selections from Cultural Writings,* trans. William Boelhower (Cambridge, MA: Harvard University Press, 1985), 241–42. Gramsci goes on to distinguish between the general elections of 1913 and 1919. He considered the later elections to be even more important, above and beyond their specific political outcome, since

> that of 1919 is the most important of all because of the proportional and provincial character of the vote, which forced the parties to group themselves and because throughout the territory, for the first time the same parties stood with (roughly) the same programmes. To a much greater and more organic extent than in 1913 (when the uninomial college limited the possibilities and falsified the mass political positions because of the constricting delimitation of the colleges), in 1919 throughout the territory, in a single day, the most active segment of the Italian population raised the same questions and sought to resolve them in its historical-political consciousness.

42. See Tullio De Mauro, *Storia linguistica dell'Italia unita* (Bari: Laterza Editori, 1979), 43.

43. Howard Moss, "Language and National Identity," in *The Politics of Italian National Identity: A Multidisciplinary Perspective,* ed. Gino Bedani and Bruce Haddock (Cardiff: University of Wales Press, 2000), 99–100.

44. This concept of the *relays of information* is particularly suggestive. In later chapters we will in fact attempt to construct a map of such relays as a means of bridging between textual production and social authorities. David Forgacs, "The Mass Media and the Question of a National Community in Italy," in Bedani and Haddock, *The Politics of Italian National Identity,* 142.

45. Brunetta, *Storia del cinema italiano: 1895–1945,* 51.

46. Despite the massive project of "reducing" literary classics to the screen, the articulation of cinematic style in this period owes a larger debt to theatrical and operatic practices of scenic construction than to any narrativization of space based on literature. See Bernardini, "Industrializzazione e classi sociale nel primo cinema italiano," 160. For the stylistic influences of literature on early Italian film, see Gian Piero Brunetta, "La migrazione dei generi dalla biblioteca alla filmoteca dell'italiano," *Italian Quarterly* 21, no. 81 (Summer 1980): 83–90; and Ernesto Guidorizzi, *La narrativa italiana e il cinema* (Firenze: Sansoni, 1973).

47. Gabriele D'Annunzio (1863–1938), novelist, poet, and dramatist, was one of the leading literary figures in fin-de-siècle Italy.

48. Maria Adriana Prolo, *Cabiria: visione storica dell III secolo a. C.* (Torino: Museo Nazionale del Cinema, 1977), 5–15. Prolo reconstructs the limits of D'Annunzio's contribution to *Cabiria* through the correspondence between D'Annunzio and Pastrone. For treatments of his relationship to the cinema in general, see T. Antognini, *Vita segreta di Gabriele D'Annunzio* (Milano: Mondadori, 1938); Mario Verdone, *Gabriele D'Annunzio nel cinema italiano* (Roma: Edizioni dell'Ateneo, 1963); L. Bianconi, "D'Annunzio e il cinema," *Bianco e Nero* (February 1942); Francesco Soro, "L'opera cinematografica di Gabriele D'Annunzio," *Cinema* 3, no. 42 (25 March 1938): 186–87; and F. Zangrando, "Gabriele D'Annunzio e il documentario," *Bianco e Nero* 18, no. 2 (January 1964).

49. Bernardini, "Industrializzazione e classi sociali nel primo cinema italiano," 160–64.

50. The emphasis is mine. Reprinted in Davide Turconi, ed., *La stampa cinematografica in Italia e negli Stati Uniti d'America dalle origini al 1930* (Pavia: Amministrazione Provinciale di Pavia, 1977), 11.

51. A good place to start for an overview of periodical film publications during this formative period is Riccardo Redi, *Cinema scritto: Il catalogo delle riviste italiane di cinema 1907–1944* (Roma: Associazione Italiana per le Ricerche di Storia del Cinema, 1992).

52. Ruth Ben-Ghiat, *Fascist Modernities: Italy, 1922–1945* (Berkeley: University of California Press, 2001).

53. For a discussion of ticket prices in relationship to wage income during the years 1901–1910, see Salvagnini, "Luoghi dello spettacolo," in *La meccanica del visibile,* 56.

54. Giuseppe Prezzolini, "Paradossi educativi," *La Voce,* 22 August 1914.

55. Mario Dall'Olio in *La Gazzetta del Popolo,* 4 February 1908. Reprinted in Prolo, *Storia del cinema muto italiano.*

56. For a detailed discussion of an audience's textual and extratextual recruitment as a public in relation to the evolution of genre conventions, see my collaborative essay with Gregory Lukow, "The Audience Goes Public: Intertextuality, Genre, and the Responsibilities of Film Literacy," *On Film* (Spring 1984): 29–36.

57. Brunetta notes that a number of films remade theatrical works during the period, capitalizing on their popular success and their publicity. Brunetta, *Storia del cinema,* 140.

58. Antonio Gramsci in *Avanti!,* Piedmont edition, 26 August 1916, reprinted in Forgacs and Nowell-Smith, *Selections from Cultural Writings,* 54–56.

59. *La Presa di Roma* (1905, Alberini and Santoni) should also be mentioned along with the other Risorgimento-themed films. It precedes the "industrialization" of Italian cinema and is often referred to as the first fully scripted Italian fiction film.

60. Literary adaptations and historical costume films do not exhaust the period's collective filmography. They do, however, represent the two major trends in genre filmmaking during the period. Further, "historical" films, in particular,

are subject to continual remakes until, at least, the advent of sound. Examples include *Quo Vadis?* (1924, Georg Jacoby and Gabriellino D'Annunzio), *Gli ultimi giorni di Pompei* (1926, Carmine Gallone), and *Nerone* (1930, Alessandro Blasetti).

61. Bernardini, "Industrializzazione e classi sociali nel primo cinema italiano," 160.

62. Translated and reprinted in Dennis Mack Smith, *Italy: A Modern History* (Ann Arbor: University of Michigan Press, 1959), 301.

63. Jacques Le Goff, "Il peso del passato nella coscienza colletiva degli italiani," in *Il caso italiano,* ed. Fabio Luca Cavazza and Stephen R. Graubard (Milano: Garzanti, 1974), 534–52.

64. For a synthetic discussion on prewar civil society and the formation of the Italian public sphere, see Victoria de Grazia, *The Culture of Consent: Mass Organization of Leisure in Fascist Italy* (New York: Cambridge University Press, 1981).

65. The government's position vis-à-vis the cinema is described as "discursive" in the sense that economic intervention and industrial regulation were sporadic up to this point. It was only in the late 1920s that the state under fascism consolidated its policies and began its major "material" intervention in cinematic practices. Chapter 2 outlines the history of the institutional relationship between the fascist state and the cinema industry.

66. Reprinted in Ernesto Laura, ed., *La censura cinematografica* (Roma: Edizioni Bianco e Nero, 1961), 4–17. For extended accounts of the shifts in Italian censorship, see Mino Argentieri, *La censura nel cinema italiano* (Roma: Editori Riuniti, 1974); R. Brancati, *La porpora e il nero* (Milano: Edizioni Bianco e Nero, 1961); Jean Gili, *Stato fascista e cinematografia: repressione e promozione* (Roma: Bulzoni Editori, 1981); Giacomo Martini, ed., *Strategie e pratiche della censura* (Ferrara: Conference Proceedings, 1980); and Leopoldo Zurlo, *Memorie inutili: la censura teatrale nel ventennio* (Roma: Edizioni dell' Ateneo, 1952).

67. The role of the Catholic church and its associations in relation to censorship practices in Italy remains a promising yet largely unexplored terrain of study.

68. Laura, *La censura cinematografica,* 4–17. Brunetta lists a number of additional provisos, including "scenes or facts which can compromise political and economic interests, scenes or facts which can compromise the prestige and decorum of the army and the navy." Brunetta, *Storia del cinema,* 65.

69. De Grazia, *The Culture of Consent,* 7.

CHAPTER TWO. THE POLITICAL ECONOMY OF ITALIAN CINEMA, 1922–1943

1. The Acerbo Laws granted an automatic two-thirds of the seats in Parliament to whichever party or alliance of parties received the most votes in general elections providing that they polled at least 25 percent of the total votes cast.

2. For a detailed study of the early years of Fascism, see Adrian Lyttelton, *The Seizure of Power: Fascism in Italy, 1919–1929* (Princeton, NJ: Princeton University Press, 1973).

3. Victoria De Grazia, *The Culture of Consent: Mass Organization of Leisure in Fascist Italy* (New York: Cambridge University Press, 1981), 24–60.

4. The best treatment of this subject is Franco Monteleone, *La radio italiana nel periodo fascista, studio e documenti: 1922–1945* (Venezia: Marsilio Editori, 1976). See also Antonio Papa, *Storia politica della radio* (Napoli: Guida, 1978), and Phillip Cannistraro, *La fabbrica del consenso: fascismo e mass media* (Roma: Laterza Editori, 1975). It should be noted that state monopoly over radio was common in Europe during this period.

5. David Forgacs, *Italian Culture in the Industrial Era, 1880–1980* (Manchester: Manchester University Press, 1990), 60.

6. As I will discuss later, the state did in fact become quickly involved in nonfiction films, e.g., in newsreels and documentaries.

7. Elaine Mancini, *Struggles of the Italian Film Industry during Fascism, 1930–1935* (Ann Arbor, MI: UMI Research Press, 1985), 173.

8. See Claudio G. Segrè, *Italo Balbo: A Fascist Life* (Berkeley and Los Angeles: University of California Press, 1987), 114–43; Italo Balbo, *Diario, 1922* (Milano: Mondadori, 1932); Alberto Aquarone, "La milizia volontaria nello stato fascista," in *Il regime fascista*, ed. Alberto Aquarone and Maurizio Vernassa (Bologna: Mulino, 1974); and Manlio Cancogni, *Storia dello squadrismo* (Milano: Longanesi, 1959).

9. Lyttelton, *The Seizure of Power*, 268. Even after 1925, it could be argued that it wasn't until the Lateran pacts (between the government and the Catholic church) were signed in 1929 that fascism had truly consolidated its hold over state affairs. Even after the liquidation of the Liberal-dominated constitutional parliament and the suppression of left-wing and trade union opposition, the church remained as a potentially major source of institutional resistance to the regime.

10. "La politica degli struzzi," *Kines*, 9 September 1920. Cited in Gian Piero Brunetta, *Storia del cinema italiano, 1895–1945* (Roma: Editori Riuniti, 1979), 210.

11. Forgacs, *Italian Culture in the Industrial Era*, 56.

12. Brunetta, *Storia del cinema*, 221.

13. *Lo spettacolo in Italia* (Roma: SIAE, 1942), 91.

14. *La vita dello spettacolo in Italia nel decennio 1924–1933* (Roma: SIAE, 1934).

15. *L'eco del cinema* 2, no. 1 (January 1924).

16. Stefano Pittaluga, "Memoriale del II Congresso-Federazione Industriali e Commercianti," *Il Cinema Italiano*, 1 October 1925.

17. The concept of "consensus" is addressed at length by historian Renzo de Felice. See, in particular, *Mussolini il duce: gli anni del consenso, 1929–1936* (Torino: Einauldi Editore, 1974). In general terms, it signifies the hegemonic construction of agreement with and conformism to fascist policy. The building of a national consensus attempts the erasure of class, sexual, and regional differences and stipulates no position for "legitimate" dissent. See also Gabriele

Turi, *Il fascismo e il consenso degli intellettuali* (Bologna: Il Mulino, 1980); Benito Mussolini, "Cinematografia educativa," in *Scritti e discorsi di Benito Mussolini* (Milano: Hoepli, 1934), 271–72; and Alessandro Blasetti, "S.O.S.," *Lo spettacolo d'Italia*, 5 February 1928.

18. Regio Decreto-Legge no. 2275, 26 Oct. 1923. *Il cinematografo e il teatro nella legislazione fascista* (Roma: 1936).

19. Giampaolo Bernagozzi, *Il mito dell'immagine* (Bologna: Cooperativa Libraria Universitaria, 1983), 12. *Italianità* might be translated as "Italianness." In this context, it refers to the specific form of fascist idealization of national character. An excellent institutional history of LUCE can be found in Mino Argentieri, *L'occhio del regime: informazione e propaganda nel cinema del fascismo* (Firenze: Vallechi, 1979).

20. Regio Decreto-Legge no. 1000, 3 Apr. 1925. *Il cinematografo e il teatro nella legislazione fascista.*

21. Though passed on June 16, 1927, this law (Regio Decreto-Legge no. 1121) did not go into effect until October. *Il cinematografo e il teatro nella legislazione fascista.*

22. The number of Italian films over 1,000 meters in length released in 1929 = 20, 1930 = 8, 1931 = 2. Aldo Bernardini, *Archivio del cinema italiano*, vol. 1: *Il cinema muto, 1905–1931* (Roma: ANICA, 1991).

23. *Lo spettacolo in Italia nel 1936* (Roma: SIAE, 1936).

24. The representation of the strongman derives from the character of Maciste as originally portrayed by Bartolomeo Pagano in Pastrone's *Cabiria* (1914). The only substantial examination of the character and the genre is Alberto Farassino and Tatti Sanguinetti, eds., *Gli uomini forti* (Milano: Mazzotta, 1983).

25. Brunetta, *Storia del cinema*, 226.

26. Cited in Denis Mack Smith, *Italy: A Modern History* (Ann Arbor: University of Michigan Press, 1959), 418.

27. Cited in Simonetta Falasca-Zamponi, *Fascist Spectacle: The Aesthetics of Power in Mussolini's Italy* (Berkeley: University of California Press, 1997), 106. See also Sergio Raffaelli, *Le parole proibite: purismo di stato e regoloamentazione della pubblicità in Italia, 1812–1945* (Bologna: Mulino, 1982); Augusto Simonini, *Il linguaggio di Mussolini* (Milano: Nuovi Saggi Italiani, 1978); Gabriella Klein, *La politica linguistica del fascismo* (Bologna: Il Mulino, 1983); and Valentina Ruffin and Patrizia D'Agostino, eds., *Dialoghi di regime* (Roma: Bulzoni Editori, 1997).

28. From 1931 to mid-1932, a number of Hollywood studios, including MGM, experimented with the dubbing of Italian films. By the summer of 1932, Cines/Pittaluga had begun dubbing in Rome.

29. Mario Quargnolo, "La censura cinematografica da Giolitti a Mussolini," *Osservatore politico letterario*, July 1970.

30. As far as I can determine, the dubbed version of this film no longer exists. It has been reported, however, that the Italian version simply transposes Cooper's references to Italy with Scotland, to the Venetian lagoons with the Scottish lochs, etc. For a detailed account of the development of censorship under fascism, see Jean Gili, *Stato fascista e cinematografia: repressione e*

promozione (Roma: Bulzoni Editori, 1981). Gili also discusses the mechanisms for the negotiations between the private sector and the state.

31. Regio Decreto-Legge no. 1414, 5 Oct. 1933. *Il cinematografo e il teatro nella legislazione fascista*, 42.

32. Philip Cannistraro, *La fabbrica del consenso: fascismo e mass media* (Roma: Laterza, 1975), 422.

33. Raffaelli, *Le parole proibite*, 153. There were exceptions to this prohibition, most notably Alessandro Blasetti's *1860* (1934). But here, since the very topic of the film was the participation of nationwide representatives in the country's unification, dialect-speaking characters from different regions were indeed included as among Garibaldi's one thousand.

34. The term *rebirth* is used to describe this period in Italian film history in virtually all the literature, including Aprà, Brunetta, Hay, Landy, Leprohon, and Mancini.

35. In 1939 the 10 percent of box-office bonus was increased to 12 percent, and by 1942 the total number of released feature films would increase to 119.

36. Lorenzo Quaglietti, *Storia economica-politica del cinema italiano, 1945–1980* (Roma: Editori Riuniti, 1980), 12. It is also true that very few postwar Italian films are set outside Italy. But in the period immediately after World War II, the limitation was based less on ideological constraints than on the lack of financial resources. By the time of Italy's economic boom in the late fifties, the geographic scope of fiction films had considerably expanded.

37. Giuseppe Bottai, "Dichiarazioni a favore della legge," *Lo spettacolo italiano* 7, July/August 1931. Cited in Brunetta, *Storia del cinema*, 308.

38. Luigi Freddi, *Il cinema: Miti, esperienze e realtà di un regime totalitario* (Roma: L'Arnia, 1949), 66.

39. Pittaluga died in March 1931. For the next two years, Cines was administered by Ludovico Toeplitz, with Emilio Cecchi as its artistic director.

40. Lorenzo Quaglietti, "Il cinema degli anni trenta in Italia: primi elementi per una analisi politico-strutturale," in *Materiali sul cinema italiano, 1929–1943* (Roma: Quaderni della Mostra del Nuovo Cinema, 1975), 294–95; also cited in Jean Gili, *Stato facista e cinematografia*, 102–3.

41. Paulucci di Calboli was president of both agencies until 1940.

42. Freddi, *Il cinema*, 159. The most complete treatment on film censorship during fascism is Gili, *Stato fascista e cinematografia*. See also Ernesto G. Laura, *La censura cinematografica* (Roma: Edizioni Bianco e Nero, 1961).

43. Regio Decreto-Legge no. 1389. The law was named after Dino Alfieri, the head of the Ministry of Popular Culture. Brunetta, *Storia del cinema*, 296.

44. Libero Bizzari, "Lo stato e il cinema italiano," in *Sull'industria cinematografica italiana*, ed. Enrico Maghrelli (Venezia: Marsilio Editori, 1986), 290.

45. Bernardini, *Archivio del cinema italiano*, vol. 1, 112.

46. The project started as an idea by G. W. Pabst for another film with Louise Brooks. The screenplay was written by René Clair, who was also originally planned as director. Sergio Grmek Germani and Vittorio Martinelli, *Il cinema di Augusto Genina* (Gemona: Edizioni Biblioteca dell'Immagine, 1989), 218.

47. Quaglietti, "Il cinema degli anni trenta in Italia," 289, 303.

48. For a broad overview of the genre groupings of Italian fiction features during the thirties, see Sergio Grmek Germani, "Introduzione a una ricerca sui generi," in *Cinema italiano sotto il fascismo,* ed. Ricardo Redi (Venezia: Marsilio Editori, 1979), 81–98. See also the annotated filmography by Francesco Savio, *Ma l'amore no: realismo, formalismo, propaganda e telefoni bianchi nel cinema italiano di regime (1930–1943)* (Milano: Casa Editrice Sonzogno, 1975). According to Adriano Aprà and Jean Gili, 722 features were produced between 1929 and 1943; "Elenco di reperibilità," in *Nuovi materiali sul cinema italiano: 1929–1943,* vol. II (Roma: Mostra Internazionale del Nuovo Cinema, 1976), 141.

49. The Battle for Grain was a major attempt to modernize farming techniques to increase productivity and thereby reduce Italy's need to import basic foodstuffs.

50. In 1931, illiteracy was still above 20 percent nationally. In the rural areas, it was much higher. See Gastone Tassinari, *Contributo all definizione del concetto dei "analfabetismo"* (Milano: Istituto per gli Studi Economici e Sociali, 1962).

51. C. Legras, "Il cinema e l'esodo rurale," *Rivista internazionale del cinema educatore,* July 1932. The *Rivista* was published by the League of Nations' International Institute of Educational Cinema. Headquartered in Rome, it regularly featured Italian-authored editorials on the best educational and propagandistic role for newsreels.

52. De Grazia, *The Culture of Consent,* 152.

53. Claudio Fogu, *The Historic Imaginary: Politics of History in Fascist Italy* (Toronto: University of Toronto Press, 2003), 33–35. Barbara Spackman, *Fascist Virilities: Rhetoric, and Social Fantasy in Italy* (Minneapolis: University of Minnesota Press, 1996).

54. The highest number of American feature films imported into Italy in a single year was 220 in 1930. Quaglietti, "Il cinema degli anni trenta in Italia," 312.

55. Will H. Hays, *The Memoirs of Will H. Hays* (Garden City, NY: Doubleday & Company, 1955), 517–18.

56. Freddi, *Il cinema,* 66.

57. Gili, *Stato fascista,* 45–46.

58. The rare representations of criminality in Italian films are situated abroad. For example, Mario Camerini's *Batticuore* (1939) is set in France, and Carmine Gallone's *Harlem* (1943) is set in New York.

59. Cited in Gili, *Stato fascista,* 48.

60. Freddi, *Il cinema,* 177. More generally, two recent studies of the relationship between Italy and Hollywood make convincing cases for the interdependence of the two "national" cinemas. On the contribution of Italian Americans to *both* cinemas, see Giuliana Muscio's *Piccole italie, grandi schermi: scambi cinematografici tra Italia e Stati Uniti, 1895–1945* (Roma: Bulzoni Editori, 2004). On the regime's cinematic attempts to inculcate fascist values with the Italian American community, see Stefano Luconi and Guido Tintori, eds., *L'ombra lunga del fascio: canali di propaganda fascista per gli italiani d'America* (Milano: M & B Publishing, 2004).

CHAPTER THREE. LEISURE TIME, HISTORIOGRAPHY, AND SPECTATORSHIP

1. Renata Bianda, *Atleti in camicia nera: lo sport nell'italia di Mussolini* (Roma: Giovanni Volpe Editore, 1983), and Felice Fabrizio, *Storia dello sport in Italia: dalle società ginnastiche all'associazionismo di massa* (Rimini-Firenze: Guaraldi Editore, 1977).

2. Omar Calabrese, ed., *Modern Italy: Images and History of a National Identity*, vol. 2, *From Expansionism to the Second World War* (Milano: Electa Editrice, 1983), 500.

3. Victoria De Grazia, *The Culture of Consent: Mass Organization of Leisure in Fascist Italy* (New York: Cambridge University Press, 1981), 178-79.

4. Simonetta Falasca-Zamponi, *Fascist Spectacle: The Aesthetics of Power in Mussolini's Italy* (Berkeley: University of California Press, 1997), 25.

5. The Italian *squadristi* foreshadowed the deployment of street terror in Germany and Spain. Their campaigns consisted of ostentatious armed processions, murders, beatings, and fire-bombings targeted at both the socialist agrarian associations in the countryside and trade unions in the city. The first recognized manifestation of *squadrismo* was the burning of the offices of the socialist journal *Avanti!* on April 15, 1919. After the regime took power, they were formally incorporated into a Fascist Party Militia. See Adrian Lyttelton, *The Seizure of Power: Fascism in Italy, 1919-1929* (Princeton, NJ: Princeton University Press, 1973), and Mimmo Franzinelli, *Squadristi: protagonisti e tecnice della violenza fascista, 1919-1922* (Milano: Mondadori, 2003).

6. Karen Pinkus, *Bodily Regimes: Italian Advertising under Fascism* (Minneapolis: University of Minnesota Press, 1995), 87.

7. Gian Piero Brunetta, *Storia del cinema italiano, 1895-1945* (Roma: Editori Riuniti, 1979), 235-36.

8. The muscle-man films would resurface during Italy's economic boom of the early sixties in films such as *Ercole al centro della terra* (1961), *Ercole alla conquista di Atlantide* (1961), *Ercole contro i figli del sole* (1964), *Ercole contro Roma* (1964), *Ercole l'invincibile* (1965), *Ercole, Sansone, Maciste e Ursus gli invincibili* (1965), *Maciste contro il vampiro* (1961), *Maciste contro i mostri* (1962), *Maciste all'inferno* (1962), *Maciste contro Ercole nella valle dei guai* (1962), *Maciste alla corte dello Zar* (1964), and others. Unlike their predecessors, these films underscored the international identities of their stars, featuring either American actors or Italian actors with Americanized names, including Mark Forest, Rock Stevens, Alan Steel, Kirk Morris, and Gordon Mitchell. The most widely recognized of the group was, of course, Steve Reeves.

9. See Jean Gili, "Film storico e film in costume," in *Cinema italiano sotto il fascismo*, ed. Riccardo Redi (Venezia: Marsilio Editori, 1979).

10. It would be misleading to suggest that these films share identical ideological orientations. They are noted here primarily to map the representations of the state's official military presence, especially toward the end of the regime.

11. Falasca-Zamponi, *Fascist Spectacle*, 40.

12. "Mussolini sulla piana di Sabaudia," *Il Resto del Carlino*, 19 December 1936, front page.

13. Mabel Berezin, *Making the Fascist Self: The Political Culture of Interwar Italy* (Ithaca, NY: Cornell University Press, 1997), 99.

14. Though published in *Bianco e Nero* in 1939, the essays were written after special screenings of the film at a Roman grade school on November 16, 1937. *Bianco e Nero*, August 1939, 18–22.

15. In Italian the wedding ring is a *fede*, which also literally translates as "faith."

16. *Bianco e Nero*, August 1939, 6.

17. See the excellent comparison between Italian fascist and American New Deal urban planning in Diane Ghirardo's *Building New Communities: New Deal America and Fascist Italy* (Princeton, NJ: Princeton University Press, 1989).

18. Borden W. Painter, *Mussolini's Rome: Rebuilding the Eternal City* (New York: Palgrave Macmillan, 2005), 33.

19. Carlo Lizzani, *Il cinema italiano* (Firenze: Parenti, 1961), 69.

20. Galeazzo Ciano, "Speech to the Senate on Fascist Cinematography," 22 May 1936. Cited in Claudio Carabba, *Il cinema del ventennio nero* (Firenze: Vallecchi Editore, 1974), 124–25.

21. See A. Crispo, *Le ferrovie italiane: storia politica e economica* (Milano: Dottor A. Giuffre Editore, 1940).

22. Berezin, *Making the Fascist Self*, 66.

23. In 1933, the luxury liner *Rex* established the world record for the fastest Atlantic crossing.

24. Michel de Certeau, *The Practice of Everyday Life* (Berkeley: University of California Press, 1984), 111.

25. Given especially the paucity of new Italian features at the end of the twenties, re-release of silent films with added sound was not an entirely uncommon occurrence.

26. James Hay, *Popular Film Culture in Fascist Italy: The Passing of the Rex* (Bloomington: Indiana University Press, 1987), 44.

27. De Certeau, *The Practice of Everyday Life*, 114.

28. De Grazia, *Culture of Consent*, 180–81.

29. This scene recalls a previous performance of an American character by Vittorio De Sica. Six years earlier, he had played a Mr. Brown, an American automotive industrialist, in Baldassare Negroni's extremely popular *Due cuori felici* (1932). In this earlier film De Sica signifies *American* by affecting a pronounced American accent as he speaks Italian.

30. The team of De Sica/Norris starred in six feature films from 1932 to 1937. With publicity strategies similar to those of the Hollywood star system, their presence as a couple in each of the individual films was highlighted in fan magazines, posters, and trailers.

31. Stephen Gundle, "Film Stars and Society in Fascist Italy," in *Re-viewing Fascism: Italian Cinema, 1922–1943*, ed. Jacqueline Reich and Piero Garofalo (Bloomington: University of Indiana Press, 2002), 333.

32. Victoria De Grazia, *How Fascism Ruled Women: Italy, 1922–1945* (Berkeley: University of California Press, 1992), 211–12.

33. I will discuss other sites of supratextual dialogue between the Italian and American cinemas in the following chapters.

CHAPTER FOUR. ITALY AND AMERICA

1. Antonio Stella, *Some Aspects of Italian Immigration to the United States* (New York: G. P. Putnam's Sons, 1924).

2. Lorenzo Quaglietti, "Il cinema degli anni trenta in Italia: primi elementi per una analisi politico-strutturale," in *Materiali sul cinema italiano, 1929–1943* (Roma: Quaderni della Mostra Internazionale del Nuovo Cinema a Pesaro, 1976), 288, 312.

3. The seminal studies of film publications during the fascist period include Lucilla Albano, "Volontà-impossibilità del cinema fascista: riviste e periodici degli anni trenta in Italia," and Vito Zagarrio, "Tra intervento e tendenza: le riviste culturali e il cinema del fascismo," in *Nuovi materiali sul cinema italiano, 1929–1943*, vol. 2 (Roma: Mostra Internazionale del Nuovo Cinema, 1976); Anna Pannicali, *Le riviste del periodo fascista* (Messina: Tangenti, 1978); and Davide Turconi and Camillo Bassotto, *Il cinema nelle riviste italiane dalle origini ad oggi* (Venezia: Edizioni della Mostra del Cinema, 1973). One of the most useful examinations of the Hollywood star system is Richard deCordova, *Picture Personalities: The Emergence of the Star System in America* (Urbana: University of Illinois Press, 1990).

4. David Forgacs, *Italian Culture in the Industrial Era, 1880–1980* (Manchester: Manchester University Press, 1990), 44.

5. In a letter to Mussolini dated March 17, 1923, Arnaldo Mondadori explained that the magazine was "intended to illustrate chronologically the great Fascist movement and which, subsequently collected in a volume, will constitute the most perfect documentation." Cited in Forgacs, *Italian Culture*, 58.

6. Ibid., 27.

7. Cited in Gian Piero Brunetta, *Cinema italiano tra le due guerre: fascismo e politica cinematografica* (Milano: Mursia Editore, 1975), 37.

8. The subject of the relationship between neorealist films and realist literature has received exhaustive attention. Some of the principal studies include Guido Fink, "Parlare Americano," in *Cinema e letteratura del neorealismo,* ed. Giorgio Tinazzi and Marina Zancan (Venezia: Marsilio Editori, 1983); David Overbey, ed., *Springtime in Italy: A Reader in Neorealism* (Hamden, CT: Archon Books, 1978); Lino Miccichè, ed., *Il neorealismo cinematografico italiano* (Venezia: Marsilio Editori, 1975); Massimo Mida and Lorenzo Quaglietti, eds., *Dai telefoni bianchi al neorealismo* (Roma: Laterza Editori, 1980); Donald Heiney, *Three Italian Novelists: Moravia, Pavese, Vittorini* (Ann Arbor: University of Michigan Press, 1968); and Giovanni Falaschi, ed., *Realtà e retorica: la letteratura del neorealismo italiano* (Firenze: G. D'Anna, 1977).

9. Giaime Pintor, *Il sangue d'Europa* (Torino: Einauldi, 1950), 159.

10. Each of these films was very successful when released in Italy. Guglielmo Giannini, "Dobbiamo morire? [Do we have to die?]," *Kines* 1, 5 January 1930.

11. The best study of the American reception of Italian fascism is John Diggins, *Mussolini and Fascism: The View from America* (Princeton, NJ: Princeton University Press, 1972).

12. Irving S. Cobb, "A Little Big Man," *Cosmopolitan* (January 1927), 145–46, cited in Diggins, *Mussolini and Fascism*, 63.

13. See Gianni Bertone, *I figli d'Italia si chiamano Balilla* (Firenze: Guaraldi, 1975). The letter to Mussolini is cited in Adelaide Frabotta, "Emigrati italiani e propaganda fascista attraverso la Produzione Americana," in *Il cinema dei dittatori: Mussolini, Stalin, Hitler*, ed. Renzo Renzi (Bologna: Grafis Edizioni, 1992), 113.

14. Although the film's credits do not name a director, Ulmer claimed to have directed the film for Columbia in 1932. The reference is located in Ulmer's biographical file at the Margaret Herrick Library of the Academy of Motion Picture Arts and Sciences (Beverly Hills, California).

15. The notion that the goals of the overall project were shared between the fascist regime and Columbia can also be seen in the organization of the promotional contest. Whereas the government paid for the costs of the transatlantic cruise aboard the *Rex*, the studio covered the living expenses of the twenty-four winners during their two weeks in Italy.

16. The emphasis is mine. *Columbia Beacon*, 4 January 1933.

17. Luigi Freddi, *Il cinema: Miti, esperienze e realtà di un regime totalitario* (Roma: L'Arnia, 1949), 169.

18. Adelaide Frabotta describes the campaign based on actual letters written to the Foreign Ministry, a selection of which are held in its archive under the category "Affari Politici Inventario 1931–1945." *Il cinema dei dittatori*, 112, 114.

19. "Giovanezza" was the anthem of the *arditi*, originally D'Annunzio's assault troops during the occupation of Fiume. The *arditi* later formed the backbone of the fascist *squadristi* and were responsible for introducing a number of fascist icons and customs, including the cudgel, the black shirts, the dagger, and the Roman salute. A. V. Savona and M. L. Straniero, *Canti dell'Italia fascista (1919–1945)* (Milano: Aldo Garzanti Editore, 1979), 53.

20. As I previously discussed, the representation of the state as social engineer, as literal architect of new urban topographies, opens up a range of provocative issues. How, for example, can we characterize the fascist social order in relationship to the regime's deployment of new urban plans? Again, see Diane Ghirardo's comparison of fascist urban design with New Deal reconstruction programs: *Building New Communities: New Deal America and Fascist Italy* (Princeton, NJ: Princeton University Press, 1989).

21. Another case is the short documentary *Mussolini: A Character Study in Motion Pictures* (circa 1935). A Hullinger Production, directed by John Pauls, the film is particularly interesting for its inclusion of Mussolini family home movies.

22. Ghirardo, *Building New Communities*, 41.

23. David Forgacs, "The Mass Media and the Question of a National Community in Italy," in *The Politics of Italian National Identity: A Multidisciplinary Perspective*, ed. Gino Bedani and Bruce Haddock (Cardiff: University of Wales Press, 2000), 144.

24. A good overview of his acting and directing career is Francesco Bolzoni, *Quando De Sica era Mister Brown* (Torino: Edizioni Radiotelevisione Italiana, 1984).

25. The film was scripted by Guglielmo Giannini, who in 1930 decried the importation of *American Kultur*, which would turn Italy into an "intellectual colony." Giannini, "Dobbiamo morire?"

26. The literal translation of the title would be *Red Joe*. In both films, the principal character is a gangster named Joe.

27. Sergio Grmek Germani, *Mario Camerini* (Firenze: La Nuova Italia, 1980), 1–10.

28. See the excellent filmography in Germani's *Mario Camerini*. For a more extensive study of Camerini's relationship to the Hollywood cinema, see my "Camerini et Hollywood: questions d'identité (nationale)," in *Mario Camerini,* ed. Alberto Farassino (Bruxelles: Editions Yellow Now, 1992). This career of exchange between the two cinemas led up to an extraordinary collaboration between Kirk Douglas as Hollywood star and Camerini as director in his 1954 version of *Ulysses.*

29. Geoffrey Nowell-Smith, "The Italian Cinema under Fascism," in *Rethinking Italian Fascism: Capitalism, Populism, and Culture,* ed. David Forgacs (London: Lawrence and Wishart, 1986).

30. *Los Angeles Examiner,* 3 September 1937. The print in question was part of the Fox studio collection, which was acquired by the UCLA Film and Television Archive in 1972.

31. The issue of star systems would prove highly significant for the formation of the Italian film industry immediately after World War II. The neorealist movement attempted, at least for a time, to establish its cultural specificity in part by avoiding the use of actors recognizable as Italian stars. The nonprofessional actors were selected, instead, for their recognizability within the social realities of postwar Italy. In the early 1960s, the cinema would turn to a new form of international competition with the Hollywood cinema by importing American actors into Italian film productions, including Broderick Crawford, Aldo Ray, Anthony Quinn, Clint Eastwood, and Richard Basehart, among others.

32. Paul Willemen, "Notes on Subjectivity: On Reading Edward Branigan's 'Subjectivity under Siege,'" *Screen* 19, no. 1, Spring 1978. This passage from Willemen's article is cited by Sue Clayton and Jonathan Curling in their "On Authorship," *Screen* 20, no. 1, Spring 1979. Clayton and Curling's discussion of independent cinema in Great Britain leverages conceptual distinctions regarding authorship made by Michel Foucault in "What Is an Author?" which was also published in this issue of *Screen.* While Willemen and Clayton and Curling begin with the subject as inscribed within the text and move outward, the process is actually bidirectional and much more dynamic. The audience becomes a spectator equally as it is prepared and addressed prior to its entry as subject into the text.

CHAPTER FIVE. THE FASCIST CODEX

1. David Horn, *Social Bodies: Science, Reproduction, and Italian Modernity* (Princeton, NJ: Princeton University Press, 1994), 77–78.

2. Victoria De Grazia, *How Fascism Ruled Women: Italy, 1922–1945* (Berkeley: University of California Press, 1992).

3. Claudia Lazzaro, "Forging a Visible Fascist Nation: Strategies for Fusing Past and Present," in *Donatello among the Blackshirts: History and Modernity*

in the Visual Culture of Fascist Italy, ed. Claudia Lazzaro and Roger Crum (Ithaca, NY: Cornell University Press, 2005), 16.

4. Carl Ipsen, *Dictating Demography: The Problem of Population in Fascist Italy* (Cambridge: Cambridge University Press, 1996), 119.

5. Ibid., 88.

6. It would be interesting to pursue how the orchestration of discourse under fascism addressed gender differences. Several valuable points of departure for such a study include Maria Antonietta Macciocchi, *La Donna Nera: "consenso" femminile e fascismo* (Milano: Feltrinelli, 1976), and Victoria De Grazia, *How Fascism Ruled Women.*

7. Michael Warner, "The Mass Public and the Mass Subject," in *Habermas and the Public Sphere,* ed. Craig Calhoun (Cambridge, MA: MIT Press, 1992).

8. Ennio Di Nolfo, "Intimations of Neorealism in the Fascist *Ventennio,*" in *Re-viewing Fascism: Italian Cinema, 1922–1943,* ed. Jacqueline Reich and Piero Garofalo (Bloomington: Indiana University Press, 2002), 83–104.

9. Lorenzo Quaglietti, *Storia economica-politica del cinema italiano, 1945–1980* (Roma: Editori Riuniti, 1980).

10. Di Nolfo, 97.

11. Angelo Restivo, *The Cinema of Economic Miracles: Visuality and Modernization in the Italian Art Film* (Durham, NC: Duke University Press, 2002), 23.

12. Mino Argentieri, *L'occhio del regime: informazione e propaganda nel cinema del fascismo* (Firenze: Vallecchi Editore, 1979), 184–85.

13. Quaglietti, *Storia economica-politica,* 38.

14. Ibid., 245.

15. Stephen Gundle, *Between Hollywood and Moscow: The Italian Communists and the Challenge of Mass Culture, 1943–1991* (Durham, NC: Duke University Press, 2000), 32.

16. Mira Liehm, *Passion and Defiance: Film in Italy from 1942 to the Present* (Berkeley: University of California Press, 1984), 57.

17. In English-language versions, this process is literalized by the superimposition of a graphic map of the peninsula that is progressively filled in as the film's narrative moves northward.

18. It is interesting to note that *Paisà* was produced and released at a time when left-wing labor groups began to reclaim their role in the organization of leisure-time activities. And, as part of an overall trend to rename fascist institutions, the Opera Nazionale del Dopolavoro (OND) was renamed E.N.A.L, the National Workers' Assistance Board.

19. Giuliana Muscio, "Paisà/Paisan," in *The Cinema of Italy,* ed. Giorgio Bertellini (London: Wallflower Press, 2004), 37.

20. David Forgacs, *Italian Culture in the Industrial Era, 1880–1980: Cultural Industries, Politics and the Public* (Manchester: Manchester University Press, 1990), 96. The fundamental study of Italian radio history is Franco Monteleone, *La radio italiana nel periodo fascista: studio e documenti, 1922–1945* (Venezia: Marsilio Editori, 1976).

21. Quaglietti, *Storia economica-politica,* 243.

22. See Kris Ravetto, *The Unmasking of Fascist Aesthetics* (Minneapolis: University of Minnesota Press, 2001).

EPILOGUE

1. In 1993 the Italian Communist Party (PCI) became the Democratic Party of the Left (PDS).

2. The phrase *panem et circenses* literally means "bread and circuses." It was first used by Juvenal in his tenth satire to refer to the Roman public's distraction from social responsibilities by its involvement with mass entertainment. For a sociological overview of its usage as a concept of cultural criticism, see Patrick Brantlinger, *Bread and Circuses: Theories of Mass Culture* (Ithaca, NY: Cornell University Press, 1983).

3. Over three hundred officially recognized film festivals are held each year in Italy.

4. Representations and reappropriations of the Historical are very common over the entire history of Italian cinema. From the very outset, films such as Alberini's *La presa di Roma* (1905), Guazzoni's *La caduta di Troia* (1910) and *Quo Vadis?* (1912), Caserini's *Gli ultimi giorni di Pompei* (1913), and Pastrone's *Cabiria* (1914) serve as benchmarks in the evolution of film language in Italy. Indeed, the strongman Maciste-Sansone-Ercole cycle often selected historical settings for its narrative framework and was the only continually successful grouping of Italian films from the teens and throughout the industry's complete decline in the 1920s. As I discussed earlier, the cycle was born with Bartolomeo Pagano's 1914 performance as Maciste in *Cabiria*. Some of its films that employ historical backdrops include *La trilogia di Maciste* (1920), *Il ponte dei sospiri* (1921), *Ursus* (1922), and *Maciste imperatore* (1924).

The explicit evocation of History continued throughout the period of fascism, even as some of the films inserted themselves into an ideological re-evocation and revision of classical Roman history. The muscle-man film had a pronounced resurgence in the early 1960s, with Steve Reeves taking over the mantle of Bartolomeo Pagano. The insistent reconstruction of classical settings even found its way into television commercials with Sergio Leone's paean to a Renault chained to the floor of the Colosseum.

5. Eric Partridge, *Origins: A Short Etymological Dictionary of Modern English* (New York: Greenwich House, 1983), 99.

6. Steven Heath, "Narrative Space," in *Questions of Cinema* (Bloomington: Indiana University Press, 1981), 44.

7. Davide Turconi, *La stampa cinematografica in Italia e negli Stati Uniti d'America dalle origini al 1930* (Pavia: Amministrazione Provinciale di Pavia, 1977).

8. Marla Stone, *The Patron State: Culture & Politics in Fascist Italy* (Princeton, NJ: Princeton University Press, 1998), 246.

Selected Bibliography

Alicata, Mario. *Ambiente e società nel racconto cinematografico*. Roma: Cinema Nuovo, 1942.

Allardyce, Gilbert. *The Place of Fascism in European History*. Englewood Cliffs, NJ: Prentice Hall, 1971.

Almanacco degli almanacchi: potere e cultura in Italia, 1925–1942. Milano: Bompiani, 1976.

Althusser, Louis. *Lenin and Philosophy and Other Essays*. New York: Monthly Review Press, 1971.

Anderson, Benedict. *Imagined Communities: Reflections on the Origin and Spread of Nationalism*. London: Verso, 1983.

Angotti, Rosario. *Osservazioni sul cinema*. Roma: Cinestudio ABC, 1943.

Anni Trenta: arte e cultura in Italia. Milano: Nuove Edizioni Gabriele Mazzotta, 1982.

Antonicelli, Franco. *Trent'anni di storia italiana (1915–1945)*. Torino: Reprints Giulio Einauldi Editore, 1975.

Aprà, Adriano, ed. *Alessandro Blasetti: scritti sul cinema*. Venezia: Marsilio Editori, 1982.

Aprà, Adriano, and Patrizia Pistagnesi, eds. *The Fabulous Thirties: Italian Cinema 1929–1944*. Milano: Gruppo Editoriale Electa, 1979.

Aprà, Adriano, and Riccardo Redi, eds. *Sole: soggetto, sceneggiatura, note per la realizzazione*. Roma: Di Giacomo Editore, 1985.

Aquarrone, Alberto. *L'organizzazione dello stato totalitario*. Torino: Einauldi Editore, 1965.

Araldi, Vinicio. *Cinema, arma del nostro tempo*. Milano: La Prora, 1939.

Arbizzani, Luigi, and Alberto Caltabano, eds. *Storia dell'antifascismo italiano*. Roma: 1964.

Argentieri, Mino. *La censura nel cinema italiano*. Roma: Editori Riuniti, 1974.

———. *Il cinema italiano e il risorgimento: passato ridotto*. Firenze: La Casa Usher, 1982.

———. *L'occhio del regime: informazione e propaganda nel cinema del fascismo*. Firenze: Vallecchi Editore, 1979.

Aristarco, Guido. *Miti e realtà nel cinema italiano*. Milano: Il Saggiatore, 1961.

———. *Storia delle tematiche del film*. Firenze: Einauldi Editore, 1963.

Baffico, Mario. *Dei e semidei del '900*. Milano: Armondo Gorlini, 1930.

Baldelli, Pio. *Bottai: il fascismo come rivoluzione del capitale*. Bologna: Cappelli, 1978.

Barbera, Alberto, and Roberto Turigliatto, eds. *Leggere il cinema*. Milano: Mondadori, 1978.

Barthes, Roland. *The Pleasure of the Text*. Paris: Éditions du Seuil, 1973.

———. *S/Z*. Paris: Éditions du Seuil, 1970.

Bedani, Gino, and Bruce Haddock, eds. *The Politics of Italian National Identity: A Multidisciplinary Perspective*. Cardiff: University of Wales Press, 2000.

Ben-Ghiat, Ruth. *Fascist Modernities: Italy, 1922–1945*. Berkeley: University of California Press, 2001.

Berezin, Mabel. *Making the Fascist Self: The Political Culture of Interwar Italy*. Ithaca, NY: Cornell University Press, 1997.

Bernagozzi, Giampaolo. *Il mito dell'immagine*. Bologna: Cooperativa Libraria Universitaria, 1983.

Bernardini, Aldo. *Archivio del cinema italiano*, vol. 1: *Il cinema muto, 1905–1931*. Roma: ANICA, 1991.

———. *Cinema muto italiano: arte, divismo e mercato*. Bari: Editori Laterza, 1981.

Bertellini, Giorgio, ed. *The Cinema of Italy*. London: Wallflower Press, 2004.

Bertieri, Claudio. *30 anni di cinema italiano*. Genova: Circolo Conigliano, 1960.

Bertone, Gianni. *I figli d'Italia si chiamano Balilla*. Firenze: Guaraldi, 1975.

Bianchi, Pietro, and Franco Berutti. *Storia del cinema*. Milano: Garzanti, 1961.

Bianda, Renata. *Atleti in camicia nera: lo sport nell'Italia di Mussolini*. Roma: Giovanni Volpe Editore, 1983.

Binchy, Daniel. *Church and State in Fascist Italy*. London: Oxford University Press, 1941.

Biondi, Dino. *La fabbrica del duce*. Firenze: Vallecchi, 1973.

Bolzoni, Francesco. *Un anno di cinema italiano: la teoria e la pratica*. Venezia: Edizioni La Biennale di Venezia, 1976.

———. *Il progetto imperiale: cinema e cultura nell'Italia del 1936*. Venezia: Edizioni La Biennale di Venezia, 1976.

———. *Quando De Sica era Mister Brown*. Torino: Edizioni Radiotelevisione Italiana, 1984.

Bondanella, Peter. *Italian Cinema: From Neorealism to the Present*. New York: Frederick Ungar Publishing Co., 1983.

Bordoni, C. *Cultura e propaganda nell'Italia fascista*. Messina-Firenze: D'Anna, 1975.

Brancati, R. *La porpora e il nero*. Milano: Edizioni Bianco e Nero, 1961.

Brantlinger, Patrick. *Bread and Circuses: Theories of Mass Culture.* Ithaca, NY: Cornell University Press, 1983.

Brunetta, Gian Piero. *Cinema italiano tra le due guerre: fascismo e politica cinematografica.* Milano: Mursia Editore, 1975.

———. *Intelletuali, cinema, e propaganda tra le due guerre.* Bologna: Casa Editrice Patron, 1973.

———. *Storia del cinema italiano, 1895–1945.* Roma: Editori Riuniti, 1979.

Calabrese, Omar, ed. *Modern Italy: Images and History of a National Identity,* vol. 2, *From Expansionism to the Second World War.* Milano: Electa Editrice, 1983.

Caldiron, Orio. *Il lungo viaggio del cinema italiano.* Padova: Marsilio Editori, 1965.

Calendoli, G. *Materiali per una storia del cinema italiano.* Parma: Macari, 1967.

Calhoun, Craig, ed. *Habermas and the Public Sphere.* Cambridge, MA: MIT Press, 1992.

Cannistraro, Philip V. *La fabbrica del consenso: fascismo e mass media.* Roma: Laterza Editori, 1975.

Carabba, Claudio. *Il cinema del ventennio nero.* Firenze: Vallecchi Editore, 1974.

———. *Il fascismo e fumetti.* Firenze: Guaraldi, 1973.

Carsten, F.L. *The Rise of Fascism.* Berkeley: University of California Press, 1967.

Casadio, Gianfranco. *Il grigio e il nero: spettacolo e propaganda nel cinema italiano degli anni trenta, 1931–1943.* Ravenna: Longo Editore, 1989.

Caudo, Ernesto. *Il film italiano.* Roma: Nuova Europa, 1932.

Cavazza, Fabio Luca, and Stephen R. Graubard, eds. *Il caso italiano.* Milano: Garzanti, 1974.

Cecchi, Emilio. *America amara.* Milano: Mondadori, 1940.

Chabod, Federico. *A History of Italian Fascism.* New York: Fertig, 1975.

Chemotti, Saveria, ed. *Gli intellettuali in trincea: politica e cultura del dopoguerra.* Padova: CLEUP, 1977.

Chiarini, Luigi. *Cinema quinto potere.* Bari: Laterza Editori, 1954.

———. *Il film nella battaglia delle idee.* Milano: Fratelli Bocca, 1954.

Clough, Shepard B. *The Economic History of Modern Italy.* New York: Columbia University Press, 1964.

Colombini, Umberto. *Hollywood: visione che incanta.* Milano: La Prora, 1930.

Corducci, N. *Gli intelletuali e l'ideologia americana nell'Italia degli anni 30.* Manduria: Lacaita, 1973.

Costa, Antonio, ed. *La meccanica del visibile: il cinema delle origini in Europa.* Firenze: La Casa Usher, 1983.

Crispo, A. *Le ferrovie italiane: storia politica e economica.* Milano: Dottor A. Giuffre Editore, 1940.

Deakin, F.W. *The Brutal Friendship.* London: Penguin Books, 1962.

Debord, Guy. *La société du spectacle.* Paris: Éditions Buchet-Chastel, 1967.

de Certeau, Michel. *The Practice of Everyday Life.* Berkeley: University of California Press, 1984.

DeCordova, Richard. *Picture Personalities: The Emergence of the Star System in America*. Urbana: University of Illinois Press, 1990.

De Felice, Renzo. *Mussolini il duce: gli anni del consenso, 1929–1936*. Torino: Einauldi Editore, 1974.

———. *Storia fotografica del fascismo*. Roma: Laterza Editori, 1982.

De Grazia, Victoria. *The Culture of Consent: Mass Organization of Leisure in Fascist Italy*. New York: Cambridge University Press, 1981.

———. *How Fascism Ruled Women: Italy, 1922–1945*. Berkeley: University of California Press, 1992.

Del Buono, Oreste, and Lietta Tornabuoni. *Era Cinecittà: vita, morte e miracoli di una fabbrica di film*. Milano: Bompiani, 1979.

Delzell, Charles. *Mussolini's Enemies: The Italian Anti-Fascist Resistance*. New York: Fertig, 1971.

De Mauro, Tullio. *Storia linguistica dell'Italia unita*. Bari: Laterza Editori, 1979.

DiCarlo, Carlo. *Il cortometraggio italiano antifascista*. Torino: Istituto di Cinema, 1951.

Diggins, John P. *Mussolini and Fascism: The View From America*. Princeton, NJ: Princeton University Press, 1972.

Doletti, Mino. *Almanacco del cinematografo 1931*. Bologna: Cappelli, 1930.

Ebenstein, William. *Fascist Italy*. New York: American Book Company, 1939.

L'economia italiana tra le due guerre. Milano: IPSOA, 1984.

Fabrizio, Felice. *Storia dello sport in Italia: dalle società ginnastiche all'associazionismo di massa*. Rimini-Firenze: Guaraldi Editore, 1977.

Faenza, R., and M. Fini. *Gli americani in Italia*. Milano: Feltrinelli, 1976.

Falasca-Zamponi, Simonetta. *Fascist Spectacle: The Aesthetics of Power in Mussolini's Italy*. Berkeley: University of California Press, 1997.

Falaschi, Giovanni, ed. *Realtà e retorica: la letteratura del neorealismo italiano*. Firenze: G. D'Anna, 1977.

Faldini, Franca, and Goffredo Fofi. *L'avventurosa storia del cinema italiano raccontata dai suoi protagonisti 1935–1959*. Milano: Feltrinelli, 1979.

Farassino, Alberto, ed. *Mario Camerini*. Bruxelles: Editions Yellow Now, 1992.

Farassino, Alberto, and Tatti Sanguinetti, eds. *Lux Film: esthétique et système d'un studio italien*. Locarno: Edizione du Festival International du Film Locarno, 1991.

———, eds. *Gli uomini forti*. Milano: Mazzotta, 1983.

Fermi, Laura. *Mussolini*. Chicago: University of Chicago Press, 1961.

Fernandez, D. *Il mito dell'america negli intellettuali italiani*. Caltanisetta: S. Sciascia Editore, 1969.

Ferrara, Giuseppe. *Il nuovo cinema italiano*. Firenze: Le Monier, 1964.

Finer, Herman. *Mussolini's Italy*. London: Frank Cass and Co., 1964.

Fogu, Claudio. *The Historic Imaginary: Politics of History in Fascist Italy*. Toronto: University of Toronto Press, 2003.

Forgacs, David. *Italian Culture in the Industrial Era, 1880–1980: Cultural Industries, Politics and the Public*. Manchester: Manchester University Press, 1990.

Forgacs, David, and Robert Lumley, eds. *Italian Cultural Studies: An Introduction*. Oxford: Oxford University Press, 1996.

Forgacs, David, and Geoffrey Nowell-Smith, eds. *Antonio Gramsci: Selections from Cultural Writings*. Translated by William Boelhower. Cambridge, MA: Harvard University Press, 1985.

Franzinelli, Mimmo. *Squadristi: protagonisti e tecnice della violenza fascista, 1919–1922*. Milano: Mondadori, 2003.

Fraser, J. *Italy: Society in Crisis/Society in Transformation*. London: Routledge and Keegan Paul, 1981.

Freddi, Luigi. *Il cinema: Miti, esperienze e realtà di un regime totalitario*. Roma: L'Arnia, 1949.

Furno, Mariella, and Renzo Renzi, eds. *Il neorealismo nel fascismo*. Bologna: Edizioni Tipografi Compositori, 1982.

Garibaldi, Andrea, and Roberto Giannarelli, eds. *Qui comincia l'avventura del signor*. Firenze: La Casa Usher, 1984.

Geller, Ernst. *Nations and Nationalism*. Ithaca, NY: Cornell University Press, 1983.

Germani, Gino. *Authoritarianism, Fascism, and National Populism*. New Brunswick, NJ: Transaction Books, 1978.

Germani, Sergio Grmek. *Mario Camerini*. Firenze: La Nuova Italia, 1980.

Germani, Sergio Grmek, and Vittorio Martinelli. *Il cinema di Augusto Genina*. Gemona: Edizioni Biblioteca dell'Immagine, 1989.

Gerosa, Guido. *Da Giarabub a Salo: il cinema durante la guerra*. Milano: Edizione di Cinema Nuovo, 1963.

Ghione, Emilio. *Le cinema italien*. Paris: Alcan, 1930.

Ghirardo, Diane. *Building New Communities: New Deal America and Fascist Italy*. Princeton, NJ: Princeton University Press, 1989.

Gilberti, G. *Legislazione italiana per la cinematografia*. Sienna: Edizioni Ex-combattenti, 1942.

Gili, Jean A. *Stato fascista e cinematografia: repressione e promozione*. Roma: Bulzoni Editori, 1981.

Ginsborg, Paul. *A History of Contemporary Italy: Society and Politics, 1943–1988*. London: Penguin Books, 1990.

———. *Italy and Its Discontents: Family, Civil Society, State, 1980–2001*. New York: Palgrave Macmillan, 2003.

Giuliani, Gianna. *Le strisce interiori: cinema italiano e psicoanalisi*. Roma: Bulzoni Editori, 1980.

Gori, Gianfranco. *Alessandro Blasetti*. Firenze: La Nuova Italia, 1983.

———. *Patria Diva: la storia d'Italia nei film del ventennio*. Firenze: La Casa Usher, 1988.

Grammantieri, Tullio. *Pubblicità cinematografica*. Roma: Cordelia, 1938.

Gregor, James A. *The Ideology of Fascism*. New York: Free Press, 1969.

Guarnieri, F. *50 anni di narrativa in Italia*. Firenze: Parenti, 1955.

Guerin, Daniel. *Fascism and Big Business*. New York: Pathfinder Press, 1973.

Guidorizzi, Ernesto. *La narrativa italiana e il cinema*. Firenze: Sansoni, 1973.

Gundle, Stephen. *Between Hollywood and Moscow: The Italian Communists and the Challenge of Mass Culture, 1943–1991*. Durham, NC: Duke University Press, 2000.

Habermas, Jürgen. *The Structural Transformation of the Public Sphere: An Inquiry into a Category of Bourgeois Society.* Cambridge, MA: MIT Press, 1989.

Hall, Stuart, Dorothy Hobson, Andrew Lowe, and Paul Willis, eds. *Culture, Language, Media: Working Papers in Cultural Studies 1972–1979.* Birmingham, UK: Centre for Contemporary Cultural Studies, 1980.

Hamilton, Alistair. *The Appeal of Fascism: Intellectuals and Fascism.* New York: MacMillan, 1971.

Hay, James. *Popular Film Culture in Fascist Italy: The Passing of the Rex.* Bloomington: Indiana University Press, 1987.

Hays, Will H. *The Memoirs of Will H. Hays.* Garden City, NY: Doubleday & Company, 1955.

Heath, Steven. *Questions of Cinema.* Bloomington: Indiana University Press, 1981.

Heiney, Donald. *America in Modern Italian Literature.* New Brunswick, NJ: Rutgers University Press, 1964.

———. *Three Italian Novelists: Moravia, Pavese, Vittorini.* Ann Arbor, MI: University of Michigan Press, 1968.

Holquist, Michael, ed. *The Dialogic Imagination: Four Essays by Mikhail Bakhtin.* Austin: University of Texas Press, 1992.

Horn, David. *Social Bodies: Science, Reproduction, and Italian Modernity.* Princeton, NJ: Princeton University Press, 1994.

Hughes, H. Stuart. *The United States and Italy.* Cambridge, MA: Harvard University Press, 1965.

Ipsen, Carl. *Dictating Demography: The Problem of Population in Fascist Italy.* Cambridge: Cambridge University Press, 1996.

Jarrat, Vernon. *The Italian Cinema.* London: Falcon Press, 1971.

Jemolo, Carlo A. *Church and State in Italy: 1850–1950.* Oxford: Blackwell, 1960.

Jones, Tobias. *The Dark Heart of Italy: Travels through Time and Space across Italy.* London: Faber and Faber, 2003.

Kelly, John D., and Martha Kaplan. *Represented Communities: Fiji and World Decolonization.* Chicago: University of Chicago Press, 2001.

Klein, Gabriella. *La politica linguistica del fascismo.* Bologna: Il Mulino, 1983.

Lanaro, Silvio. *L'Italia nuova: identità e sviluppo 1861–1988.* Torino: Einauldi Editore, 1988.

Landy, Marcia. *Fascism in Film: The Italian Commercial Cinema, 1931–1943.* Princeton, NJ: Princeton University Press, 1986.

Laura, Ernesto. *La censura cinematografica.* Roma: Edizioni Bianco e Nero, 1961.

Lazzaro, Claudia, and Roger Crum, eds. *Donatello among the Blackshirts: History and Modernity in the Visual Culture of Fascist Italy.* Ithaca, NY: Cornell University Press, 2005.

Lega, Giuseppe. *Settant'anni di cinema: cronache, documentazione, panoramiche.* Milano: Gastaldi, 1967.

Leprohon, Pierre. *The Italian Cinema.* New York: Praeger Publishers, 1972.

Liehm, Mira. *Passion and Defiance: Film in Italy from 1942 to the Present.* Berkeley: University of California Press, 1984.

Lizzani, Carlo. *Il cinema italiano.* Firenze: Parenti, 1961.

Luconi, Stefano, and Guido Tintori, eds. *L'ombra lunga del fascio: canali di propaganda fascista per gli italiani d'America.* Milano: M & B Publishing, 2004.

Lyttelton, Adrian. *The Seizure of Power: Fascism in Italy, 1919–1929.* Princeton, NJ: Princeton University Press, 1973.

———, ed. *Italian Fascisms: From Pareto to Gentile.* New York: Harper and Row, 1973.

Macciocchi, Maria Antonietta. *La Donna Nera: "consenso" femminile e fascismo.* Milano: Feltrinelli, 1976.

MacGowan, Kenneth. *Behind the Screen: The History and Techniques of the Motion Picture.* New York: Dell Publishing Co., 1965.

Mack Smith, Dennis. *Italy: A Modern History.* Ann Arbor: University of Michigan Press, 1959.

———. *Mussolini's Roman Empire.* New York: Penguin Books, 1976.

Madaro, L. *Bibliografia fascista.* Milano: Mondadori, 1935.

Maggi, Raffaello. *Film industria: riflessi economici.* Pianezza: Busto Arsizio, 1934.

Malvano, Laura. *Fascismo e politica dell'immagine.* Torino: Bollati Boringhieri Editore, 1988.

Mancini, Elaine. *Struggles of the Italian Film Industry during Fascism, 1930–1935.* Ann Arbor, MI: UMI Research Press, 1985.

Marinese, L. *Andiamo al cinema.* Palermo: Flaccovio, 1941.

Marinucci, Vinicio. *Tendenze del cinema italiano.* Roma: Unitalia Film, 1959.

Martinelli, Vittorio. *Il cinema muto italiano: i film degli anni venti, 1921–1922.* Roma: Edizioni Bianco e Nero, 1981.

———. *Il cinema muto italiano: i film degli anni venti, 1923–1931.* Roma: Edizioni Bianco e Nero, 1981.

———. *Il cinema muto italiano: i film del dopoguerra, 1919.* Roma: Edizioni Bianco e Nero, 1980.

———. *Il cinema muto italiano: i film del dopoguerra, 1920.* Roma: Edizioni Bianco e Nero, 1980.

Martinelli, Vittorio, and Mario Quargnolo. *Maciste and co: i giganti buoni del muto italiano.* Gemona: Edizioni Cinepopolare, 1981.

Martini, Andrea, ed. *Bibliocinema: elementi per una bibliografia cinematografica.* Roma: Bulzoni Editore, 1982.

Martini, Giacomo, ed. *Strategie e pratiche della censura.* Ferrara: Conference Proceedings, 1980.

Miccichè, Lino, ed. *De Sica: autore, regista, attore.* Venezia: Marsilio Editori, 1992.

———, ed. *Il neorealismo cinematografico italiano.* Venezia: Marsilio Editori, 1975.

Mida, Massimo, and L. Quaglietti, eds. *Dai telefoni bianchi al neorealismo.* Roma: Laterza Editori, 1980.

Mignone, Giangiacomo. *Gli stati uniti e il fascismo: alle origini dell'egemonia americana in Italia.* Milano: Feltrinelli, 1980.

Monteleone, Franco. *La radio italiana nel periodo fascista: studio e documenti, 1922–1945.* Venezia: Marsilio Editori, 1976.

Morley, David. *The "Nationwide" Audience: Structure and Decoding.* London: British Film Institute, 1980.

Mostra Internazionale del Nuovo Cinema. *Cinecittà 1: industria e mercato nel cinema italiano tra le due guerre.* Venezia: Marsilio Editori, 1985.

———. *Cinecittà 2: sull'industria cinematografica italiana.* Venezia: Marsilio Editori, 1985.

———. *Materiali sul cinema italiano 1929–1943.* Vol. 1. Roma: Mostra Internazionale del Nuovo Cinema, 1975.

———. *Nuovi materiali sul cinema italiano 1929–1943.* Vol. 2. Roma: Mostra Internazionale del Nuovo Cinema, 1976.

———. *Risate di regime: la commedia italiana 1930–1944.* Venezia: Marsilio Editori, 1991.

———. *Titanus: modi di produzione del cinema italiano.* Pesaro: DiGiacomo Editore, 1985.

———. *Tra un film e l'altro: materiali sul muto italiano 1907–1920.* Venezia: Editori Marsilio, 1980.

Muscio, Giuliana. *Piccole italie, grandi schermi: scambi cinematografici tra Italia e Stati Uniti, 1895–1945.* Roma: Bulzoni Editori, 2004.

Mussolini, Benito. "Cinematografia educativa." In *Scritti e discorsi di Benito Mussolini.* Milano: Hoepli, 1934.

Nolte, Ernst. *Three Faces of Fascism.* New York: Holt, Rinehart and Winston, 1969.

Ottavi, N. *L'industria cinematografica italiana e la sua organizzazione.* Roma: Edizioni Bianco e Nero, 1940.

Overbey, David, ed. *Springtime in Italy: A Reader in Neorealism.* Hamden, CT: Archon Books, 1978.

Painter, Borden W. *Mussolini's Rome: Rebuilding the Eternal City.* New York: Palgrave Macmillan, 2005.

Paolella, Roberto. *Storia del cinema muto.* Napoli: Giannini, 1956.

———. *Storia del cinema sonoro 1926–1929.* Napoli: Giannini, 1966.

Papa, Antonio. *Storia politica della radio.* Napoli: Guida, 1978.

Papa, Raffaele. *Storia di due manifesti.* Milano: Feltrinelli, 1968.

Pasinetti, Francesco. *Mezzosecolo di cinema.* Milano: Poligono, 1946.

———. *Storia del cinema: dalle origini ad oggi.* Roma: Edizioni Bianco e Nero, 1939.

Pavese, Cesare. *La letteratura americana e altri saggi.* Torino: Einauldi Editore, 1962.

Pellizzari, Lorenzo. *Hollywood, anni trenta.* Venezia: La Biennale di Venezia, 1972.

Perrella, Giuseppe. *L'economico e il semiotico del cinema italiano.* Roma: Teorema Edizioni, 1981.

Pickering-Iazzi, Robin, ed. *Mothers of Invention: Women, Italian Fascism, and Culture.* Minneapolis: University of Minnesota Press, 1995.

Pinkus, Karen. *Bodily Regimes: Italian Advertising under Fascism.* Minneapolis: University of Minnesota Press, 1995.

Pintor, Giaime. *Il sangue d'Europa*. Torino: Einauldi Editore, 1950.

Portelli, Alessandro. *Taccuini Americani*. Roma: Manifestolibri, 1991.

Poulantzas, Nicos. *Fascism and Dictatorship*. Translated by Judith White. London: Verso Editions, 1970.

Prinzhofer, Renato. *Le città galleggianti: navi e crociere negli anni '30*. Milano: Longanesi, 1978.

Prolo, Maria Adriana. *Cabiria: visione storica dell III secolo a. C.* Torino: Museo Nazionale del Cinema, 1977.

———. *Storia del cinema muto italiano*. Milano: Poligono, 1951.

Prolo, Maria Adriana, and L. Carluccio, eds. *Catalogo del Museo Nazionale del cinema*. Torino: Casse di Risparmio, 1978.

Quaglietti, Lorenzo. *Il cinema italiano del dopoguerra: leggi, produzione, distribuzione, esercizio*. Pesaro: Mostra del Nuovo Cinema, 1974.

———. *Storia economica-politica del cinema italiano, 1945–1980*. Roma: Editori Riuniti, 1980.

Quargnolo, Mario. *Luciano Albertini, un divo degli anni venti*. Udine: CSU, 1977.

———. *La parola ripudiata: l'incredibile storia dei film stranieri in Italia nei primi anni del sonoro*. Gemona: La Cineteca del Friuli, 1986.

———. *Qui comincia l'avventura del signor. . . .* Firenze: La Casa Usher, 1984.

Rabagliati, Alberto. *Quattro anni fra le stelle*. Milano: Alberto Rabagliati, 1932.

Raffaelli, Sergio. *La lingua filmata: didascalie e dialoghi nel cinema italiano*. Firenze: Casa Editrice Le Lettere, 1992.

———. *Le parole proibite: purismo di stato e regoloamentazione della pubblicità in Italia, 1812–1945*. Bologna: Mulino, 1982.

Randone, B., and G. Solito, eds. *Guida film: tutto l'ambiente cinematografica di Roma*. Roma: Agenzia Film, 1932.

Ravetto, Kris. *The Unmasking of Fascist Aesthetics*. Minneapolis: University of Minnesota Press, 2001.

Redi, Ricardo, ed. *Cinema italiano sotto il fascismo*. Venezia: Marsilio Editori, 1979.

———. *Cinema scritto: il catalogo delle riviste italiane di cinema 1907–1944*. Roma: Associazione Italiana per le Ricerche di Storia del Cinema, 1992.

———. *La Cines: storia di una casa di produzione italiana*. Roma: CNC Edizioni, 1991.

———. *Ti parlerò d'amor: cinema italiano fra muto e sonoro*. Torino: ERI, 1986.

Reich, Jacqueline, and Piero Garofalo, eds. *Re-Viewing Fascism: Italian Cinema, 1922–1943*. Bloomington: Indiana University Press, 2002.

Renzi, Renzo, ed. *Il cinema dei dittatori: Mussolini, Stalin, Hitler*. Bologna: Grafis Edizioni, 1992.

Restivo, Angelo. *The Cinema of Economic Miracles: Visuality and Modernization in the Italian Art Film*. Durham, NC: Duke University Press, 2002.

Rogger, Hans. *The European Right: An Historical Profile*. Berkeley: University of California Press, 1965.

Rondi, Brunello. *Cinema e realtà*. Roma: Edizioni Cinque Lune, 1957.

Rondolino, Gianni. *Torino come Hollywood*. Bologna: Cappelli, 1980.

Ruffin, Valentina, and Patrizia D'Agostino, eds. *Dialoghi di regime*. Roma: Bulzoni Editori, 1997.

Saladino, Salvatore. *Italy from Unification to 1919: Growth and Decay of a Liberal Regime*. New York: Thomas Y. Crowell Company, 1970.

Salvatorelli, Luigi. *Storia d'Italia nel periodo fascista*. Torino: Einauldi Editore, 1956.

Salvemini, Gaetano. *The Fascist Dictatorship in Italy*. New York: Harper and Row, 1927.

———. *The Origins of Fascism in Italy*. New York: Harper and Row, 1973.

———. *Under the Axe of Fascism*. New York: Citadel Press, 1971.

Sardi, Alessandro. *Cinque anni di vita dell'Istituto Nazionale L.U.C.E*. Roma: Grafica, 1930.

Savio, Francesco. *Cinecittà anni trenta: parlano 116 protagonisti del secondo cinema italiano 1930–1943*. Roma: Bulzoni Editore, 1979.

———. *Ma l'amore no: realismo, formalismo, propaganda e telefoni bianchi nel cinema italiano di regime (1930–1943)*. Milano: Casa Editrice Sonzogno, 1975.

Savona, Virgilio, and Michele L. Straniero, eds. *Canti dell'Italia fascista (1919–1945)*. Milano: Aldo Garzanti Editore, 1979.

Seton-Watson, Christopher. *Italy from Liberalism to Fascism*. London: Metheun and Co., 1967.

Silva, Umberto. *Ideologia e arte del fascismo*. Milano: Gabriele Mazzotta Editore, 1975.

Simonini, Augusto. *Il linguaggio di Mussolini*. Milano: Nuovi Saggi Italiani, 1978.

Smith, Anthony D. *National Identity*. London: Penguin Books, 1991.

———. *Nationalism and Modernism*. London: Routledge, 1998.

Solaroli, L., and L. Bizzari. *L'industria cinematografica italiana*. Firenze: Parenti, 1958.

Soldati, Mario. *America: Primo Amore*. Roma: Einauldi Editore, 1945.

Soro, Francesco. *Splendori e miserie del cinema*. Milano: Consalvo, 1935.

Spackman, Barbara. *Fascist Virilities: Rhetoric and Social Fantasy in Italy*. Minneapolis: University of Minnesota Press, 1996.

Spinazzola, Vittorio. *Cinema e pubblico: lo spettacolo filmico in Italia 1945–1965*. Roma: Bulzoni Editore, 1985.

Staiger, Janet. *Interpreting Films: Studies in the Historical Reception of American Cinema*. Princeton, NJ: Princeton University Press, 1992.

Stone, Marla. *The Patron State: Culture & Politics in Fascist Italy*. Princeton, NJ: Princeton University Press, 1998.

Tannenbaum, Edward R. *The Fascist Experience: Italian Society and Culture 1922–1945*. New York: Basic Books, 1972.

Tasca, Angelo. *Nascita e avvento del fascismo*. Firenze: Bollati Boringhieri, 1950.

Thompson, Kristin. *Exporting Entertainment*. London: BFI Publishing, 1985.

Tinazzi, Giorgio, ed. *Il cinema italiano dal fascismo all'antifascismo*. Venezia: Marsilio Editori, 1966.

Tinazzi, Giorgio, and Marina Zancan, eds. *Cinema e letteratura del neorealismo.* Venezia: Marsilio Editori, 1983.

Tozzi, Leonardo, ed. *Il mito di Hollywood e l'Italia degli anni '30.* Firenze: Centro Editoriale Florence Press, 1981.

Turconi, Davide, ed. *La stampa cinematografica in Italia e negli Stati Uniti d'America dalle origini al 1930.* Pavia: Amministrazione Provinciale di Pavia, 1977.

Turconi, Davide, and Camillo Bassotto. *Il film e la sua storia.* Bologna: Cappelli Editore, 1964.

Turconi, Davide, and Antonio Sacchi, eds. *Bianconero rosso e verde: immagini del cinema italiano 1910–1980.* Pavia: La Casa Usher, 1983.

Turi, Gabriele. *Il fascismo e il consenso degli intellettuali.* Bologna: Il Mulino, 1980.

Vittorini, Elio. *Diario in pubblico.* Milano: Bompiani, 1957.

Vittorio, Giuliano. *C'era una volta il duce.* Roma: Savelli, 1975.

Weber, Eugen. *Varieties of Fascism.* Princeton, NJ: Von Nostrand, 1964.

Williams, Alan, ed. *Film and Nationalism.* New Brunswick, NJ: Rutgers University Press, 2002.

Wiskerman, Elizabeth. *Fascism in Italy: Its Development and Influence.* London: MacMillan and Co., 1969.

Zangrandi, Ruggero. *Il lungo viaggio attraverso il fascismo.* Milano: Feltrinelli, 1962.

Zanotto, Piero, and Fiorello Zangrando, eds. *L'Italia in cartone.* Padova: Liviana Editrice, 1973.

Zurlo, Leopoldo. *Memorie inutili: la censura teatrale nel ventennio.* Roma: Edizioni dell'Ateneo, 1952.

Index

Italicized page numbers refer to illustrations.

protectionism, 34–35, 57–58, 157–58,
168, 193n38
public, 18; and dissolution of fascist
order, 174–75; and heuristic codes,
161, 163; and historical narration
shift, 104; and Massenzio, 186;
and *Mussolini Speaks,* 140; and
national identity, 42–43, 47; and
representation of transportation,
124; and rise of fascism, 72, 75; and
sports, 80. *See also* audiences
publicity: for *Cabiria,* 39–40, 40; and
historical amnesia, 39–40, 40,
43, 47; and influence of American
culture, 127; for *Mussolini Speaks,*
135–36; for *Scipione l'africano,*
102; and star system, 43. *See also*
propaganda
public sphere, 12–13, 188n17; and heuristic codes, 159, 161, 164–65; and
national identity, 36–38, 47, 50–51;
and relationship to Hollywood
cinema, 155; and representation of
transportation, 123; and rise of fascism, 72–73; and sports, 80
purity, cultural: influence of American
culture, 130; and Italian language,
62–64, 158; and relationship to
Hollywood cinema, 153; and
strongman cycle, 15, 83, 87

Quargnolo, Mario, 63
Quattro passi tra le nuvole (1942), 165
Quinn, Anthony, 204n31
Quo Vadis? (1913), 32–33, 44, 206n4
Quo Vadis? (1924), 69

racism, 79, 84, 188n14
radio, 53, 71, 97, 102, 133, 175, *175,*
176–77, 196n4
Radio Audizioni Italia (RAI), 24–25,
175
Radio Londra (BBC), 176
Radio Torino, 175, *175*
Raicevich, Giovanni, 81
rail transport, 16, 34, 36, 71, 139,
192n36. *See also* trains
Ras (local fascist leaders), 54
Ray, Aldo, 204n31
readership, 3, 7–11, 14, 16–18, 20,
188n14; and dissolution of fascist
order, 174, 176; and heuristic
codes, 159, 164, 169; and historical narration shift, 98, 104; and
influence of American culture,
126, 130–31; and relationship to
Hollywood cinema, 154–55; and

representation of transportation,
116, 124; and rise of fascism, 73
realism, 22, 105, 114, 130, 165
rebirth of Italian cinema *(rinascita),* 4,
65, 198n34
Reeves, Steve, 200n8, 206n4
Regio Decreto-Legge (R.D.L.): (no.
918), 65; (no. 1000), 60; (no. 1121),
60, 197n21
regional differences: and dissolution
of fascist order, 169, 174; and
heuristic codes, 163–64, 169; and
historical narration shift, 98; and
Massenzio, 186; and national identity, 36–38, 41, 46–47, 50, 188n14,
191n22; and rise of fascism, 64,
196–97n17, 198n33; and sports, 80
Il Regno (journal), 45
relays of information, 38–39, 141–42,
186, 193n44
remakes, 146–50
Renaissance, 91, 93, 95–96, 104, 161
Renault, 206n4
resistance, 178–86; and Catholic
church, 196n9; and heuristic codes,
18, 165; and historical amnesia, 23;
and influence of American culture,
130; and national identity, 47
Restivo, Angelo, 166
retrospectives, 24–26, 28, 191n16
return to origins: and dissolution of fascist order, 174; and heuristic codes,
163; and relationship to Hollywood
cinema, 146, 148; and representation of transportation, 16, 111–12,
113, 118, 122–24
revisionist studies, 23, 26–27, 190n8
Rex (Italian luxury liner), 134, 203n15
Riefenstahl, Leni, 29
Righelli, Gennaro, 69, 142
Risi, Dino, 106
Riso amaro (1948), 169, 170, 174–76,
175
Risorgimento (national unification):
and historical narration shift,
88, 91, 98; and national identity,
36–38, 44–47, 194n59, 198n33; and
strongman cycle, 81
La riva dei bruti (1930), 146
*Rivista internazionale del cinema edu-
catore,* 199n51
RKO, 168
Rogers, Ginger, 148–49
Roma città aperta (1945), 165–66, 170
Roman antiquity: and heuristic codes,
160–62, 171–73; and historical
narration shift, 87–88, 95–104,

101; and Massenzio, 179–85, 206n2; and national identity, 44–47; and rise of fascism, 62–63; and sports, 79; and strongman cycle, 81
romance, 21, 81, 83
Roncoroni, Carlo, 66
Roosevelt, Theodore, 9, 75, 132
Rossellini, Roberto, 88, 170–72
Rossi, Carlo, 32, 53, 55
Rossi-Itala (production company), 31
Rota, Nino, 115
Rotaie (1929), 107–13, *109, 110, 111, 113,* 150, 173; and *Il signor Max,* 117, 123; and *Treno popolare,* 114–16
Royal Decree #532, 49
rural-urban migration, 36, 137, 141, 162–63
Ruttman, Walter, 105

Saetta, 61
SAFFI-Milano Films, 32
Salimei, Francesco, 31
Salò, republic of, 167
salute, fascist, 93, *94,* 171
Sansone (filmic character), 61, 81, 85, 206n4
Sarfatti, Margherita, 9
Saroyan, William, 129
SASP (Società Anonima Stefano Pittaluga), 61, 66
satire, 144–45
Saturday Evening Post, 132
Scarface (1932), 75, 135, 144
Lo Schiavo di Cartagine (1910), 44
Scipione l'africano (1937), 28–29, 73, 87–90, *89,* 95–104, *101,* 138, 201n14
Sciuscià (1946), 166, 170–72, *172,* 174
Uno scozzese alla corte del Gran Khan (1938), 64, 197–98n30
Seconda B (1934), 28
Serao, Matilde, 39
sets, 41, 46, 65, 69, 102
sexuality: and censorship, 48–49, 130; and dissolution of fascist order, 169–70; and heuristic codes, 158, 163; and influence of American culture, 130, 158; and national identity, 48–49; and representation of transportation, 16, 115–16, 122, 124
sexual orientation, 188n14
Il signor Max (1937), 107, 116–24, *118, 120, 121,* 173
silent films, 19, 107

socialism, 37, 76, 200n5
Socialist Party, 53–54
social mobility, 16, 112, 122, 154, 170
social realism, 114, 176
Società Anonima Stefano Pittaluga. *See* SASP
Società Italiana per il Cinematofono, 192n24
socioeconomic status: and dissolution of fascist order, 169; and heuristic codes, 163, 169; and national identity, 42; and relationship to Hollywood cinema, 146–50, 154; and representation of transportation, 106–7. *See also* class
Solaroli, L., 189n7
Soldati, Mario, 142
Il sole sorge ancora (1946), 170
Sordi, Alberto, 106
Il sorpasso (1962), 106
sound technologies, 4, 61, 63–64, 105, 107
source material, 40–41
Soviet totalitarianism, 2–3
Spackman, Barbara, 72
Spada, Marcello, 115
Spagnoletti, Giovanni, 190–91n13
Spartacus (1913), 44, 104
spectacle, 181–83; and heuristic codes, 161–62; and historical narration shift, 15, 104; and Massenzio, 182; and national identity, 43, 46, 49; and representation of transportation, 106, 123; and sports, 80–81, 104
spectatorship: and heuristic codes, 161; and historical narration shift, 102–4; and Hollywood cinema, 126, 204n32; and Massenzio, 183; and national identity, 42, 46; and rise of fascism, 73; and sports, 80–81, 85
speedboat races, 109
Sperduti nel buio (1941), 165
sports, 15, 77–81, *78;* and heuristic codes, 161; and historical narration shift, 101, 103–4; and Mussolini, 5, 77–79, *79,* 106; and rise of fascism, 57, 71; and youth culture, 133
Sports Charter (1929), 80
squadristi (fascist terror squads), 203n19; and historical narration shift, 93; and *Mussolini Speaks,* 138; and rise of fascism, 53–54, 72; and strongman cycle, 85, 200n5
Squadrone bianco (1936), 87–88
Staiger, Janet, 8

Text: 10/13 Sabon
Display: Franklin Gothic
Compositor, printer, and binder: Integrated Book Technology